A new imperative for leadership in a disruptive age

THINKING *the* UNTHINKABLE

Nik Gowing & Chris Langdon

D0434352

First published 2018

by John Catt Educational Ltd,
12 Deben Mill Business Centre, Old Maltings Approach,
Melton, Woodbridge IP12 1BL

Tel: +44 (0) 1394 389850 Fax: +44 (0) 1394 386893
Email: enquiries@johncatt.com
Website: www.johncatt.com

ISBN: 978 1 911 382 74 4

Set and designed by John Catt Educational Limited

THINKING THE UNTHINKABLE

by Nik Gowing and Chris Langdon

'This is an amazing piece of work! It deals with the little known irony that those with the most decision-making power often feel under the most pressure to conform to the systems and norms around them. This explains why our institutions – whether national, regional or international – have been caught off guard. And why we are stuck in reactive – rather than proactive – mode. The need for a strategic overhaul in our thinking is widely acknowledged, though few know how to go about it. I think giving a copy of this book to every world leader would be a good place to start.'

Miroslav Lajčák, President of the UN General Assembly, Foreign Minister of Slovakia

'I can say, very genuinely, that what you're working on is hugely important. But it is also difficult because it is human nature to react to crises but not to prepare for and pre-empt them. It is also very different today from what it used to be because of the multiplicity of possible crisis events that can overlay each other. We simply do not have the capacity to deal with more than one crisis at a time. I was very impressed by the work Nik presented when he came to the Bank. . . . At that time it was a provocative discussion actually; people did refer to it a number of times.'

Kristalina Georgieva, CEO of the World Bank

'This book is timely, scary and important. One hopes it will be widely read – and that it will resonate with those in demanding senior roles in both public and private sectors who are overwhelmed by the fast-changing and complex challenges they confront. Still more importantly, one hopes that it will trigger wide debate and thereby help to reduce the probability of the 'unthinkable' setbacks that threaten our current civilisation – threats about which too many people are still in denial.'

Lord Martin Rees, Astronomer Royal, Co-founder, Centre for the Study of Existential Risk, Cambridge University

'With so much change in business and in the political arena, you can either play safe in responding, or – as this wonderful book encourages the reader – you can "thrive on change". *Thinking the Unthinkable* urges leaders to engage with ideas that may appear – or may be in the short run – disruptive but will lead to innovative outcomes, products and services. This is a must read for all leaders in all sectors!'

Professor Sir Cary Cooper CBE, Alliance Manchester Business School, Co-author of *The Myths of Management* (2017)

'In *Thinking the Unthinkable*, Nik and Chris will challenge and inspire you in equal measure to do just this. Every modern leader should both read it and embrace it.'

Katherine Garrett-Cox, CEO of Gulf International Bank (UK) Ltd

'Organisations and governments are usually poor at adapting to sudden change and *Thinking the Unthinkable* helps explain why and what can be done to address the leadership pathologies that lead to missing the signs of coming disruption or trouble in the organisation.'

Professor Sir Lawrence Freedman, Emeritus Professor of War Studies, King's College London. He was a member of the Iraq (Chilcot) Inquiry, 2009–2016

'There is constant change and many seismic events have swung the course of history. However as a student of history I believe that viewed in 100 years' time the issues of today will be seen as a landmark.

Globalisation and its perceived unfairness to people and planet is leading to calls for change. Capitalism, at its rawest, is being challenged as the preeminent economic model. At the same time the dawning of the digital era is creating new paradigms in how we live and work.

Fear, uncertainty and discontent is growing. Politicians and businesses are struggling for the answers. The age of the power of nation states is drawing to a close. But what will replace it? In this thoughtful book the issues are explored, and a well reasoned case put forward to Think the Unthinkable.'

Lord Mark Price, Author of *Fairness for All* (2017), Managing Director of Waitrose (2007–2016), Minister for Trade and Investment (2016–2017)

'A connected world is a complex world. Once stable sand piles are cascading all around us in the economic, social and political and strategic domains. As some of today's most important government and corporate leaders confess to authors Nik Gowing and Chris Langdon, they feel helplessly behind the pace of change. And yet: we are all price takers, but we are not helpless. Read this important book for guidance on navigating a world of unthinkables.'

Dr Parag Khanna, Author of *Connectography: Mapping the Future of Global Civilization* (2016)

PREFACE

This book is the product and direct result of an ongoing, dynamic research project with the title **Thinking the Unthinkable**.

It started in 2014 with a simple question. Why were so many leaders in government, business, major institutions and non-governmental organisations evidently struggling in the face of the start of what is now recognised as a new normal of disruption globally?

For four years we have interviewed and had conversations with hundreds of top leaders. The interviews are mostly off the record, but often recorded by agreement. Throughout we have been astonished by the candid revelations about new fears and being overwhelmed. The process has demonstrated the power of the open question. The project now has thousands of pages of transcripts and a database described to us by others as unrivalled.

The trove of insights and findings has led to significant invitations worldwide for the findings and implications to be shared at thought leadership gatherings for both top executives and aspiring leaders. There is a hunger among leaders to discover why they feel so overwhelmed and even scared by the new disruptions. There is an anxiety among millennials that leadership is out of touch with the new realities of the new purpose and values that they expect. It is challenging most and possibly all of their powers to lead as effectively as expected by those they work for.

Thinking the Unthinkable (TTU) started with a calculated hunch by Nik Gowing. He initiated the first conversations as part of the Churchill 21st Century Global Leaders Programme to mark 50 years since Sir Winston Churchill's death. It has since developed and expanded into much more. Chris Langdon joined at the end of 2014. By mid 2018 it became a seven-person social enterprise company that is independent, self-funded and non-partisan.

For easy access to our research, the book's footnotes are also published online on www.thinkunthink.org. You will find clickable links to sources. We recommend that as you read the book, you simultaneously open our web platform on your mobile or tablet. Then you can read the original sources and watch the videos as you go.

We will be regularly updating the information as new disruptions emerge. We will provide more case studies and more examples of what leaders are doing to handle the unthinkable challenges they face.

The experience should be two way. As well as reading and watching, you can contribute your thoughts, ideas and challenges via the web platform in real time.

CONTENTS

FOREWORDS

Thinking the Unthinkable bridges the generations.

It reflects how much the older generation and the next generation are in sync with fears about the scale of disruption, and its unthinkable impacts on our society. Why are leaders being wrong-footed and failing to cope?

So we are delighted to offer two forewords.

Lord Nicholas Stern (born 1946) is the distinguished British economist who has worked in many national and international institutions. He wrote the Stern Review (2006) which detailed why the world must be seized of the growing, imminent threats from climate change.

Aniket Shah (born 1987) is an extraordinary talent. Before reaching the age of 30 he already has a career in the worlds of finance, the human rights sector and at the United Nations to match someone much older. His work focuses on financing a sustainable global future.

Both reflect here the concerns about why leadership is ill equipped to handle the new unthinkables from disruption at a crucial time for humanity.

Foreword by Lord Nicholas Stern

When we have to cope with or respond to difficult or damaging large-scale disruption we will do far better if we have previously thought about its possibility, about why and how it might occur, and about how we can shape the forces at work. Even better, we can create positive radical changes or good disruptions if we both recognise their necessity and imagine what might be.

As an economist, two examples of immense importance have had a profound effect on my own thinking about the unthinkable over the last two decades. The world in general, and economists in particular, did not, in the main, see the great financial crisis of 2008 coming. Many policy-makers and economists spoke of the 'great moderation'. They thought or claimed that the era of boom and bust had gone. They built models where only small shocks could happen and where systems re-adjusted fairly smoothly to cope with them.

This thinking largely excluded the possibility of major crises. We have now discovered that the thinking, models and policies were robust against small change but not against large change. Complacency of approach made crises more likely.

When the crisis occurred, powerful reaction from citizens took a long time coming. But it did come after nearly a decade – in terms of Brexit, the election of Donald Trump and now the pushback against leaderships and systems in other countries too. There was increasing concern about the competence of leaders, policy-makers, institutions and received ways of thinking. We have now witnessed a deepening corrosion of confidence in systems and those who lead them.

The next two decades will see a doubling of the world economy. In those two decades we have to cut greenhouse emissions by around 20% to have a chance of avoiding dangerous climate change. The investments we make in the next two decades will define our future for this century and beyond. The choice is stark. We can, for example, build cities and their infrastructure which allow us to move, breathe and be productive. Or we can leave our children and grandchildren facing a profoundly hostile environment that would cause hundreds of millions to move, leading potentially to lasting and widespread societal unrest and conflict.

We must recognise the unthinkable consequences of inaction, whilst also seeing how attractive the alternative paths could be in terms of rising living standards and more cohesive societies. But are we capable of doing this? Again, economists build models which in large measure ignore or make light of the risks that the scientists are describing. Policy-makers are all too often unable or unwilling to face up to the radical decisions that are necessary.

This book is full of powerful and vital examples where the failure to think the unthinkable has led and could lead to deeply damaging disruption. All too often there is an asymmetry. Those benefiting from what looks like a stable status quo are those who have the strongest belief in its stability. They are in most need of this book.

But it can and must concern all of us. The successes of the last seven decades across the world – and there have been many in terms of strongly rising life expectancy and major reductions in poverty, for example – seem to have lulled many into thinking that things 'can only get better'. That confidence has been deeply shaken over the last decade and for good reason.

We are, at last, beginning to recognise that we have to think and act differently. That is not to jettison analysis and rationality, but to apply these in a much deeper, more open, and imaginative way. This book makes a vital step in that process.

I have been talking to Nik Gowing and Chris Langdon throughout the four years that this book has been in the making. I did not know how it would turn out – and, I suspect, neither did they. At the start I wondered whether it would be mainly a cry of warning that we must think differently. It has become much more than that. It shows us how to begin to do our thinking differently. We owe them a great debt.

Lord Nicholas Stern, is Professor of Economics and Government at the London School of Economics. He was President of the British Academy 2013-2017. He headed the Stern Review on the Economics of Climate Change in 2006. He has previously served as Chief Economist at the World Bank and Second Permanent Secretary at HM Treasury.

Foreword by Aniket Shah

The 'older' I get the more I believe in the conversations that I had with Nik and Chris in 2015 on thinking the unthinkable, and the driving impulse behind the **Thinking the Unthinkable** project.

There is a double challenge. Leadership needs to be redefined and leaders have to redefine themselves for the new disrupted, 'non-normal' world that we now live in. The shortcomings of leadership are now becoming more and more stark.

There is an incredible schizophrenia about the world today and where it may go in the future. On any given day you can go from extreme optimism to enormous pessimism. Are we living in the best of times or the worst of times? Technology gets better by the day and so does our ability to make progress. But at the same time there are some structures in this world that are out of sync with what we actually need. The institutions that have governed the world are very much now under question. So are leaders – especially the relevance of their qualities and their awareness of how profound the changes from disruption are.

I am amazed at our lack of ability to think outside the box. The box has also lost definition. When you dig under the surface we are still operating within a system that is incredibly slow moving. It is unable to respond to the times we are living in.

We know that there is a better way of doing things. Whenever I need to be energised I go and teach a class or give a guest talk at Columbia University or NYU, or even better go to a community college. There's just so much excitement and optimism about the world and there's so much energy to live in a better world. If there is a way that, with all of this technology, people can become more independent in their thinking, that would be great. But I worry that we're not moving in the right direction. I think people are becoming less independent-thinking and more conformist in order to get on and keep a way of making a living.

You should read *__Thinking the Unthinkable__* because we live in a world where the unthinkable is not just possible – it is happening. We have the ability to do anything that we want to do; technology enables us to do so much and we are aware of so many more things than we were in the past. Put simply: the technology, the ability, those are not the limiting factors. The limiting factor, for some, is imagination. So, if you train yourself to keep thinking the unthinkable, you can actually turn imagination into reality. I think that's a really powerful thing.

You have to think the unthinkable because for certain problems that the world is facing, we will require such massive changes. There has to be the total transformation in the global energy system in the next 40 years – in a way that we've never done before. We're going to have to figure out ways to accommodate hundreds of millions of refugees per annum leaving North Africa and the Middle East. The challenges that we may be confronted with will require us to think through the unthinkable today. Because without that, we won't be able to continue. That needs new approaches to leadership.

I don't think it's a choice. It's a necessity. ***Thinking the Unthinkable*** lays out new ways to be that brave so we can do that.

Aniket Shah is a global practitioner in sustainable finance. He is currently the Chair of the Board of Amnesty International USA and is a Senior Advisor on SDG Financing for the UN Sustainable Development Solutions Network. He has written this foreword in his personal capacity.

1
RED ALERT...FOR UNTHINKABLES

'There isn't a single CEO out there that doesn't appreciate this strange new world that they're trying to lead through.'

Aron Cramer, President, Business for Social Responsibility.

This book has a red cover. Why so? It is a red alert for leaders confronted by an end to the conformity that got them to the top.

Ignore the colour and the warning at your peril.

How 'woke' are you to the implications of the new disruption and turbulence you are facing?[1]

For so many reasons and in so many ways, this is a call to action because of the new struggles facing those at the top. This is not imagination. Leaders and leaderships have confirmed confidentially to us the scale of their concerns. They are enduring great difficulties in the business of leading. They have described how they are looking for new solutions and ways forward.

Thinking unthinkables is what this book sets out to do. We reveal here how a number of smart leaders are finding ways to handle them. We analyse the challenges from disruption using a host of examples. Those we are sharing come from the hard-won lessons of leaders at the top who have taken big risks, and been willing to be open about them. Importantly, having shown courage, humility and flexibility, most are still in their jobs. They still relish the challenges they have been confronting and found ways to overcome.

The lessons are clear. The aim must be to thrive on change, not be derailed by it. Your aim should be to disrupt yourself. Your ambitions should create a new **culture, mindset** and **behaviour,** with new **purpose, values, courage** and **humility.** Bear in mind these seven words at all times as you read the book. But how can culture, mindset and behaviour be changed in a world of new disruption which is 'zig-zagging towards the future',[2] and where 'negative economic and political forces are … unleashing a global revolt'?[3]

Our main finding is this. The conformity which gets leaders to the top disqualifies most of them from gripping the scale of disruption and knowing what to do about it. This is the spine which binds together everything that follows. It underpins our findings and analysis.

We are in a time of 'zombie orthodoxies'[4] which are no longer fit for purpose. A new, ill-defined normal has put those orthodoxies under deep stress. We report and audit the **human capacity** of leaders to handle all that is being hurled at them, often in unprecedented form from unpredictable directions. How can leaders learn to cope and manage such unthinkables? It is the question many have told us they keep asking themselves. Are you one of them?

This book is designed to embolden and empower leaders – both current and aspiring – to embrace the massive scale of disruption. It will identify the enormous, almost superhuman scale and pace of what must be done at a necessarily high speed.

One top leader graphically describes the enormity of the challenge as like 'eating an elephant in one mouthful'. Will it be done? Can it be done? Can the elephant be eaten at all? We argue that it must be, even at a slower pace by eating smaller bites, however formidable the prospect.

Thinking the Unthinkable is for everyone worried about whether leaders can handle this. And if not, why not? Leadership has not necessarily failed when judged by the qualities and skills that qualified it for the top. Instead the world has moved on dramatically. 'We need to create a new form of thinking for business, away from orthodoxies.'[5] 'We must adapt and not in nostalgic, sentimental ways.'[6]

This book is for 'you' if you are already a top leader, an aspiring leader, an anxious member of the next generation, or one of the zillions of concerned citizens alarmed by apparent failings of leaders in this disrupted world. That means almost everyone. All of us are impacted if leaders are struggling. All of us have an interest in first understanding and accepting what is going on, then defining the problems, assessing what can be done, and finally calibrating which 'solutions' might work, and which have little or no chance.

Are you an aspiring leader, a millennial or member of Generations Y or Z?[7] If so, have you assumed that a career path in a corporate or government was your way ahead in life? But are you now disillusioned by what you see? Alternatively, are you somebody who does not understand why the highest paid executives or officials cannot see what is obvious to you?

Are you an angry citizen or consumer who feels misled or betrayed, and expects leaders to pay a price? If you are none of these, then you may think this book is not about you, that it is about someone else, that it is only for and about 'them up there' who are somehow screwing up the system and leaving the world an even more resentful place.

Wrong! It is about you too. It will help you understand why, if we are heading for some kind of 'hell in a handbasket', many of those at the top are finding they cannot cope. That may astonish and anger you. But those at the top have human weaknesses too, and they are becoming remarkably more frank about them – as we have discovered and reveal here.

So stick with us. There is a much-improved chance that you will be able to eat the elephant of disruption and uncertainty. We will lift the veil on how you might achieve it.

In this book we analyse the embedded and failing leadership processes which mean unthinkables are not actively thought about. What we report and write is not about criticism. It is about making a cold analysis. We challenge whatever orthodoxy we have found. Then find positive ways to face up to new realities, however intimidating they might seem. Overall, for so many reasons and in so many ways, those processes are no longer fit for purpose. They need to be dispensed with. Yet they remain firmly entrenched.

Recalibrating those zombie orthodoxies is a necessary and exciting prospect. But it is also a formidable one. Can leaders do it? They have to, even though there are plenty of myths about what makes good leaders and what they get wrong.[8]

Hence the urgency of this **Thinking the Unthinkable** analysis and ongoing work.

But trying to do all this by way of a book carries a high risk. In principle, a book captures the spirit and detail of the drop-dead moment when it is submitted, then published. Traditionally that impact is long delayed by months of editing. This means the content can easily be out of date and overtaken by developments. For a project like **Thinking the Unthinkable**, that would be pointless.

So in tune with the high-speed disruptive changes highlighted by Brexit, Trump, Putin and all the findings of our ongoing research so far,[9] we are disruptors too. This book challenges many tenets of publishing. It will have been printed within days of the current text being submitted. It will also be a living digital book. As well as the book there is a dynamic web platform – www.thinkunthink.org – which will be regularly updated as new issues and insights develop or emerge. The platform will also be expanded to reflect what we expect to be the fast-growing leadership community of what we call 'lily pads'.

When reading this book, just like buying a subscription to computer software, you will buy into a living process of Thinking the Unthinkable research, analysis and documentation that is updated by an ever-expanding team. You will be passing frequently through a digital door. Beyond it we expect to reveal the ongoing human impact on top executives of the intense pressures and stresses from the current disruption and resulting turbulence. This is because all the evidence is that the process and realities will become even more troubling. As it analyses unthinkables, our output will be both immediate and at times perhaps rough and ready. Don't always expect perfection, but it will be up to date. And as a result, so will you be.

So we urge that you are not just passive in your reading and engagement.

For leaders: you and your corporate or government institution could be active partners in our living process of research and capacity building on unthinkables. The scale and nature of the problem does not automatically lend itself to a swift, ready-made one-off solution. It is about developing

Joining together for the Leadership challenge . . . ?

what we are labelling a community and a process. The salutary experiences and anxieties of being a leader can be shared. The value of that sharing is already clear. 'It is incredibly cathartic to talk about what isn't working with another CEO,' tweeted one Chief Executive.[10] Then options can evolve. This two-way process will benefit everyone. Into the future you can help us audit experiences, find common factors and then converge all your challenges with the experience of others. All confidences will be respected. If requested, we will of course sign a Non-Disclosure Agreement.

Join us at www.thinkunthink.org. We hope you will.

Please even consider inviting us to hear and share your own C-suite perspectives, anxieties or experiences as others have already done. Please also think how you, and we, can engage the millennials and Generation Z or 3.0 in this process. They hold in their hands the future of organisations like yours. Then their concerns and even resentment of conformity can be reflected in the ongoing iterations of our research. They have a voice and views that are just as important as the leaders already at the top, and arguably more so.

So this **Thinking the Unthinkable** book is a call to arms at a moment of mass, destabilising turbulence for us all. Having detailed in this book the scale and nature of the problem for you, we will analyse and signal what many at the top would hope can be solutions.

Solutions?

Technical problems have technical solutions, of course. But we do not yet see compelling evidence of neat overarching solutions to the many profound problems from disruption that leaders in government, business and the non-government sector confirm they are desperate to find.

Why is that? Is the natural expectation of finding 'solutions' in itself a product of conformity? Is it as conformist as the mindset that causes so much heart-searching for leaders who are having to confront unthinkables?

A doyen of radical strategic thinking believes that is the case. Peter Ho's career path to the top of Singapore's civil service was blooded by embracing the often-uncomfortable implications of risk across government and beyond. We heard him argue that trying to break down today's challenges in the expectation of neat solutions misses the point. Solving what many now describe as 'wicked problems'[11] cannot be achieved in a world of extraordinary uncertainty and change. 'Their causes and influencing factors cannot easily be determined. Furthermore, they have multiple stakeholders who see these problems from different perspectives, and who have divergent goals. This means there are no immediate or obvious solutions, because nobody can agree on what the problems are in the first place, never mind what the solution should be.'[12] Another doyen of the impact of risk on leaders agrees. Ronald Heifetz of Harvard University calls them 'adaptive challenges', 'often murky, systemic problems with no ready answers.'[13]

So while you struggle with disruption and unthinkables, don't be overoptimistic that the solutions are out there somewhere, hidden from your view but ready to be picked like ripe fruit. In the push to embrace unthinkables there has been blossom and some fruit is showing positive signs of ripening well. But tender young fruits are readily blown off the branches by the wind from unexpected storms, meaning there is no crop to harvest. In this world of new disruptions there continue to be plenty of unexpected storms.

So how can you move ahead productively in the search for new insights and possible solutions? We urge you to conceptualise and visualise the challenges of how to think unthinkables in the following way.

Please picture the 3D image of an enormous, limitless pool of water that is dotted with a huge number of lily pads.

You are likely to be one of those lily pads in this infinite ocean of anxiety. Each pad represents a concerned leader or institution of the legacy era, or a frustrated millennial, or a member of the Next Gen.

The surface of the pool soon becomes hidden as the number of lily pads of anxiety multiplies dramatically. This is indicative of the mounting scale of concerned leaders, institutions and millennials who become willing to share their leadership worries about the scale of the unthinkable problem. Soon, the water is no longer visible because it is covered by the proliferation of green pads of concern. You are probably one of them. This lily pad process is designed to share anxieties you have so far been keeping to yourself.

But how to get there? How to build among leaders a consensus on the scale of disruption and options for solutions?

The ride could be as rough as the new torrent of unthinkables emerging all over the place in ways no one ever imagined, let alone predicted, expected or feared. Ask yourself: did you see this scale of disruption and unthinkables coming?

Leaders are struggling. How do we know? We did not just ask them. An extraordinary number of them carved out significant amounts of time from their mad schedules to unburden themselves and tell us. Then they volunteered many more details. We will share with you a good part of what they told us. You will be both astonished and reassured.

Hold on tight.

End notes

[1] 'Woke' was originally African-American slang. The Black Lives Matter movement gave it a new, massive, common, popular conversational profile globally in 2017. For a better understanding of its implications and relevance see 'He's trying to be woke*. Are you? How one word became ubiquitous', The Times 2, 12 March 2018.

[2] 'Zig-zagging toward the future' (2017) by Gregory R Copley, *Defense and Foreign Affairs Strategic Policy* 45 (3) p. 4.

[3] 'Brexit was just the start of a global revolt, IMF warns' by Philip Aldrick, *The Times*, 5 October 2018.

[4] 'The core phrase is from Geoff Mulgan, Chief Executive of NESTA, (National Endowment for Science, Technology and the Arts), in a speech to the ESPAS (European Strategy and Policy Analysis System) conference at the European Commission, Brussels, 16 November 2016.

[5] Interview with Norman Pickavance, CEO of Tomorrow's Company, 6 February 2018.

[6] Speech by Air Chief Marshal Sir Stuart Peach, UK Chief of Defence Staff, Royal United Services Institute (RUSI), 14 December 2017. To watch the video of the event, go to www.thinkunthink. org/digital-footnotes.

[7] Millennials or Generation Y are born after 1980. Generation Z are post-millennials born after 2000.

[8] See for example: *Myths of management: what people get wrong about being the boss* (2017) by Stefan Stern and Cary Cooper. London: Kogan Page.

[9] See www.thinkunthink.org

[10] See the potential for this in the Twitter stream sparked by Ryan Caldbeck, the CEO and co-founder of @CircleUp, 25 March 2018.

[11] Wicked problems are problems that are not easily defined or solved. The term was developed in the 1970s. See: 'Dilemmas in a general theory of planning' (1973) by Horst Rittel and Melvin Webber, *Policy Sciences* 4 (2) pp. 155–169.

[12] Peter Ho, opening remarks to the International Risk Assessment and Horizon Scanning Symposium (IRAHSS 2017), Singapore, 17 July 2017.

[13] 'The work of leadership' by Ronald A Heifetz and Donald L Laurie, *Harvard Business Review* January–February 1997, pp. 124–134.

2
'OUR MAGIC IS FAILING'

This book does not take a view that disruption is bad. After all, history confirms how often 'shit happens' and leaders have read things wrong or made a miscalculation. Nor does it suggest it is wrong to challenge the comfort zone of a political and economic status quo that has benefited many, but which huge numbers of people believe is failing them.

Who can argue against the sudden and welcome disruption created by the #MeToo movement highlighting sexual abuse?

#MeToo was not unthinkable. So please reflect. Would you have been putting this on your priority risk agenda as late as – say – mid 2017? Yet surely it was inevitable that one day the unpalatable truths of long-tolerated sexual abuse would be revealed. In 2017 the shock waves of disgust spread at lightning speed well beyond Harvey Weinstein or Hollywood. Swiftly they burrowed deep into corporate and public life everywhere, plus more widely into the media, schools and religious institutions. Even the Nobel committee in Sweden, which recognises professional distinction in multiple disciplines, was rocked by the unthinkable of resignations. It was 'in a state of crisis'.[14] This was after it emerged that complaints of sexual harassment had been ignored for 20 years.[15] Suddenly the scandal put the future of the Nobel Prize for Literature in doubt.[16] Then extraordinarily, the prize for 2018 was cancelled to 'safeguard the long term reputation of the Nobel Prize'.[17] No longer was it taboo to speak of the appalling scale of abuse, with the fear that careers would be cut short by revealing long hidden truths.

The long-hidden pain and resentments of abused women had found both a voice and profile.[18] Many men at the top had long believed they could exploit their position of power and abuse their victims with impunity. It was unthinkable to them that eventually they would be named or shamed. They were wrong. The result has been the unthinkable of the summary end to their careers and acclaimed status, and the bankrupting of companies and sky-high statuses that most assumed were untouchable. The unthinkable brought them down, sometimes in a matter of minutes in ways they never believed possible. The US veteran comedian Bill Cosby had been super confident as he entered the Pennsylvania courtroom for his retrial on a specimen charge of indecently assaulting a woman. His foul-mouthed outrage after a jury found him guilty[19] epitomised the shock at what to him over decades had been the unthinkable of discovery and one day being held accountable.

#MeToo reinforces our overarching focus, which is clear and broad. It is about culture change. We examine the ability of leaders to handle every kind of impact from disruption, and then the personal and professional trauma that is created for those at the top. There is also the corporate and political cost of such an unthinkable shock. Most leaders are 'myopic, viewing it as a public relations blip that will not alter a firm's operations or its competitive position,' The Economist concluded when it calculated the impact of Facebook's data security crisis on its value long term. Those leaders are wrong. Corporate crises since 2010 'were deeply injurious to the companies' financial health, with the median firm losing 30% of its value since its crisis, compared with a basket of its peers'.[20]

Yet remarkably, the vast majority of people – those conditioned to believe that there is natural entitlement to a better life and improved fortunes – somehow still assume that such upheavals are a blip. They cannot accept there is a new normal that is marked by a profoundly different shape and reality. Somehow they continue to assume that the old normal and a new optimism will return, that fractures will be healed, and value will be restored. They say that cyclical change always happens. They try to find comfort in an 'obsession with patching up the present'[21] in an era of 'deferring risk'.[22]

So they ask: why is it different this time? Why worry? 'The future is not an extension of the past, but a re-invention of everything we have ever been.'[23] And the lessons of history hold little comfort. 'Forces of change release forces of change, which were disastrous. ... The worldview we had is no longer secure. Our magic is failing.'[24]

The new scale of disruption, uncertainty and curve balls means we are enduring an inflection point of massive proportions. All your assumptions about your capacities and skills are at stake. What secured your job and role is being challenged and found wanting. The challenge might easily intimidate and overwhelm. Yet it is also a challenge brimming with those positives and opportunities of the kind that history has long primed us to expect from moments of adversity and 'shit' happening.

The rate of change is not gradual and measured. It is ferocious, rapid, harsh, destabilising and above all unexpected. The moral and institutional compass of good governance and a certain predictability has been imploding. The height of public fashion has been to push back on the established ways of doing politics and business by challenging the system and those who run it. There seems to be a new (if undefined) moral code. Overall 'we have never experienced so many simultaneous tugs at the fabric of everyday life.'[25]

'Normal' in politics and business has not only been questioned and confronted. It has been forced into a somersault, catching out and blindsiding those at the top who assume they have both the wisdom and capacity to know what is coming and what to do about it. After all, surely that is what leaders are elected or appointed to do. They are assumed to be wise, visionary and able to impress with their leadership. Or had the unthinkables been signalled by some who are the more enlightened and farsighted, yet whose views were rejected as too unpalatable or irrational?

Overall, you must assume that the past you believed you understood will not return. There is still progress in many areas. But, 'at the same time we must recognise that in some fundamental ways our world is going backwards,' we heard the UN Secretary General, Antonio Guterres, warn publicly – not just once but twice in one morning, at a meeting on peacebuilding at UN headquarters in New York.[26] He added over lunch that, in his view, disruption the world is currently confronting 'is more difficult than I remember at any stage of my life'.

Secretary General Guterres is one of the few leaders to articulate publicly the potentially overwhelming scale of the changes we are facing. This goes a long way to explain why for so many reasons the new normal is an existential threat to both corporates and systems of government. It is engulfing and destabilising all you assume you understand and have a grip on. 'We are not sure where we are heading. There is a struggle over how to respond' is how we heard one leader confirm the predicament to hundreds of colleagues. 'We suck at confronting the skeletons in our own closet. We are dreadful at it,' said another about the scale of problems.[27] 'We do not have consensus visibility on what we are getting wrong. Our models are inadequate.'

Behind closed doors, we discovered a large number of leaders anguishing privately over the new loneliness and vulnerabilities they were experiencing at the top in these suddenly hyper-turbulent and unstable times of anti-globalisation, populism and nationalism. 'The lifestyle is shit,' said one highly regarded chairman.[28] 'At the top of the organisation you are not normal.'

Another described a 'huge number of balls' to juggle with the constant worry: 'are you going to drop them?' One compared himself to a boiled frog: 'The conformity just boils you. I mean, you just get overweight. And so, the temperature goes up, and up, and up. . . You're reading compliance and regulatory reports, and anything else. . . You lose perspective. You get railroaded into a narrow set of tracks because that's how the game's played. The ability to stand back and think: what if? You know, the broader implications, it's completely . . . You're completely reacting to historical data. You're not anticipating anything of the future. That's why it's become form over substance. You analyse one set of data, which is a reflection on the past, the past month, the past quarter, the past year. Nothing is about anticipating what's coming next.'[29]

So under sometimes-acute pressures from unthinkables, all too often the default is to assume you can return to the way it has been. 'Sooner or later everyone wants or expects their past back.'[30] But they delude themselves. This is not just an era of change; it is 'increasingly a change of era'[31] at a dramatic pace. The direction of travel now must be assumed to be clear and inexorable. It should not conveniently be assumed to be a projection of the recent past.[32] 'The lessons learned from 75 years creating wealth and stability are [being] attacked from all quarters.'[33] There is 'rising intolerance, hate speech, escalating rhetoric, and more and more disregard for the principles and systems we have spent seven decades building up', we heard the President of the UN General Assembly, Foreign Minister Miroslav Lajčák of Slovakia, warn at a UN high level meeting convened to find ways to build peace globally.[34]

It is a time of profound alert: 'All over the world the ghosts of conflict past ... have reappeared in modern but no less vicious or dangerous guise. ... Do not diminish or forget the danger of this moment', warned John Kerry, the former US Secretary of State, 'Do not forget for an instant what happens when fear about economic circumstances is exploited by rank demagoguery and a combination of sectarian, ethnic and religious distortion.'[35] As a result, there is a 'combustive cocktail of challenges that are confounding western leadership' in what is the 'greatest period of global uncertainty since the Cold War's end, and perhaps since World War Two'.[36]

Overall, emboldened by the conformity which got them there, far too many leaders have made the profound and costly error of thinking only they know best. The global push back by populists, demagogues and nationalists against leaders and the establishment is the outcome. Here is a warning from former US President Barack Obama: 'I think a great danger that often befalls leaders is that the people they are supposed to be serving become abstractions. They are not abstractions. And if you don't understand that what you do every day has a profound impact on somebody else, then you should not be there.'[37]

Can leaders' minds, attitudes and behaviour change? The insights of those, like ex-President Obama, just out of office, have consistently been the most valuable and revealing for finding answers to the 'thinking the unthinkable' conundrum. 'It is not just a generational divide. It is about the bias of those who are comfortable with power as it is currently exercised. People get invested in the old ways of doing things, because in part that is where their power has come from,' said Obama, reflecting a year after he left office.[38]

Remarkably, a huge number of leaders indicated to us that they are at least unsettled. Many of them went much further and used the word 'scared'. But in contrast a huge number seem to see no dramatic scenarios unfolding which require equally dramatic action. Indeed, too many don't seem to see this. Here is the former top corporate leader and UK government minister[39] Lord Mark Price: 'We are now petrified at a lot of the things. ... In my limited experience of change management, the one thing that is difficult to do is achieve change when there is no particular burning platform or reason to do it. Yet we now have some serious, potentially existential, threats and other things where Chief Executives are going: "OK, I'm now absolutely petrified.'"

All of us have built-in assumptions that things will conform to what we expect from the present and our recent past. On balance things will just keep getting better because that is what has always happened in recent decades. We assume the upward path of stability, improvement, growth and a general upward progression will…well…just keep happening! The best-selling cognitive psychologist Steven Pinker captures that spirit of unbounded optimism in his new study 'Enlightenment Now'. Every global measure of human flourishing is on the rise, he argues. So, what justifies pessimism? If there are problems, then they can be solved.[40]

But there is an equally powerful counter view emerging. It is that the last 70 years – from World War Two through to the end of the Soviet empire in 1989 and the Soviet Union in 1991, plus what we now know to be the temporary loosening of communist shackles in China[41] – have not been a normal situation. Instead, the growing signs are that they have been disruptions and an aberration or freak of history.

Hence the sober reasons to assume that the waters of instability, rivalry and confrontation are closing in on us. We are enduring a 'world in disarray'[42] where there is a 'crisis of the old order'. There is a 'crisis of small thinking' and 'global irresponsibility' which means global governance has 'catastrophically collapsed'.[43] Europe is even facing the prospect of a 'civil war' between liberal democracy and authoritarianism, the French President Emmanuel Macron has warned. Europe must recommit to democracy. 'I don't want to belong to a generation of sleepwalkers that has forgotten its own past.'[44] The former US Secretary of State Madeleine Albright – herself a refugee from totalitarianism – warns of a new fascism in the 21st century.[45] It is distorting the liberal morals and enabling structures we have assumed we can take for granted.[46] Overall, there are new 'threats to democracy within the democratic system', warns Francis Fukuyama.[47] It is leading to 'illiberal democracy without rule of law, without constraints on executive powers' and a growing number of 'charismatic, anti-institutional leaderships'. It is 'ossifying political correctness' and the problem is 'going to get worse' as skills are eroded, and immigration increasingly becomes 'a dirty word'.[48]

This was already tough stuff. But new threats to democracy have now opened a second flank.

In 2018, evidence suddenly emerged of digital tampering with elections and democratic processes on an industrial scale. This was not just the misuse during the 2016 US Election of vast amounts of private data held by Facebook. It emerged that the data hijacking was probably repeated to some extent in at least Kenya's presidential election in 2017 and other elections such as in Nigeria. It may also have happened in the UK's Brexit referendum in 2016. A whistleblower and data scientist from the company, Cambridge Analytica, at the heart of the allegations, said, 'It makes me so angry. To irrevocably alter the constitutional settlement of this country on fraud is a mutilation of the constitutional settlement.'[49]

In a new study, The Jungle Grows Back, the neoconservative American historian Robert Kagan argues that while 'it has been a democratic era … when democracies appear it is an accident'.[50] The norm we have taken for granted for 70 years 'is in defiance of human nature'. When people feel weak or insecure they are 'prone to want to seek strong leadership'. That is what is happening now: a return to type, a return to geopolitical competition, with potentially 'an almost endless cycle of conflict', especially in Europe and Asia-Pacific. There is a 'pretty profound geopolitical recession'.[51] The established US determination to put right global wrongs has had its day because historically 'it was a big and unusual load to carry. … Normal nations don't have global responsibilities … they have much narrower definitions of their interests.'[52]

So the message is this. Don't take cosy comfort in the belief that on balance the curve of life, opportunity and prospects will just keep rising. It appears we are in the early but dramatic stages of twisting and jerking towards an increasingly uncomfortable downward spiral of increasing shocks.

Are you still holding on tight?

End notes

[14] Press Release from the Swedish Academy, 24 April 2018.

[15] 'Nobel chief quits as anger over sex scandal worsens' by David Charter, *The Times*, 13 April 2018.

[16] 'Nobel literature prize may be postponed after reports that Swedish princess and others were harassed' by Rick Noack, *Washington Post*, 30 April 2018.

[17] 'Nobel literature prize cancelled this year following academy's own #MeToo scandal', *Washington Post*, 4 May 2018.

[18] 'How #MeToo became a global movement' by Pardis Mahdavi, *Foreign Affairs Snapshot*, 6 March 2018.

[19] 'Bill Cosby found guilty of sexual assault in retrial, *BBC News* website, 26 April 2018.

[20] 'Getting a handle on a scandal', Schumpeter column in *The Economist*, 31 March–6 April 2018.

[21] Conversation with Richard Hames, strategic futurist and editor, *The Hames Report*, Melbourne, 30 October 2017.

[22] Conversation with Mike McCallum, foresight practitioner, Melbourne, 30 October 2017.

[23] Presentation by futurist Chris Riddell to The Big Ideas Summit, Melbourne, organised by Procurious, 30 October 2017.

[24] Ian Goldin and Chris Kutarna in a joint presentation about their book *The age of discovery: navigating the risks and rewards of our new renaissance* (2016, London: Bloomsbury), The British Museum, 6 November 2017.

[25] 'In defence of globalism' by John Kerry, former US Secretary of State (2013-17), Ditchley Annual Lecture, 8 July 2017.

[26] Remarks to the UN High Level Meeting on Peacebuilding and Sustaining Peace, UN Headquarters, New York City, 24 April 2018.

[27] Confidential proceedings at the Australian Leadership Retreat, Gold Coast, 18 May 2017.

[28] Sir Peter Gershon at Centre for the Study of Existential Risk seminar at Cambridge University, 5 August 2016.

[29] Private remarks by a newly retired C-suite executive, 13 March 2018.

[30] Gregory R Copley, President of the International Strategic Studies Association, in conversation at Australian Leadership Retreat, Gold Coast, 18 May 2017.

[31] General Sir Nick Carter, Chief of the General Staff (head of the British Army), at his conference of top staff, 12 January 2017.

[32] From remarks at COP23 in Bonn, Germany, on 13 November 2017 by Bertrand Piccard, pilot, innovator and co-inspiration for the Solar Impulse aircraft, which circumnavigated the world fuelled only by solar power 2016-17. The success defied the sceptics who said the challenge was unachievable.

[33] Dominique Moïsi, French political scientist, closed remarks to the Oslo Energy Forum 2018, 14 February 2018. Released by agreement.

[34] Opening speech to the UN High Level Meeting on Peacebuilding and Sustaining Peace, UN Headquarters, New York, 24 April 2018.

[35] op cit. John Kerry, 8 July 2017.

[36] 'Inflection Points' by Fred Kempe, President and CEO of the Atlantic Council, 3 March 2018.

[37] US President Barack Obama, interviewed by Prince Harry, Today, BBC Radio 4, 27 December 2017.

[38] ibid.

[39] Interview on 25 July 2017.

[40] *Enlightenment now: the case for reason, science, humanism and progress* (2018) by Steven Pinker. New York: Allen Lane.

[41] Confirmed by the robust, often uncompromising new tone in President Xi's remarks to the National People's Congress, 20 March 2018.

[42] *World in disarray: American foreign policy and the crisis of the old world order* (2018) by Richard Haas. New York: Penguin.

[43] Robert Legvold, professor emeritus at Columbia University, and Wolfgang Ischinger, chairman of the Munich Security Conference, speaking at the International Forum of the Primakov Institute in Moscow, 30 November 2016.

[44] Speech by President Macron to the European Parliament, Strasbourg, 17 April 2018.

[45] 'Will we stop Trump before it is too late?' by Madeleine Albright, *The New York Times*, 6 April 2018.

[46] *Fascism: a warning* (2018) by Madeleine Albright. New York: Harper Collins.

[47] Francis Fukuyama is Professor of Political Science at Stanford University. Closed remarks to the Oslo Energy Forum 2018, 14 February 2018. Released by agreement.

[48] ibid.

[49] Evidence by Christopher Wylie under parliamentary privilege to the Digital, Culture, Media and Sport Committee of the House of Commons, 27 March 2018.

[50] *The jungle grows back: the case for American power* by Robert Kagan. New York: Knopf. (Publication forthcoming September 2018.)

[51] Recorded remarks by Ian Bremmer, Founder and President of the Eurasia Group, to the ESPAS conference in the European Commission, Brussels, 22 November 2017.

[52] Summary of remarks taken from Robert Kagan's presentation at the Brussels Forum, 8 March 2018. To watch the video of the event, go to www.thinkunthink.org/digital-footnotes.

3
THE NEW WORLD THAT'S 'COMING RIGHT AT ALL OF US'

This book and our research continue to look for what many have urged us to come up with: 'solutions, please, guys!' We have already made clear how difficult that is. But as you will see we have identified some.

'Recognising that the world is changing, and engineering a very complicated systemic change to the basis on which we power our prosperity. That's a very heavy lift,' said Aron Cramer, of Business for Social Responsibility. As a result, so many at the top find it hard to break with what they know and what got them there. 'Too many things are scripted and programmed, and people are not willing to speak up anymore,' Paul Polman, CEO of Unilever, told us.[53]

For all the reasons we list below (and please do share more with us via www.thinkunthink.org), what is needed to address the new nature of disruption and uncertainty must be assumed to be extreme. The need for leadership to embrace them is just as extreme. But so are the obstacles and the creaking mindsets. Hoping against hope cannot be an option.

'What are your solutions?' 'Do you have a framework for me?' The questions keep coming to us from concerned leaders. But to repeat: we don't believe there are neat, easily defined 'solutions'. This conclusion is based on our case studies and the huge number of interviews. Then it comes from our closed-door work rattling the cages of businesses and organisations who invite us to embolden them to first understand then embrace these unthinkable challenges,

No 'solutions' then, at least for the moment. But there is a process of steps which we know can move you and your organisation in the kind of positive, forward direction needed. These steps can be dainty, risk averse and cautious in the style of the fictitious detective Hercule Poirot.[54] Or they can be far bolder in the kind of giant Colossus strides that Shakespeare evoked to describe Julius Caesar.[55] Certainly we recommend that these are more appropriate to the scale and pace of disruption.

Whichever style is chosen, the steps chosen must firstly calibrate the impact of disruption. Then they must offer options for consideration as solutions so that leaders can thrive on change. We call them 'the TTU progressions'. The progressions are a series of five sequential stages through which you and your organisation can travel.

1. **Status quo.** This is the situation most people and businesses find themselves in. Conformity, short-term thinking and other embedded traits of behaviour that we detail in this book stop them from understanding and embracing the scale of the disruption, then what to do about it.

2. **Audit the external reality.** Understand and embrace the new realities of the extraordinary, disrupted world we now live in. This is what has driven the **Thinking the Unthinkable** project, and now this book that captures our work.

3. **Audit the internal reality.** Understand and define frankly the nature and impact of what confronts you as a leader. What behaviour, cultures, mindsets and structures prevent you and your organisation dealing successfully with the new, fast evolving external and internal challenges you face?

4. **Address your challenges.** With a new awareness of the scale of what you face, and the resources available to handle it, discover and scope your own ways to deal with disruption and change. Assess your own abilities to embrace disruption and adapt to it. Be inspired by the details in the case studies we have found and reported for you.

5. **Thrive on change.** There is no one-size-fits-all solution. So through these progressions this process of adaptation must be iterative, loosely structured, flexible and inspiring. It must become a core way through which you and your organisation think and work. As our case studies highlight, the need to be super sensitive and flexible is

of paramount importance. But ask yourself: are you brave enough? Do you have the necessary capacities and skills? Through what we liken to that community of lily pads, you will discover this by staying up-to-date through linking up with like-minded leaders. Via this lily pad community of mutual concerns you will be able to share each others' experiences and learning in real time.

What you read later in our case studies brings together what leaders themselves shared with us after months and sometimes years of experimentation. There is much for you to learn from this that should stiffen your resolve. Like you, they have been following their own often frustrated processes in order to identify and hunt down positives. There have been many false trails and culs de sac. Like them, you will need to dip or plunge your toes into the increasingly hot tar of disruption in order to learn how to adapt and find new approaches. Frequently, good progress has been derailed by new unthinkables! The new world is merciless and unrelenting.

Are you still struggling to accept how profound the impact of disruption is, and will be? To frame the positives and possibilities, let us quote this sobering, up-to-the-minute alert and assessment from Steve Schwarzman. He leads one of the world's largest and most cash-rich companies. He is Chairman and CEO of the Blackstone Private Equity Group, which he founded in 1985. It is now a leading global asset manager worth $434 billion.[56] It owns around 120 companies. It employs up to 600,000 people and is the second- or third-biggest corporation in the US. Schwarzman's personal fortune is said to be $11.2 billion. We heard him give this advice to 3500 of the world's top corporate leaders sitting in a giant gilded hall alongside the Crown Prince of Saudi Arabia.[57] His sage words struck at the heart of the challenge for leaders in both corporates and governments, or those manoeuvring to become one of them.

'There are now no more conventional types of investments. Technology is affecting almost everything we know. … **Nothing remains the same. And this is a warning to all of you who live your lives and think everything is going to be the same the next day. It is changing so fast. … It is happening everywhere.** And we are sending our people in effect back to school so they can learn. ... Even as more conventional investors you have to learn, you have to know or else your children won't be able to inherit businesses that you have. They will be damaged. ... It will not happen if you don't engage and understand the different things that are going to be affecting your life. You can't see those. I am starting to see them. ... **But it is a world that is coming right at all of us. There are big benefits. And there are dangers for not knowing and adapting.**'

Dangers for not knowing and adapting!

You will read shortly that as leaders themselves told us, none have ever got everything right. Most have travelled down those dead-end streets, sometimes with a high cost due to excessive optimism and expectations. At least they have tried. In doing so they have created a new resilience. They have stiffened institutional spines for the inevitability of unthinkables hitting them from left field or right field. They have established the urgency for a new, embedded culture of change. Universally the risks and setbacks have been worth it under the principle 'nothing ventured, nothing gained'.

Is there a greater willingness to show that new courage and humility? 'We are seeing the rise of the new "humble CEO" – someone who talks about "we" rather than "I",' one leading Chairman told our study. Patricia Seemann agrees. She founded the 3am Group. It advises CEOs who are willing to air their new anxieties that – as the name suggests – keep them awake at night.[58] 'There are now some leaders who admit they do not have all the answers and are asking "Do I get the right set of skills capabilities, to come up with a couple of solutions that we can try out and see what works?" But we do not have a workforce who knows how to "follow" such leaders – with some exceptions. It is not that they are stupid; they have been beaten into that mould since the dawn of industrialisation.'

That is the troubling question: how to break the armlock created by the cost of challenging conformity and risk aversion. Our tracking down of examples has revealed important possibilities.

The imperative for new will, speed, agility and a positive attitude to risk is paramount, whether in corporates or governments. Both face the same superhuman challenge. 'The demands of frankness and honesty here are austere,' said Professor Michael Ignatieff.[59] 'Careerists and "yes men" who are not warning their ministers are not doing their job. But the penalties for "Chicken Little, the sky is falling"[60] – and then it not happening – are huge. So our systems reward "Keep calm, don't make a crisis." Our systems don't reward Cassandras. Our systems don't reward whistleblowers. Our systems punish them. Our systems don't reward people who say, "This could be much worse than you imagine."'

In those words Ignatieff confirms the imposing nature of the cliff face of disruption to be climbed. One former official revealed the scale of the dilemma. 'There is a fine line to be trodden – and I was very conscious of this when I was [job title redacted] – between saying the difficult things (but have an impact because they make people think differently) and just saying it so often and so wildly in areas that they're not going to be able to do anything about that you just lose credibility because you're banging on again, like Cassandra, about things that there is no capacity, resource, will or political willingness to do.'

Our search for examples of solutions was driven by significant evidence of caution and greater concern about taking responsibility. The fear of making a CLM – a career-limiting move – was cited time and again as a massive psychological swerve for those below the leadership level to negotiate. If they dare, how can leaders inspire those who work for them to reverse this totally justifiable fear? This prompted the question we now address to all of you. How can you put in place a newly energised determination to overcome the default to the bureaucratic imperative of 'managerialism' when you are being 'demotivated' and 'do not feel empowered'?

Many have described how what was once inspirational leadership acting on insight and vision has been replaced by that 'managerialism'. Where is the space for the maverick? Why are those with ideas which are regarded by conformist minds as 'wacky' not given air, space and encouragement? After all, there is a good chance that they could be right!

Why all these suspicions and negatives?

Managerialism has in too many cases taken precedence over what should be the political priorities for understanding and action. This is especially true within public and government service.[61] It constrains clarity of analysis. In turn this handicaps the radical thinking needed for action. In governments this is compounded by acute strains from multiple pressures, including austerity and spending cuts. Ever-tighter budget restrictions constrain the ability to think the unthinkable too. These cash-strapped ministries in particular are no longer equipped to handle the scale of multiple disruptive threats to their operational effectiveness with the kind of capacity, insight and commitment needed.

Which means we turn to that ugly but important word invented by one senior public sector insider: 'de-responsibilisation'. Too many shared with us how 'de-responsibilisation' heightens fears that the personal cost of standing ground on facts and arguments is real, and therefore a big limiter for first imagining then tabling any unthinkables. This helps us to understand how risk-taking is discouraged. It stops dead the airing of what some view as the kind of maverick but well-informed analysis that is required to identify unthinkables. 'This blame culture ... has gone to the top,' said a Whitehall observer. 'This helps to explain why, increasingly, civil servants see it as career-limiting to be seen to go off-piste,' explained one top business leader who has previously been a key player in civil service reform. Ngaire Woods, Dean of the Blavatnik School of Government at Oxford University, told us: 'If you're asked to write a policy brief, and you know that the minister's not really going to read it, and that the minister's actually asked his or her advisors to write a brief that's more likely [to get a hearing], how much effort are you going to make on your own policy brief? You tell me!'[62]

These are big hurdles. But what follows are examples we have found of how they can be jumped with inspirational vigour and determination, both for the highest C-suite[63] levels and – just as important – the Next Gen levels.

The barriers to the profound changes needed in mindset, culture and behaviour were openly crystallised for us by Lord Mark Price. He was in business for 33 years. He rose to become managing director of the supermarket giant Waitrose. He left the John Lewis Group as Deputy Chairman in 2016. Then for 17 months he was Minister for Trade and Investment in the UK government. He is now a prolific author and commentator and campaigner for change in the workplace.[64] Now he can speak without corporate or government restrictions on what stands in the way of leaders doing what is needed to recalibrate leadership.

'It's about turning a whole company on its head and saying the answers are with our people, not with our management. … [But] people that are running our big companies have given their heart and soul for decades to get to that position. And once they have got there, their instinct is to preserve the status quo. It's human to want to do that,' Lord Price told us.[65] 'Where they are struggling is they can't make their numbers add up any more. I think that's causing them real angst. … CEOs are really struggling for an answer to the challenges of squeezed profitability and they are all opting for faster horses. … I think they're getting an increasing amount of pressure. [In the UK] they have a pressure to deal with Brexit. They have a pressure to deal with shareholders and profitable returns. They've got a pressure from government saying that the system we have got isn't working. They have a pressure from their workers who are saying this doesn't feel fair to us. So they are managing multiple pressures and they are really struggling to find an answer for it. That is their challenge. If they had a more-engaged business they should be turning to the workers and saying, "Look, we have got some challenges here. How can we work through this together?" But they can't do that, so what they will feel is a sense of isolation.'

Lord Price says inclusive leadership and management is still alien to most organisations. Management attitudes are rigid. They obstruct instead of empowering and emboldening. 'That's what's happening in business, you know. This is our plan. This is your part of the plan. This is what you will do. It's almost that military element that is coming into business where – if you are fighting a battle in the Second World War – frankly you don't want your soldiers doing whatever they fancy. You want them to get stuck in … [But] you have to get all of your stakeholders involved and say what is fair and acceptable.'

Are leaders – are you – willing to be this brave? Maybe! Or at least we have recently heard increasing numbers of you start talking as if you are. But don't linger and procrastinate. Time is not on your side. Shareholders, the high-net-worth investors, the employees, contractors, voters and stakeholders are all starting to show anxiety, and if necessary a determination to show their displeasure by swiftly withdrawing their money or switching their votes. And like so many unthinkables, as with #MeToo's dramatic revelations on sexual abuse or Facebook's disaster with revelations of huge data breaches, the guillotine of public patience can fall amazingly fast. Confidence can vaporise with devastating consequences in days, hours or even minutes. Clawing back confidence can then take on Everest-like proportions. And on that mountain many ill-prepared or unlucky climbers have perished.

Do you have the steel for this?

'We're stuck in a mindset in which you still think that – even if we did think straight – we would have the capability to deal with it,' admitted one former senior government official with a hint of despondency. Others said the same thing, albeit expressed differently. Paul Polman, the CEO of Unilever, said: 'So first you have to find your inner compass, what you're strong about. If that is so important, you'll be able to take more risks. And we have become risk-averse.'[66]

Are you still on board and holding tight?

End notes

[53] Paul Polman, interview, 6 July 2015.

[54] The cautious gait of Hercule Poirot – the fussy, meticulous Belgian detective invented by the crime writer Agatha Christie – has been made famous by the actor David Suchet in the *Poirot* TV films.

[55] 'Why, man, he doth bestride the narrow world / Like a Colossus, and we petty men / Walk under his huge legs and peep about', *Julius Caesar* by William Shakespeare. 1.2:226–228.

[56] Value as at 31 December 2017.

[57] Remarks at 'Future Investment Initiative' in Riyadh, 25 October 2017.

[58] www.the3amgroup.org/

[59] Michael Ignatieff was Professor of Practice at Harvard University at the time of the interview; 14 April 2015.

[60] *Chicken Little* is an old European folk tale about the risks of warning of an approaching calamity, real or imagined. In 2005, it was made into a film by Walt Disney Feature Animations.

[61] Interview with Professor Chris Donnelly, Director of the Institute for Statecraft, 6 July 2015.

[62] Interview, 21 April 2015.

[63] C-suite describes the cluster of top officers in an organisation whose titles include 'chief'. For example, Chief Executive Officer (CEO), Chief Operations Officer (COO), Chief Financial Officer (CFO).

[64] *Fairness for all* (2017) by Mark Price. Oxford: Stour Publishing.

[65] Interview on 25 July 2017.

[66] op cit. Paul Polman, 6 July 2015.

4
BLACK SWANS, BLACK ELEPHANTS AND BLACK JELLYFISH

Let's pause for a reality check. What is an unthinkable? It has dictionary definitions. It is 'beyond the scope of thought' or 'incapable of being framed or grasped by thought'.[67] In other words, no! Unthinkables can't be thought about!

But we argue that they still need to be.

That definition certainly fits the impression left by events and the associated non-actions which were revealed when we started asking questions. The project title Thinking the Unthinkable was inspired by Herman Kahn's thought experiment from 1962 and beyond on the possibilities for nuclear war.[68] That was the year when the world went to the nuclear brink during the Cuban missile crisis. The prospect seemed unthinkable and beyond comprehension. But it was stark and real.

Why had the possibility of events during and after 2014 apparently not even been thought about by those at the top, or those working for them? Were the unthinkable events really so unthinkable? Why were risk registers so narrow and limited? Or was this a failure of imagination, will, courage, insight and above all process? Our conclusion is that it is all of those and many more. Those events could have been foreseen. For all of them there was evidence of what was coming down the track. But for whatever reasons it was either denied or rejected.

This is why the phrase 'thinking the unpalatable' is probably more appropriate for much that we write about. 'Unpalatable' is defined by the Oxford English Dictionary as 'unpleasant, distasteful, disagreeable'.[69] This well describes something that it is known about, but too risky or dangerous or unattractive to think about or engage with.

It is this that creates the urgent human imperative for profound self-examination by the leadership class which this book and process are about. Because of so many pressures their minds are framed too narrowly, based on their experiences and the past. But both have routinely been overtaken by massive new realities and the new normal.

The frequent self-justification sounds more like an excuse than an explanation. It goes something like this: 'Well we did not see it coming.' It was a surprise. It was a Black Swan. Or a Black Elephant. Or even a Black Jellyfish, they said.

Black swans don't exist in the real world, except in Australia and New Zealand. Hence the global association with unthinkables. 'Black Swans' are events or developments which 'we don't realise that we don't realise'.[70] Yet they occur with ever-increasing regularity and high global visibility. They are, indeed, what the former US Defense Secretary Donald Rumsfeld memorably referred to as 'unknown unknowns.' Among interviewees there were different views as to whether such 'unthinkables,' 'Black Swans' or 'unknown unknowns' can ever be thought about and predicted. That is especially if, by their very nature, they occur due to either strategic calculation or miscalculation by others.

'Black Elephants' are usually well known and present 'in the room,' wherever and whatever that is defined as.[71] They are 'known unknowns' in Rumsfeld-speak. Why an elephant as opposed to a black dog, cat, mouse or squirrel? Because an elephant is too big and therefore too obvious to miss. So how can something so enormous and visible be ignored, discounted, bypassed or not reported up the line? This is despite it being logged, present and known about because 'one day it might have enormous Black Swan consequences'.

The concept of 'Black Elephants' helps explain why a significant number of interviewees – especially those from public service – suggested that the phrase 'thinking the unpalatable' is more appropriate for confronting what they face. The Black Elephant is in the room, but it is ignored or 'not seen' by those who should know better. It defines with greater precision why abnormal developments have been ignored or not taken into account in the way events require.

Finally come the 'Black Jellyfish'. They seem to be a recent additional creation of fertile minds within NATO. It is 'all about scale'. Black Jellyfish are 'simultaneous, predictable developments causing disruption when [they] converge through innovation'.[72]

What must be understood most urgently are the failings of modern leadership and current management culture to grip this world of black creatures that is changing so dramatically fast. Black Swans are flying around out there; Black Elephants have their giant trunks wrapped around institutional processes; and Black Jellyfish are lurking ready to emit their toxins to generate a painful and surprise sting. What makes it so hard for leaders to think the unthinkable (or the unpalatable) and just accept without question the sinister threats from these animals with the darkest of appearances?

Peter Ho says 'the Black Swan reminds us that we will be surprised from time to time. And sometimes that surprise is strategic and game changing. The Black Elephant and the poor frog in boiling water tells us that, even if we can somehow reduce the complexity of our operating environment and locate the Black Swans, we can still be shocked and surprised. [This is] because of our cognitive biases.'[73]

In what is fast becoming a new disruptive age of digital public empowerment, big data and metadata, leadership finds it hard to recognise these failings, let alone find answers and solutions. The challenges are sharpened by the frustrations and instinctive over-the-horizon vision of millennials. They centre on the appropriateness and configuration of management systems, plus the human capacity of those at the highest levels to both cope with, and respond to, 'unthinkables'. This is because most organisations are increasingly afflicted by a 'frozen middle' that 'lacks muscle' and has little scope to risk addressing the scale of the 'wicked problems' and 'strategic gap'.

These are frailties that large numbers of executives do not want to admit to publicly, even to their fellow C-suite executives or their board. This is why there is a disconnect that makes even more problematic and unlikely the business of first identifying unthinkables and then taking action to prevent or pre-empt them.

End notes

[67] *The Shorter Oxford English Dictionary* (1970) London: Oxford University Press, p. 2315.

[68] *Thinking about the unthinkable in the 1980s* (1984) by Herman Kahn. New York: Simon and Schuster. It revisited Kahn's classic 'thought experiment' on nuclear war, *Thinking about the unthinkable* (1962) New York: Horizon Press. Kahn's work partly inspired the eccentric character Dr Strangelove, who was made infamous by Peter Sellers in the movie of the same name.

[69] op cit. *The Shorter Oxford English Dictionary*, p. 2309.

[70] Adapted from the Black Swan principle identified by Nasim Nicholas Taleb in his book *The black swan: the impact of the highly improbable* (2007) London: Allen Lane.

[71] The term was borrowed by *The New York Times* columnist Thomas Friedman from environmentalist Adam Sweidan. He is the Chief Investment Officer of Aurum Fund Management Ltd.

[72] Mehmet Kinaci, NATO Strategic Foresight Analysis Team, presentation to ESPAS conference at the European Commission, Brussels, 16 November 2016.

[73] Opening presentation to the International Risk Assessment and Horizon Scanning Symposium (IRAHSS), Singapore, 17 July 2017.

5
THE 'GREAT WAKEUP' AND A 'NEW WARTIME'

'The rate of change we are going through at the moment is comparable to that which happens in wartime. We have change at war rates, yet we think we are at peace. The global pace of change is overcoming the capacity of national and international institutions.'

Chris Donnelly, Director, Institute for Statecraft.[74]

Let's pause. How did we all get here? What led to this book with its converging of the evidence of how much the new disruptions are scaring leaders, its search for solutions, and its call to arms?

Why Thinking the Unthinkable?

That certainly fits the impression left by events and the associated non-actions which were revealed when we started asking questions. Unthinkables are proliferating in ways that few seem able to contemplate. Hence the appropriateness of the title to this project. Why had the possibility of events during and after 2014 apparently not even been thought about by those at the top, or those working for them? Were the unthinkable events really so unthinkable? Why were risk registers so narrow and limited? Or was this a failure of imagination, will, courage, insight and above all process? Our conclusion is that it is all of those and many more.

Our project started unexpectedly and tentatively in early 2014 during a conversation over a flat white coffee. 2014 was turning into the year of 'the great wake up'.[75] The label came from a dramatic set of new strategic global ruptures. It was becoming a watershed period where 'the old assumptions for making decisions are behind us'. In quick succession, crises of an unforeseen nature and scale were breaking out.

President Putin had engaged Russian forces in a sinister armed campaign of subversion in eastern Ukraine, a sovereign state bordering the European Union. Then Russia seized Crimea, which was a part of Ukraine. Such interventions in violation of international law seemed unthinkable. How had the EU, NATO and their member nations been so blindsided and wrong-footed? How had Putin managed to mislead and even deceive some of the world's most sophisticated intelligence-gathering capabilities?

Then followed a progression of what seemed like more unthinkable events. The world was being increasingly inverted by a whole series of challenges to normality.

2014 saw the rise of so-called Islamic State – apparently from nowhere – to create a digital caliphate. Then came the devastating outbreak of Ebola – the World Health Organisation rejected unthinkable warnings from Médecins Sans Frontières staff in Guinea that the disease would decimate West Africa.[76] Eleven thousand people died. Saudi Arabia suddenly slashed oil prices by 60% to try to crush low-cost oil production like shale. China strengthened its seizure of tiny islands in the South China Sea to extend its territorial influence. Sony Pictures endured a major cyber breach that targeted a new comedy movie about North Korea. Sony Pictures executives had never conceived of this unthinkable of a state-sponsored digital hack against intellectual property which a nation state did not like.[77]

The pace did not relent. It intensified. Unthinkable events continued through 2015, 2016 2017 and then into 2018.

In 2015 they were led in impact by the sudden human tsunami of refugees and migrants into Europe from Africa, Asia and the Middle East. Europe flunked its handling of a crisis which for two years the UN and International Organisation for Migration had warned was looming. This created existential threats to the EU.[78] By late 2016 even the very survival of the European Union was thought to be at risk.[79] The Commission's First Vice President, Frans Timmermans, confirmed that the EU had been 'to the brink'.[80] This was because of the political failure to embrace the apparent unthinkable of the massive migration flows which overwhelmed parts of Europe in 2015. Then came the political exploitation of public anger by newly confident radical and nationalist forces in many of the 28 member states.

Much that had always seemed assured and in place after 70 years of painstaking post World War Two construction was either wobbling or disappearing. 'The model that has dominated geopolitical affairs for more than 70 years appears increasingly fragile. Its tenets are being challenged by a surge of nationalism and its institutions are under assault from some of the very powers that constructed them — not least, the United States under President Trump.'[81]

As a result, confidence was falling. To many it seemed unreal, and most could neither explain nor understand what was unfolding.

At the start of 2016, the uncertainty created by 'unthinkables' reached ever-greater depths. Prices of oil and commodities kept tumbling. The failure of China's leadership to grip and halt the giant nation's economic slowdown catalysed the New Year downturn in global stock markets. Phrases like 'a dangerous cocktail of new threats'[82] captured the pervading mood of global fear and new, uncharted uncertainties. One well-regarded, soccer-loving hedge fund manager was in a small minority prepared to confront the scale of unthinkables. He announced to his investors in December 2015 that his fund was returning their money to them. He said that he and his team were determined to 'walk away from the pitch with our legs intact, rather than play on and risk having them broken in a bad tackle we didn't see coming.'[83] And what about the once unthinkable in the United States: the potential election of President Donald Trump?

The emerging picture was both scary and of great concern. We captured the impact of disruption at a closed door C-suite event for the consultants Deloitte in June 2016.[84] But few leaders seemed to grip the true scale, let alone have even the first clue as to what was taking place. There was a deep reluctance – an executive myopia[85] – to contemplate even the possibility that 'unthinkables' were embedding profound change, let alone how to handle them.

A mood of despair at the end of 2016 led to a sharp (if tongue in cheek), fast book, *F*ck You, 2016: A Look Back on the Worst Year Ever*. Given the deep horrors and tens of millions of deaths in World Wars One and Two, including the use of nuclear weapons, the title was way over the top. But it reflected a deep sense of anxiety. It paid homage to a 'year of unparalleled cockhattery, fuckmuppetry and shitcombobulating world events'.[86] It asked: 'it can't get any worse can it?' As the weeks of deepening disruption progressed, so did the sense of 'what the fuck is happening?'. Another far more measured and thoughtful analysis reflected this mood.[87]

And throughout this period, Russia's activities were becoming ever-more assertive and sinister. Yet leaders could only belatedly piece together the implications of what was unfolding. Finland, for example, had 'slumbered for 15-20 years'. Then Russian military activity intensified and 'we saw black clouds on the horizon'.[88] The Baltic states started experiencing 'years of harassment'. One or two 'accidental' violations of airspace became fifty in one year. These were 'not accidents: pilots showed they were doing it on purpose with international finger signs'. To this day, Finland is haunted by the Winter War with Russia in 1939–40, when it lost many thousands of soldiers killed and injured. Now there seemed to be a sombre return to old suspicions and mistrust. 'We have been there. We don't want to be there again. But [now] we have to be prepared.'

In parallel came the unexplained unthinkable of cyber-penetration of the US Democratic party during the 2016 election. There was fast-growing evidence of ever-bigger levels of e-infiltration in election processes in several countries.

Simultaneously, confidence in corporate values was being severely challenged. The credibility of the huge German automaker VW was shattered by the defeat device system which had been designed by its own engineers to mislead environmental inspectors over the true levels of diesel emissions. It was a 'criminal conspiracy'[89] born of 'VW's culture such that immoral behaviour became acceptable'.[90] VW ignored lessons in morality from the 2008 financial crash. The corporate deceit that new diesel engines were 'clean'[91] started not just a backlash against diesel. It hastened the demise of vehicles fuelled by carbon, with the additional challenge from Tesla and battery-driven vehicles.[92] The unthinkable of the end to the massive corporate bet on cars fuelled by petrol and diesel was suddenly being catapulted forward.[93][94]

Then came financial scandals like the creation of a huge number of ghost accounts at Wells Fargo bank, which was still costing billions of dollars in regulatory fines 18 months later.[95] There were heavy fines for other banks for violating ever-tighter regulations. The consulting giant McKinsey faced the unthinkable of paying back fees in South Africa. It admitted 'several errors of judgement' after being implicated in a scandal which involved the then-president Jacob Zuma, the state power utility Eskom and the Gupta brothers.[96] But they could not find anyone to return the fees to! At a time of allegedly shady business dealings by others, McKinsey had 'looked the other way for money'. It had made $73 million from one deal in nine months in 2016.[97]

Simultaneously, Deutsche Bank had been plummeting from being the world's biggest bank in 2007 to talk of a bail-out in 2016 and acting in a way which was 'only semi legal'.[98] Deutsche had been fined $55 million for false accounting after stock was grossly overvalued. The new CEO John Cryan 'brought people down to earth from too much hype'. But it ultimately it cost him his job two years later.[99] In 2018 came the sudden advertiser backlash against the 'wild west free for all'[100] by giant tech companies like Facebook and Google. They faced the unthinkable of being found to be abusing customer data and making large amounts of money from adverts linked to the streaming of vile content like child pornography and graphic violence of many kinds.

Together, events like these – and many more – did finally set alarm bells ringing for most leaders. They would swiftly generate and build momentum for a project that soon consumed our focus with an intensity that was not just 24/7, but 25/8. It is now 26/9 because of the scale and proliferation of unthinkables.

Such violations of norms could have been a simply a momentary blip of opportunism. As the weeks passed, it was clear they were not.

End notes

[74] For his detailed argument see 'Rapid reaction force for success' by Chris Donnelly, *The World Today*, June & July 2016.

[75] Interview with Carl Bildt, former Swedish Prime Minister and Foreign Minister, 20 April 2015.

[76] *Pushed to the limit and beyond*, Médecins Sans Frontières, 19 March 2015.

[77] Confirmed to this project in February 2018 by a former senior Sony Pictures executive in Hollywood.

[78] Manuel Valls, the then Prime Minister of France, at the World Economic Forum in Davos, 22 January 2016.

[79] Confirmed at a private dinner with senior European Commission officials, Brussels, 16 November 2016.

[80] '(E)U are my destiny' by Frans Timmermans, *Bled Strategic Times*, September 2017, and then on the conference platform, 4 September 2017. To watch the video of the event, go to www.thinkunthink.org/digital-footnotes.

[81] 'The post World War Two order is under threat from the powers that built it' by Peter S Goodman, *The New York Times*, 26 March 2018.

[82] George Osborne, the then UK Chancellor of the Exchequer, in Cardiff, 7 January 2016.

[83] Martin Taylor confirming Nevsky Capital's closure, 6 January 2016.

[84] Deloitte thought leadership brainstorming, 'Thinking the unthinkable: facing the new leadership challenge', 7 June 2016.

[85] 'The short long', speech by Andrew Haldane and Richard Davies to 29th Société Universitaire Européene de Recherches Financières Colloquium: New Paradigms in Money and Finance?, Brussels, May 2011.

[86] *F*ck you, 2016* by 'Bob A N Grypants'. London: Michael Joseph.

[87] *WTF* (2017) by Robert Peston. London: Hodder and Stoughton.

[88] Remarks to conference on 'Europe's strategic choices', hosted by Chatham House and the Institute for Security Policy at the University of Kiel, Berlin, 7 December 2017.

[89] 'Volkswagen, the car maker that sees no evil, loses its moral compass' by Tony Allen-Mills, *The Sunday Times*, 4 February 2018. Also 'Diesel cars built to cheat test for toxic fumes' by Jonathan Leake, *The Sunday Times*, 21 September 2014.

[90] 'The Volkswagen scandal shows that corporate culture matters' by Robert Armstrong, Financial Times, 13 January 2017.

[91] See *Faster, higher, farther: the inside story of the Volkswagen scandal* (2017) by Jack Ewing. New York: W W Norton. Also *Leadership lessons from the Volkswagen saga* (2017) by Steven Howard. Palm Springs: Caliente Press.

[92] 'Germany's car industry suffers a Tesla shock' by John Gapper, *Financial Times*, 3 August 2017.

[93] 'A change of direction key for German automakers: ministers cannot shield companies from their diesel difficulties', editorial, *Financial Times*, 3 August 2017.

[94] ESPAS Forum at the European Commission, 22 November 2017. Also 'Dodgy diesels and changing tastes do not bode well for car sales' by Neil Collins, *Financial Times*, 11 November 2017.

[95] 'Wells re-elects board amid criticism' by Emily Glazer, *The Wall Street Journal*, 25 April 2018.

[96] 'McKinsey admits to South Africa errors' by Joseph Cotterill, *Financial Times*, 17 October 2017.

[97] 'McKinsey has closed its eyes in South Africa' by John Gapper, *Financial Times*, 21 September 2017.

[98] 'Deutsche's big gamble – how a sleepy German bank bet on the world – and lost' by Patrick Jenkins and Laura Noonan, *FT Weekend Magazine*, 11/12 November 2017.

[99] 'Deutsche Bank sacks British boss John Cryan after years of losses,' *BBC News* website, 9 April 2018.

[100] Remarks by Matt Hancock, UK Secretary of State for Digital, Culture, Media and Sport, *Today*, BBC Radio 4, 22 March 2018.

6
THINKING THE UNTHINKABLE: WHY US?

We don't claim to be leadership experts or gurus. We are not business professors. We have dipped into only a tiny percentage of the tens of thousands of books on leadership. Instead we followed our decades of research and global analytical instincts. In 2014 they told us that something extraordinary was unravelling in our world. But what was it? And why?

Nik had just decided to step aside after 35 years as a high-profile news broadcaster with ITN then the BBC. His career was consumed by presenting, reporting and monitoring the achievements – but usually the horrors – of geopolitical change. It started in the stressed, often poor industrial communities of Tyneside and Merseyside in northern England. Then from 1980 it moved to reporting the drama of Solidarity's challenge to communism in Poland and the wider upheavals behind the Iron Curtain which brought down communism. Next came the war in Yugoslavia, change in China, plus the improving atmospherics between East and West.

Chris had a career watching and chronicling similar extraordinary political earthquakes with the fall of the Berlin Wall as a television producer in news and current affairs. Then he brokered closed-door conferences at the Wilton Park conference centre, co-creating new thinking on cutting-edge global affairs for 11 years, before heading the independent NGO, Oxford Research Group. His professional passion is how to foster reconciliation in global trouble spots through the use of video and other media.

Through 2014 and 2015 we both watched and logged how leaderships at many levels and in many different milieux were being wrong-footed.

We saw conformist executive mindsets being caught out by events they never imagined they might one day have to confront. As a result, they were being accused of failing in their responsibilities. Even worse, public opinion was fast becoming unforgiving.

So we asked ourselves the question: was this a weird blip, or evidence of a profound new trend? We describe our interview process later. We also followed up the issue in a great number of bar stool chats and coffee shop conversations with our good contacts inside companies and governments. Were they being unnerved and destabilised? 'Yes.' It was clear that was happening. Were leaders and leaderships adequately equipped to cope with this level of upheaval, disruption and challenge to the assumptions that helped get them to the top? Our contacts told us that 'No' they weren't.

So we asked: if not, why not? Do they have the human capacity to appreciate firstly the scale of disruption and unthinkables, then to make the profound readjustments that are needed? This human frailty of leadership at times of acute stress or change is not new.[101] But that does not excuse the ongoing inability of so many at the top to handle the latest upheavals currently underway.

Our instincts in 2014 and 2015 were spot on. Our resulting interim analysis of our early interview data then rattled cages and rocked boats. As we prepared it for publication we confronted deep conformist resentment at what our findings had uncovered about leadership's failings. Many would have preferred them to be shelved. Inevitably the pushback came from leaders themselves, those representing them, the business schools who realised we were challenging their curricula and any other vested interest which was determined to maintain the relative comfort of conformity. There was a view that we had found ways to use interviews with leaders selectively to say what we ourselves were determined to say. It was suggested that we had led them on, rather than getting them to voluntarily reveal the scale of anxiety they privately felt.

Faced with such suggestions it became a lonely struggle against many forces of conformity. We fought on, having to think and confront our own unthinkables. Months earlier, the Chartered Institute of

Management Accountants (CIMA) had kindly offered to publish our interim findings. They too could not believe what our interviews and research had uncovered. For several months they had a vigorous internal debate on whether to publish them. CIMA only did so after their own Executive Director of Education Noel Tagoe took his own risk in defying sometimes-significant internal resistance at the highest levels. He persuaded them to end their suspicions. He told CIMA executives they had to open their own eyes to our new evidence. They had become a hostage to their own mindsets. Noel won through. 'I commend the report to you without hesitation for its relevance, rigour and potential to impact how we deal with the systemic and unparalleled challenge facing leadership in the 21st century,' Noel wrote in the foreword of the findings' eventual publication in February 2016.[102] Thank you, Noel.

This interim analysis of a huge amount of data from top-level interviews led us to anticipate in an article published on 1 June 2016 that a majority of voters in the UK would vote for Brexit.[103] This was even though almost none of those voters would appreciate that a vote to leave the EU meant at least 759 agreements with 168 countries having to be renegotiated 'just for Britain to stand still'.[104] In the event, it was more than a rejection of the EU. It was an expression of widespread and deeply held public resentment against the system. But political and corporate leaderships simply did not get this. In that lead cover article for the World Today published by Chatham House 23 days before the referendum we also warned of the likely nomination – then election – of Donald Trump as US president.

Then four days before Theresa May's disastrous election result in June 2017, Nik was invited to brief 26 chairs and CEOs on our updated **Thinking the Unthinkable** findings at a smart lunch hosted by a major consulting firm. 'What will the election result be?' was one question. Press coverage in the UK was almost universally urging a vote for the Conservatives. The Labour leader Jeremy Corbyn should be consigned to the 'Cor-bin', yelled one Tory newspaper with a photo-shopped image of him in a dustbin across the front page.[105] We predicted a brutal turn against Mrs May and the Tories, a high turnout of the next generation, and then many who disliked the Tories and the UK's departure from the EU voting for Labour. This was even though many had doubts about Corbyn himself. The response from those top executives around the table was questioning. It did not fit with what they were reading. For Nik it left the impression that they thought he 'had been smoking something'. The analysis defied the predominant mood of the polls and media commentators. But it was right. Far too many had made conformist assumptions and were not prepared to think unthinkables which did not fit their mindsets.

On Brexit, Trump, and much more, our data, collected from leaders themselves, told the story. It defied conformity and orthodoxy which instinctively believed something different. That, after all, is what most minds are tuned to. It also flagged that 'what many viewed as outlandish unthinkables were not even being considered or investigated as part of corporate or political risk assessments. Now they have to be.'[106]

End notes

[101] See for example *The seventh enemy: the human factor in the global crisis* (1978) by Ronald Higgins. London: McGraw-Hill.

[102] *Thinking the unthinkable: a new imperative for leadership in the digital age* (2016) by Nik Gowing and Chris Langdon. London: CIMA.

[103] 'Want to lead? Then tear up the rule book' by Nik Gowing and Chris Langdon, *The World Today*, June & July 2016. Our findings had been first published in Germany: 'Das Undenkbare denken: Politik und Wirtschaft haben sich fundamentalen Änderungen anzupassen' by Nik Gowing and Chris Langdon, *Internationale Politik* 1, January/February 2016, pp. 8–13.

[104] 'Let the haggling begin' by Paul McClean, *Financial Times*, 31 May 2017.

[105] 'Don't chuck Britain in the Cor-bin', *The Sun*, 7 June 2017.

[106] op cit. 'Want to lead? Then tear up the rule book', Nik Gowing and Chris Langdon.

7
'ASKING A TRACK ATHLETE TO BECOME A WRESTLER'

So how are you coping? Do you have a grip on the apparently topsy-turvy scale of the combative cocktail of challenges, plus what is happening and why? Have you battened down for a turbulent journey through potentially mountainous seas compared to what you have experienced on your career path so far? Are you even prepared to contemplate that society around you is not as stable and guaranteed as you assumed? That society is 'wafer thin', requiring a 'gear change from where you are to where you need to be' because 'instability is the norm in all sectors'?[107]

Early signs of a hollowing out of society and the middle class are already there. The pace is quickening.

Traditionally people assume there is a societal contract. It works because 'everyone puts in and everyone takes out'. But now 'that contract is under threat, with widespread concern that young adults may not achieve the progress their predecessors enjoyed ... Pessimism is most marked in relation to the key economic aspects of living standards – housing, work and pensions', said the UK's Intergenerational Commission on May 8 2018 in its final report on 'A New Generational Contract'.[108] Within 48 hours, the British telecom giant BT was announcing the end of 13,000 back office and middle management jobs.[109]

These new sobering realities and dynamics go way beyond the important economic ideas and optimism promoted by Professor Klaus Schwab in his concept of a Fourth Industrial Revolution.[110] The issues are far broader and potentially more sinister. The reverberations are societal, with enormous implications for how leaders in governments and corporates handle the resulting societal disruption – that is if they are mentally prepared to confront and admit them. A new fragility threatens our communities, our lifestyles and all we take for granted in ways which 'are beyond the focus of many government efforts'. Many people are already 'very jaundiced to leaders just passing through' when the disruptive threats are so profound.[111]

We are in uncharted territory for unthinkables in every sector of global activity. Even those like Facebook who believed they enjoyed unchallenged dominance and wealth have suddenly found their image and reputation shattered and ripped apart in hours. A whistleblower exposed the alleged inappropriate harvesting of the personal data of 87 million FB users. The data was allegedly obtained via an app developed by a university lecturer in the UK. Then it was passed to Cambridge Analytica (CA) and apparently 'used for political gain'.[112] CA denied it. The company said it had assured FB that it had deleted the data. FB's Mark Zuckerberg confirmed that the tech giant did receive CA's assurance, but should have then checked for itself.[113] The whistleblower told the UK parliament: 'It's categorically untrue that CA has never used Facebook data.' The Cambridge University academic who created the app which allowed the harvesting of up to 87 million accounts also told Parliament that Facebook was aware that its platform 'was being mined by thousands of others'.[114] He claimed Facebook 'did not care'.[115] Right up to the moment when Cambridge Analytica and its associates suddenly filed for insolvency,[116] they denied allegations that they had obtained Facebook data illegally, or used it without proper permissions. They had been forced into liquidation because of 'numerous unfounded accusations' and having been 'vilified for activities that are not only legal, but also widely accepted as a standard component of online advertising in both the political and commercial arenas.'[117]

But the secret strategy had helped Trump win the 2016 US election campaign through targeting of inaccurate claims about Hillary Clinton. CEO Mark Zuckerberg went on television to express 'regret' that confidential personal data held by Facebook had been misused.[118] His COO confirmed a 'major breach of trust' and that Facebook had 'let people down'.[119] Zuckerberg repeated the apologies to two US Congressional hearings on Capitol Hill.[120] FB leaders and engineers had never considered the possibility of this kind of unthinkable profoundly damaging the brand and wiping $50 billion off the company's value in 48 hours,[121] and $70 billion in eight days.

Worse still, Facebook now faced multiple congressional enquiries and the Federal Trade Commission launching an investigation into 'concerns about the privacy practices of Facebook'.[122] Investors who had long enjoyed stratospheric rises in the value of Facebook shares suddenly turned on the company and especially Zuckerberg. They demanded a 'new structure of accountability'. 'In essence Mr Zuckerberg is not accountable to anyone. Not the board, nor the shareholders. . . Right now, Mr Zuckerberg is his own boss and it's clearly not working.'[123] The issues had not been raised before when FB's stock values and returns were barrelling along just fine. Now the unthinkable of this massive corporate reputational disaster changed some attitudes super fast.

One senior FB executive described how this giant had failed to think unthinkables. 'We have been as a tech company too focused on the positive and not nearly vigilant enough about the negative. We have been caught flat footed.'[124] And it then got even worse. Advertisers began 'pressing pause'[125] on pumping the lifeblood of huge amounts of advertising money into the company's giant cash coffers. In a matter of hours, the result of months of journalistic investigation was threatening Facebook's phenomenal wealth, global reputation and perhaps even its survival.

Then take the real estate sector. With so many professional and back office jobs being replaced by non-human algorithms and AI which require next to no space, who will occupy swanky office blocks?[126] Leaders in the sector called in Joseph Stiglitz, the Nobel economics laureate. They heard him conclude a sobering presentation to top executives: 'This is a time of unprecedented uncertainty in the global economic landscape. This is the only thing about which we can be certain! Navigating these dangerous shoals will be difficult, in both the public and private sectors.'[127]

The audience of executives and dark suits was largely inscrutable and silent. Why should they publicly reveal any of the deep fears and vulnerability which some of them had shared privately over dinner the night before?

It is unnerving enough at 'citizen' level to work out what the disruption is already doing, and what it will do next. So imagine what it is like being a leader in one of the many vulnerable sectors like real estate or retail. Top executives in retailing signed up to a conference with the dramatic title 'How to Survive Retail Armageddon'.[128] The unpalatables are that threatening. In retail they are the distressing societal implications (for city life and communities) of online shopping. Steadily the unpalatables are eliminating the concept of shops, stores and high streets as we know them.

If you are at the top in business or government then you probably feel vulnerable and scared, but don't really want to admit it, even to those you trust. 'The life of a senior executive in a company is just grim,' confided one C-suiter. 'Because you're just crisis-managing now. Incoming crises every single day. You don't get time to breathe. ... All sorts of stuff coming your way. That's just your life. It's just a series of crises. And you're just reacting to it.'[129]

Additionally there is a rainbow of unthinkables from a fast-growing societal fragility to the resulting impact on national security and stability which can be exploited by other forces like Russia or China. 'Winter is coming and approaching fast. Is Europe prepared?' asked Wolfgang Ischinger, chair of the Munich Security Conference.[130] His answer was 'a categorical "No!"' Do the public get this? Again, the answer is 'No'. Governments, political leaders and corporates who do have a grip on the deep negatives threatened by the 'coming winter' and disruption fear the impact on the public if they are as candid as they need to be. 'They are scared of this issue.'[131] There is a 'wrong mindset and [we] need to change it to challenge new threats,' said Rob Wainwright, director of the Europe-wide policing agency Europol.[132]

That is why it is helpful to so many when a small number of leaders dare to discuss publicly the scale of their anxieties about the new leadership challenges that require change and recalibration.

Iain Conn, Group CEO of the UK gas provider Centrica, reflected what so many have told us privately. 'It's moving too fast. It is revolution, not evolution. ... There are many accelerations at once. One of the biggest problems ... is the difficulty for mankind to cope with it. ... I don't know whether political leaders or business leaders can easily handle it'.[133] He urged publicly that overall, leaders must engage in a 'mindset flip'. But how to find the time, energy and space to even consider what kind of 'mindset flip' that should be?

Chey Tae-Won is the billionaire chairman of the huge SK group in South Korea. He has been working on his own version of that 'mindset flip'. But he has revealed how tough it is to achieve, even as a super-rich entrepreneur who runs the enormous conglomerate – the chaebol. He emerged from a four-year prison sentence for embezzling shareholders' funds and financial crimes, saying social responsibility and creating economic value must be SK's new dominant principles. But could he change the corporate mentality of the huge numbers of senior executives working for him? 'It is like asking a track athlete to become a wrestler,' he explained in a tone of exasperation.[134] This is 'due to the limited incentives to create social values in earnest. ... Social responsibility is like a bit of homework imposed after school.'

How so? Why this resistance?

You have progressed successfully through the political or corporate ranks over the years. You have conformed to institutional expectations. Now you find that the new 'wartime' realities you face are a whole lot different from those you prepared for. Levers that you expected to pull for one result produce something very different or nothing at all. And those working for you are flailing around, hunting for firm anchor points in turbulent seas. They are destabilised by realities they never imagined and are certainly not trained or prepared to respond to. They are intimidated by disruption. So they hunker down passively in lowest risk mode as the way to preserve their comfort zone and what they still have.

Too often we have heard this level of obstruction and foot dragging compared to thick syrup, or to permafrost that never thaws. It results from an inbuilt, institutional 'executive myopia'.[135] Remarkably, it often manages to block the expectations of radically minded CEOs. 'The biggest obstacle [to change] is mid-level leadership,' confided one chief operating officer.[136] 'We are not taking it seriously enough to get people on board. We need a cultural change. We must bring people on board.' Frequently we witnessed despair. 'After a couple of times you give up. ... We are boring and risk averse. [We] can't see easily what is coming or tracking what is happening' is a familiar expression of despair in the upper middle ranks.[137]

So the resistance to that change of culture, mindset and behaviour multiplies. There are, however, voices pushing for change. One of the most influential thinkers is Alan Murray. He uses his position as President of Fortune Magazine to oversee important initiatives and events aimed at breaking the mould. At his Brainstorm Design gathering in March 2018, he challenged senior executives: 'In a world of rapidly accelerating change, where technology threatens to remake almost every aspect of every company in every industry, how do large corporations, built for predictability and stability, adapt and innovate fast enough to survive and thrive?'[138]

New ideals relating to purpose and values, involving a new courage and humility, simply become too much when there are production and financial targets to be met. 'At a certain age they dig in their heels. It is harder to get jobs at 50 … and boards just want conformity,' said one radically minded CEO.[139] It is downright irresponsible to assume that your career and your value will progress by being loyal to the mantra that 'I managed to convince people I was a good guy'. Instead, 'you must be strong willed, resolute and don't give a damn! There must be no blame for taking new risks.'[140] And that critical new value of humility? 'Humility can be such a painful virtue,' wrote Hillary Clinton as she anguished over why she lost the 2016 presidential election.[141]

Do you recognise these conditions? If so, keep reading. If you don't recognise them, then it is probably because you are one of the many who remain in denial and not willing to face up to the enormity of upheaval that is now underway. But you too should read on for the sake of your effectiveness and reputation. Ask yourself: in this new world, are you able and willing to think the unthinkable? Or will the new realities eventually spit you out for failing to grip the enormity of change and its inexorable impact? Don't squirm or recoil. Instead, take comfort in realising you are not alone. You are normal in struggling to grip with confidence this new swirl of instability.

Recent months have confirmed how readily and swiftly such unthinkable events will now happen in defiance of what were all considered to be existing assumptions of risk. The assumed relative comfort of stability and 'tranquillity'[142] has been displaced. 'We are at the start of a march to the abyss. ... Something pretty profound is underway. ... What has gone wrong with politically democratic societies that has led to this outcome?' asked the International Crisis Group (ICG) in their most pessimistic assessment in its 21 years in operation.[143] They tabled a 'hair-raising list' of threats to business that reflect these 'dangerous times'.

Surely there must be reasons to be optimistic with warm, enlightened new possibilities ahead?

It is not just hard to find evidence that encourages optimism. It is very hard. The former president of the International Crisis Group and former Australian Foreign Minister Gareth Evans confirmed the scale of difficulty. He has always insisted on describing himself as an 'incorrigible optimist'. He accepts that his optimism is now under extreme stress. 'The environment for good public policy making, both internationally and domestically, is as desolate as I can ever remember,' he wrote in his new political memoir.[144] 'My normally incorrigible optimism has felt very corrigible indeed.'

But we have discovered fascinating examples which give grounds for optimism. In the coming pages we will reveal examples of organisations and leaders who have found ways to take new risks and transform themselves. They are rare. But they are out there. And they give reasons for hope.

Here's the first one.

End notes

[107] Alert to senior military commanders considering the new realities of national security in a private gathering, 9 January 2018.

[108] A new generational contract final report of the intergenerational commission by the Resolution Foundation, 8 May 2018.

[109] 10 May 2018.

[110] *The fourth industrial revolution* (2016) by Klaus Schwab. Geneva: World Economic Forum.

[111] See wide-ranging presentation by Linton Wells III on the scale and nature of new over-the-horizon risk at the IRAHSS 2017 (International Risk Assessment and Horizon Scanning Symposium) in Singapore, 18 July 2017. To watch the video of the event, go to www.thinkunthink. org/digital-footnotes.

[112] *Channel 4 News*, 23 March 2018. On 24 March, the UK Information Commissioner's Office issued a statement that its investigators had been inside the offices of Cambridge Analytica overnight 23/24 March. The ICO said this was 'one part of a larger investigation by ICO into the use of personal data and analytics by political campaigns, parties, social media companies and other commercial actors'.

[113] Testimony by Mark Zuckerberg to a joint session of the US Senate Judiciary and Commerce Committees, 10 April 2018.

[114] Dr Aleksandr Kogan in testimony to the House of Commons Digital, Culture, Media and Sport Committee, 24 April 2018.

[115] 'Facebook did not care, says data harvester Aleksandr Kogan', *The Times*, 26 April 2018.

[116] 2 May 2018.

[117] Cambridge Analytica statement, 2 May 2018.

[118] CNN interview re-run on *Channel 4 News*, 22 March 2018.

[119] Sheryl Sandberg interview re-run on *Channel 4 News*, 22 March 2018.

[120] 10 and 11 April 2018.

[121] This followed the exposure by Channel 4 News of how Facebook data was used by Cambridge Analytica to mislead voters to Trump's advantage using false data and allegations. Transmissions on 19 and 20 March 2018.

[122] 26 March 2018.

[123] 'Zuckerberg's dual role at Facebook helm draws fresh fire' by Hannah Kuchler, *Financial Times*, 15 April 2018.

[124] Campbell Brown, Facebook's Head of News Partnerships, opening a platform conversation at the FT conference on 'The Future of News', New York, 22 March 2018.

[125] Company announcements led by Mozilla on 22 March 2018.

[126] 'Skyscrapers rise in city's insurance hub just as demand begins to fall' by Oliver Ralph and Judith Evans, *Financial Times*, 21 February 2017.

[127] Remarks to EXPO REAL in Munich, 6 October 2017.

[128] 'How to survive retail armageddon', Axcel Company Day, Copenhagen, 23 May 2018.

[129] Private remarks, 13 March 2018.

[130] Remarks by Wolfgang Ischinger, chair of the Munich Security Conference, at the ESPAS Forum in the European Commission, Brussels, 22 November 2017.

[131] ibid.

[132] Remarks by Rob Wainwright, the then Europol Director, ESPAS Forum in the European Commission, Brussels, 22 November 2017.

[133] Iain Conn, CEO, Centrica, remarks to the Brussels Forum, 9 March 2008. Video available at www.centrica.com/news

[134] Chey Tae-Won, presentation on his new corporate philosophy after imprisonment, to the World Knowledge Forum, Seoul, 17 October 2017.

[135] Myopia as identified in 'Patience and finance', a speech by Andrew Haldane, Executive Director Financial Stability and Chief Economist at the Bank of England, at the Oxford China Business Forum, Beijing, 2 September 2010. Also op cit. 'The short long', Andrew Haldane and Richard Davies, May 2011.

[136] Private remarks. 15 February 2018

[137] Private remarks in the margins of a **Thinking the Unthinkable** presentation at the IMD Business School in Lausanne, 16 November 2017.

[138] Alan Murray is Chief Content Officer of Time Inc and President of Fortune. He writes the *CEO Daily* newsletter. He also convenes the CEO Initiative which advocates putting purpose at the heart of business. Brainstorm Design was convened from 6–8 March 2018 in Singapore.

[139] Private remarks. 26 February 2018.

[140] op cit. Alert to senior military commanders, 9 January 2018.

[141] *What happened?* (2017) by Hillary Clinton. New York: Simon and Schuster, p. 6.

[142] The belated realisation of the German Foreign Ministry in early 2016, as relayed to us by a senior diplomat.

[143] Remarks by Lord Mark Malloch Brown, Co-Chair of the ICG, at a session: 'Ten Crises to Watch for in 2017', Chatham House, London, 30 January 2017.

[144] *Incorrigible optimist – a political memoir* (2017) by Gareth Evans. Melbourne: Melbourne University Press, p. xii.

8

BLAZIN' SAFARICOM: FIGHTING BACK AFTER BEING LABELLED A 'THIEF'

Safaricom has been a cutting-edge provider of mobile phone connectivity in Kenya since 1997. It had visions of the future then, even though the fibre infrastructure in East Africa was almost non-existent. Massive investment was needed both within Kenya and for connectivity abroad. Its impact was boosted by the revolution in digital technology.

Over the years, Safaricom's path to success has at times been tortuous because of governance, shareholding and competition issues as other telco players and banks manoeuvred to secure a significant slice of East Africa's digital telecoms market. Its ability to connect people was both credited and blamed for providing organisational capacity that fuelled the post-election violence in 2008. Yet it still managed to lead significant breakthroughs in the telco market.

The unthinkables which challenged the telco in early 2016 hit unexpectedly from left field and right field together. A huge number of 'digital ninjas' wanted revenge because they believed the telco was overcharging and exploiting them. Safaricom was viewed as a corporate crook. Millennial consumers even cried 'Thief!' Yes: it was as crude as that.

Safaricom had become blinded to how they were alienating the next generation of both customers and employees. They confronted potentially existential threats by swiftly giving new influence to the next generation. Denial was not an option. It is an example of how voices of scepticism and anger had to be confronted then calmed. Waverers were largely convinced. The resulting breakthroughs have been remarkable. But they can't be taken for granted.

Safaricom's greatest pioneering success had been the digital banking system M-PESA. It was launched in 2007 as a microfinance loan scheme. It transformed commerce and business, especially for the vast majority in the Kenyan economy who had the least and always struggled to turn a few shillings to put food on the table. Quickly M-PESA became much more, as a general money-transfer scheme between anyone with a mobile phone. Everyone, including the smallest traders and merchants, could transfer money digitally via SMS messaging. No bank account was needed, just an SMS-enabled phone and SIM card for the transfer of cash deposited with an M-PESA agent.

In a country where few people have bank accounts, M-PESA dramatically revolutionised the economy. It rapidly ramped up the speed at which anyone could do business. More importantly people found they could transfer cash and get paid with full confidence and no risk. In 2000 the success was built on with the launch of the Kipokezi service, enabling email and online chat through mobile phones. It is run-of-the-mill and taken for granted now. Back then it was a market leader. This was because of the great connectivity implications for the poor who live in often slum townships with bad conditions, no phone landlines, electricity or running water. Suddenly they could communicate in a new, cost-effective way without needing access to the internet. And they could make business in new ways. The number of MPESA users is up from two million in 2008 to more than 27 million now.

Despite introducing more customer-centred schemes like E-Citizen, an unthinkable in 2016 suddenly threatened Safaricom's path to success. From literally nowhere, and with no warning, the issues became possibly existential for the company after a potentially unfavourable internal audit was leaked to the press. Urgent efforts were needed to find solutions.

'I was being labelled a thief!' was how the new CEO Bob Collymore described the new unthinkable. He conceded that under one telco bundle, 'it was not a deliberate attempt to steal, but the fact is we were stealing because we were taking money for things which people weren't using.'[145] Account holders from the millennial generation accused Collymore of running a telco which was exploiting them by charging far too much for data and connectivity. At least that was their view. And they would not be budged in their beliefs and perceptions. They were determined that Safaricom would pay a high price for its image being portrayed in the Kenyan media as a digital, financial rapist.

Safaricom's executives realised that their brand was in danger of being trashed within weeks, possibly just days. The unthinkable was that Safaricom had failed to understand the very different moral compass of the next generation. And that generation was angry. Not only did the millennials and Generation 3.0 view Safaricom as 'the brand of their parents' which was out of touch with them. They were alienated and had very different views to Safaricom's board and shareholders about what the telco's purpose and values should be. They view a mobile phone as a right that should project high social values, not just a product and convenience.

The company's executives described to us how they were wrong-footed. They found themselves shocked by how out of touch they were. The speed of millennial anger unhinged them and forced on them a 'grieving process'. While older and traditional customers were always 'just satisfied' and 'for years Safaricom could do no wrong', in comparison 'the expectations of the new generation are raw', Charles Wanjohi, head of Consumer Segments Marketing told us. 'Everyone was quite shocked.' Safaricom was 'not just a company for older people'. It made executives suddenly feel 'quite uncomfortable' with a new imperative to be 'humble' and not to believe they knew everything – the attitude of millennials proved they did not. 'When you are successful you lose touch with your consumers.'

This fitted a pattern of a new assertiveness and alienation by youth which had already been identified by Kenya's Strathmore Business School. But few in corporates or government gave its findings the time of day, let alone considered their profound implications. Trust is just not there. Even the Skiza music site, which Safaricom set up to promote musicians and help them with income, had become tainted by suspicions. Musicians claimed they 'were being screwed' because Safaricom was making money from the site, and that was money due to them.

Overall, the next generation viewed Safaricom as screwing them financially. The telco should not be pursuing profit at any cost. It should have an indispensable role and value as a service to society, not as a profit-generator for investors and shareholders. So it should not be 'stealing' the hard-earned cash of young people who regard a phone and its services like SMS texts as indispensable as human rights. The idea that profit was needed to invest in the next generation of digital equipment to ensure wider and more reliable coverage was not seen as relevant.

'They steal our shillings,' was the common millennial view. And we heard it loud and clear when two dozen of them came together at our request to share their views of Safaricom in an atmosphere that was dressed down and cool.[146] 'I was negative, completely,' complained Stephen. 'Safaricom is seen as a disappointment,' said Pinto. 'A bit stingy,' said Ian. 'Annoying,' said Dennis. 'Expensive' with the aim to 'catch out youth' using 'bundles I could not afford', said Christine. None of the millennials had a positive view.

As revenues first spluttered then fell, Safaricom realised it had to move fast. It labelled what was unravelling as a 'setback'. But how to react to this unthinkable? What to do? There was no guarantee that any fall from grace could be reversed. The telco could not assume it had some sacred right to exist. Was it conceivable that the backlash by digital millennials could destroy the company?

Potentially it could become existential for the business. So the telco could not ignore the millennial anger and dismiss it as some kind of temporary blip. There was a danger that blogs and tweets would kill the Safaricom brand irreversibly. And the reality was suddenly becoming much worse with a brutally targeted media campaign against Collymore and his new wife, Wambui Kamiru. Unidentified campaigners described as twitter 'trolls' started blaming the CEO's new marriage for the 'fast-depleting data bundles'. One named as Towett with the handle @Dmx254 tweeted that '#BeforeWambuiMarriedBob I used to spend 10 bob for unlimited texts all day, now I use the same 10 bob for 200 texts per day.' @DenoDNB tweeted 'Data was a bit lasting #BeforeWambuiMarriedBob.'[147]

How did Safaricom respond to this unthinkable that young customers – the future – were turning against the company for changing its data charges, and even that its CEO's marriage had somehow led him to screw those with mobile phones for more money?

At high speed in May 2016, it created what it christened its BLAZE initiative for 18- to 26-year-olds. In Kenyan patois, 'blaze' is colloquial for 'What's happening?' The aim was to create a new buzz for the 50% of Kenyans who are under 26. 'BLAZE celebrates the young' is the opening catchline on its web site alongside a smiling drummer and hyper-energetic skate boarder or rapper. 'Those on the road not taken are now our hope. We celebrate their passion, and its effect on the world around us. This is Blaze.'[148]

A million young Kenyans come onto the job market each year. Most – 80% – never have regular employment. Their life is a daily scrounge. 'Our millennials are hustling for a living, they have zero prospect of a job, almost zero,' Bob Collymore underlined.[149]

But they aspire to make an impact with creative purpose. For all of them – however poor and struggling – their lifeline to hope is their mobile phone regardless of how battered and ageing the device is.

In a blunt recognition of everything the millennials blame it for, BLAZE describes itself as 'more than a tariff. ... We realised that a tariff alone wouldn't cut it.' Instead BLAZE would be a 'whole new youth network powered by Safaricom' which 'supports unconventional journeys to success, and will empower youth through Be Your Own Boss [BYOB] Summits, Boot Camps and [a] TV show'. The main principle? 'You can do – and be – so much more than any other network allows.'

Why did Safaricom leaders come up with this bold concept to ensure its survival? Panic, confided one. 'We know that your needs are different. How? You told us!' says the online blurb. Within weeks BLAZE, had a million millennials signed up as subscribers. By mid 2018 there were 1.9 million. It was set up by a new generation of Safaricom millennials – 'created for young people by young people'. They were hired specially as 'guys in campus' and 'young entrepreneurs' to 'join the corporate race' in order to relate to the next generation and its deep disillusionment with the company. Mentors – young people who have made or are making it to success like that drummer or young entrepreneurs – would help energise and focus both the new possibilities and ambitions of BLAZERS.

To all outsiders, the company's image had to be changed rapidly. For insiders, Safaricom management and executive attitudes had to be transformed. There could be no ifs or buts. This was hyper-urgent. 'We had to be comfortable within our own skins,' said Sylvia Mulinge, Director for Consumer Business who had to make BLAZE work. 'Customers are getting angrier and angrier.' They related their empty pockets to Safaricom. Sylvia recalled how one customer said 'My money is disappearing. Safaricom must be stealing from me.' The BLAZE generation 'saw Safaricom getting big at their expense'.

There could be no corporate dithering because of the existential threat to the business from unthinkables. It was as serious as that. If Safaricom could not reliably restore the confidence and loyalty of the next generation – their future clients and business bedrock – then it must be assumed that the company's previously buoyant outlook, built on the pioneering brilliance of M-PESA, could fast become bleak.

For starters, the company refunded one million shillings because 'reputation trumps revenue every day'. Then it quickly took a strategic view that the new BLAZE project must be about building a much broader, compelling relationship with the next generation. It had to go far deeper and wider than just the cost of data bundles. BLAZE set out to appeal to youth in Kenya who 'are very talented and often passionate and ambitious about life'. That is how the new online BLAZE site described the come-on to the next generation. But 'passion and talent are not always enough to get ahead in life. Sometimes you need more. You need training, mentorship, funding, planning, networking and discipline (amongst other things).'

The bold Safaricom initiative was high risk. It could be likened to a commitment to a form of social engineering. There could easily be a blowback of even-deeper suspicion and resentment. For a telco this was remarkable: as remarkable as creating a new money transfer service ten years earlier which took this telco into creating a new form of banking, first in Kenya then across much of Africa. 'To be successful, you need to have a plan. A plan for yourself, your brand, your passion and your business. As BLAZE, we believe that you have something within you that can be great, and we want to offer you the tools and avenues that will teach and enable you to make a solid plan for your life. A plan that will get you where you want to be,' was Safaricom's bold promise.

So what offering would entice the disillusioned and sceptical youth to be convinced by Safaricom? It had to be more than being loved for organising a concert. 'They said: "Sure, thanks. But I am not going to love you because of that,"' Collymore told this us.[150] The engagement had to be 'relevant' and 'deeper than that'. It must be an all-in package: 'BLAZE enables the Youth to get access to the "Be Your Own Boss" mentorship summits, shop with BLAZE Bonga, buy more affordable bundles with Create Your Plan, and stand a chance to participate in the new weekly, one-hour BYOB TV show.'

There was no room for complacency or self-congratulations. Executives knew they did not have the luxury of time. To maintain the company's brand, the BLAZE initiative had to be constantly updated, modified and reconfigured.

Is BLAZE working?

'Without BLAZE things would be much worse,' said Sylvia Mulinge, Director for Consumer Business,[151] who was given the daunting task of making BLAZE work. But nothing could be taken for granted. Improvement is balanced on a knife edge. 'We must now accept it as a fact of life and live with the damage. [At least] "brand love" from youth is improving. The danger is that if two or three complain, then it becomes a mass complaint. We are held hostage by just two or three people.'

The two dozen millennials we met were all newly sceptical and resentful Safaricom customers. They sat amidst a mix of mentors, business people and executives. Do the next generation expect Safaricom to provide its telco services for something close to free? No. 'They want honest, value-based pricing. They do not want it to be free.' At least 'as they get older they become more accepting' of how much needs to be charged for data and services.

What about the embedding of a new BLAZE generation of millennials inside the company? Here is a selection of the kind of descriptions our study heard in their Nairobi headquarters.[152] 'They want to work with people who believe in them ... both motivating and frustrating, but less fearful ... exhausting and very smart. ... They want to make an impact in the world. ... Keeping up with their language is a basic challenge! ...

It is very difficult to motivate them with incentives. No cars! They don't want to have a car.'

And how do they fit in to a corporate environment which had never given their generation such a core role and responsibility? 'They struggle in a bureaucratic organisation,' said Sylvia Mulinge. This, in its own way, signals a future problem for every company: how to keep the next generation – which instinctively does not like much of what they see and experience inside – on the books.

And what about the Safaricom executives and managers who have experienced the corporate invasion of their company by the digital ninjas?

'All executives are being mentored,' says Bob Collymore, the CEO. 'They have to sit there two hours a month listening to the digital ninjas. They always say I am the dumbest person in the room!' And the ninjas do not hold back from their core message. There has to be new purpose and values. Overall: 'You have to hang out with the right people. If you hang out with thieves you become a thief!'

Above all, the human principles for being a leader have been flipped 'We have changed the way we run the company fundamentally,' said Charles Wanjohi, Head of Consumer Segments Marketing. They realised 'Safaricom needs to be more than a business', no longer is the principle one of 'top-down'. It has to be inclusive, including from the bottom up, plus embracing of the next generation as a core part of decision-making. After all, they are the new customer base. 'Now there must be young people in the room for there to be sign off. As a corporate executive, I am not used to this level of engagement with customers,' said Peter Kucia, Brand Assets Manager.

No one expects perfection. But decline and the populist millennial perception of Safaricom and their executives being 'thieves' has been arrested. Keys to maintaining momentum in the following months would be courage, humility, flexibility and above all the fullest possible sensitivity to the new reality that things will never be as even the top executives had known and assumed.

Has the BLAZE initiative had the business impact needed on the next generation? Peter Kucia says the data shows 'more are willing to give Safaricom a chance' because of the impact of BLAZE. And the millennials? Here are some views from our two hour hang out together. No one was gushing, of course. That's not the way things ever are! But the dial was moving towards positive, even if the direction could not be taken for granted. On the plus side, Alex said: 'If a company seems to be helping you, then you feel more positive. They are not just out to get your money.' Dennis said: 'They have done a good job with BLAZE. [But] I want an unlimited, affordable package.' Ian said: 'There was suspicion of BLAZE as a PR stunt. When BLAZE came out people did think as positively as they could.' Another said: 'You are listening to us. We like your packaging.' Yet the negatives persist. Pinto, a firm sceptic from the start, still dismissed Safaricom as 'opportunist'. Dennis said: 'People expected more when Blaze came out.' Christine warned: 'Too many expected more for them. They expected much more.' Rita said: 'Safaricom are still not trying their best.' One student said: 'I am still sceptical: as a student I don't earn money.' Alan said: 'Before BLAZE I was sceptical about Safaricom. … I thought Blaze was a way for Safaricom to get deeper into our pockets.' But he would not commit more positively.

Would any favourable impact be enduring? Would the 'thief' accusations vaporise? It was the obvious, first and vital question. Nothing could be taken for granted, especially in this new market. As Stephen warned, 'loyalty is temporary'. Which prompted another vital question: could a newly embedded change in executive mindset, culture and behaviour remain smart and flexible enough?

Safaricom discovered the hard and unexpected way that the tension between millennial expectations and corporate realities is brutal. If the next generation of digital ninjas wanted the 'human right' of contracts that provide unlimited data and streamed video 24/7, then Safaricom had to invest and give it to them. That required revenue and cash to fund new technology right across Kenya. It was a sobering reality which the millennials who labelled Safaricom as thieves took time to come to terms with. Most still viewed the business priority of holding cash to invest in upgraded systems as akin to theft.

Yet at least they now realised that Safaricom was willing to be much more than just a telco corporate cash cow. 'We want the young to see us as more than a telecoms company,' said Yvonne Achieng, Youth Segment Manager. By 2018, the number signed up to BLAZE was still rising well beyond 1.9 million. Regional BLAZE 'youth empowerment' summits every few months were oversubscribed. There was a core theme: GRIT – Greatness Requires Internal Toughness. On platforms as mentors were musicians, a fashion blogger, film directors, videographers, comedians, actors, a bicycle manufacturer and an agribusiness entrepreneur. At least 93,000 BLAZERS experienced the new opportunities of summits and boot camps being opened up for them. Some 2.2 million shillings was donated to startup ventures.

BLAZERS got what they wanted: a 'portfolio that allows users to control how much they spend on voice, data and SMS each time they purchase airtime'.[153] Safaricom had to 'encourage a more intimate understanding of our customers' needs'. So despite the corporate fear in 2016, numbers kept rising. Revenues were up 14.8% in 2017, the customer base was up 11.8% and the number of mobile data customers was up 16.6 million.[154] The revenue per customer was up too. It was a fuelled by a spirit of 'transformation' which resulted in a 'Year of Strong Financial Performance'.[155]

But more bold innovation, experimentation and risk-taking would be needed to ensure that the old normal and assumptions did not return to haunt Safaricom's prospects. As executives told this study: 'Bob [Collymore, the CEO] will always ask: does it address customers? Is it what the customers need?'

These are two questions that were barely asked until BLAZE had to be created at high speed to re-light Safaricom's corporate flame in mid 2016.

End notes

[145] Bob Collymore, interview in Chamonix during 'The Summit of the Minds 2017', 24 September 2017.

[146] Nairobi, 22 February 2017.

[147] *Daily Nation*, 7 February 2017.

[148] For more detail see www.blaze.co.ke

[149] op cit. Bob Collymore, 24 September 2017.

[150] ibid.

[151] Nairobi, 22 February 2017.

[152] ibid.

[153] *Safaricom annual report and financial statements 2017: where will we go next?* p. 28.

[154] ibid. p. 10.

[155] ibid. p. 23.

9
WHAT GOT US HERE?
WHY IT MATTERS

Unthinkables!

All of us pinch ourselves, either with delight or growing shock. Each day, each hour and sometimes every few minutes, you ask as a leader: is this real? How do I handle this assault on the assumptions that got me to the top? If it feels like the kind of dream you have longed for, then you punch the air with delight. If it resembles a nightmare, you shake your head with disbelief and wonder about the next unthinkables and their destructive impact.

Who do you believe? What can you believe?

Are we heading for that 'hell in a handbasket' for reasons of our own making? Or could a new 'era' emerge that justifies all the pain of this new 24/7 reality of upheaval? Could the US be a better place under Trump, as he promises and as those who elected him hope and celebrate?[156]

Suddenly, in late April 2018 came the summit of the leaders of the two Koreas at the ceasefire line, and the previously unthinkable warming of relations between North and South. It sparked the question: might Trump's unorthodox approach to geopolitics have found a new and successful way to secure new progress after the vitriol that had flowed between his Washington and Kim's Pyonyang? Might many experts and media columnists have unwittingly become slaves to their own conformist thinking? Could it be that the US and global interests are not 'tethered to a raging buffoon called Trump'? Might the way he 'rages and veers, spreading ugliness like an oil slick smothering everything in its viscous mantle' be a new way of achieving progress that conformist thinking regards as unthinkable?[157]

Certainly the former US Secretary of State Condoleezza Rice mused openly at the start of May 2018 about whether conformist thinking now carried a high price of being found to be wrong. Korea's two leaders had just met and walked back and forth across the ceasefire line at Panmunjom. It had been unthinkable even a few weeks earlier. We saw US Korea 'experts' openly shocked at Trump agreeing to meet the Korean leader. Despairingly, many predicted he was being drawn into a trap. But might Trump's gut businessman instinct for a deal prove to be a genius move? After her eight years dealing in government with fallout from intransigent regimes, Professor Rice said: 'I was the first to say, "Oh, my goodness, what's he doing?" when he accepted Kim Jong-un's invitation. And then I thought, "But you know, nothing else has worked, so maybe this will work."'[158]

In contrast it is hard to take comfort after President Trump's summary withdrawal from what he called the 'rotten' and 'defective' Iran nuclear deal, and his rejection of last minute international appeals not to.[159] The subsequent immediate threats from Iran's supreme leader Ayatollah Ali Khamenei threatened new dark times instead of the new détente that the hard won six nation agreement heralded in 2016. So did Israel's swift targeting of Iranian forces in Syria.

In a similar spirit of contrariness, might the United Kingdom defy the sceptics and doomsayers when it is economically and politically detached from a newly rejuvenated European Union? Will the UK flourish in with its new international status? And what about Russia's President Putin. After re-election for another six years, how much further will he feel he needs to go to assert Russia as a new strategic power determined to destabilise Western adversaries? "The Kremlin's confidence is growing as its agents conduct their sustained campaigns to undermine our confidence in ourselves and in one another," warned outgoing US National Security Adviser Lt. Gen H.R. McMaster.[160] And the same concerns can be raised about President Xi's China. The Chinese leader confirmed how inaccurately the West has read the People's Republic's true direction of political travel[161] for what is now known to be the president's unlimited term as leader.[162]

Had global affairs returned to whatever constitutes 'normal' then our research work for **Thinking the Unthinkable** could have been wound up in a few months. Instead it has grown and expanded exponentially in scale and capacity. Leaders themselves have routinely urged us to keep going. Such is the demand for a combination of insight and reassurance. They keep asking us to urgently identify answers or solutions. We don't believe there are neat solutions. You will find out why in our answers later in this book.

Since 2014 unthinkable events have become increasingly traumatic for those leaders reared in public or corporate life on a predictable conformity that would move in largely positive directions. Now everything is at risk. Nothing is secure or safe from disruption.

By 2016 leaders were already destabilised and struggling to reconfigure their professional satnavs in a global landscape with a whole new uncharted topography. But the satnavs were still not programmed correctly for what was unfolding. For understandable reasons their programmers did not yet have the necessary over-the-horizon vision. How could they? Yet those driving the corporate and political machines still tuned in by default. They naturally assumed new hazards, roadworks and diversions and roads were on the maps. They were not. The unthinkables had not yet been identified.

Our work anticipated the likely Brexit vote, then the nomination and election of President Trump. We also challenged the conventional wisdom of the opinion polls to correctly predict the result of Theresa May's catastrophic UK election gamble in 2017. May ignored advice from her election adviser Sir Lynton Crosby.[163] She called an election no one but her wanted. She had screwed up and been forced to reverse the deeply unpopular dementia tax she proposed. 'The main purpose of this election is to destroy two-party politics as Britain has known it since 1945.'[164] Instead, the election result reactivated it and revitalised Jeremy Corbyn's Labour Party. May did not realise that 'many voters feel disenfranchised because no party adequately represents them'.[165]

It was part of a pattern which was emerging relentlessly. Traditional politics and established structures were being dismembered in France, Germany, Italy, Austria, Poland and Hungary. Populism. Nationalism. 'Democracy in crisis ... battered and weakened ... its most serious crisis in decades,' concluded Freedom House for its 2018 review.[166]

Everywhere, 'patriots on the march'.[167] The deep resentments towards globalisation, which has generated so much new wealth. 'The end of liberal international order,' arguably caused by the West itself?[168] Indeed, it was asked, 'will the West survive?'[169] The populist anger has good reason, which has long been overlooked. 'Today's frustration and anger is completely justified, and frankly far too long sidelined or ignored, sometimes … with an arrogance that pours fuel on the fire. The anger and frustration is as real as it gets.'[170] As evidence of that, Hungary's Victor Orban gets overwhelmingly re-elected by relentlessly shutting down any voice or media outlet against him. He secures a thumping victory by presenting himself as the defender of Europe against being invaded. He also portrays himself as the saviour of an EU nation from Muslim migrants.[171]

Behind closed doors, war games scoped an increasingly possible military or cyber war between Europe and Russia. Planning for a nuclear conflict is now centre stage again because there is 'vulnerability' and a 'new risk to our life,' said the Chief of the UK's Defence Staff.[172]

'The Russian threat is definitely intensifying and diversifying,' the UK National Security Adviser warned.[173] Even Vladimir Posner – one of the most well-known Russian voices who articulated in perfect American English the views of the Kremlin in the pre-Putin era – has revealed he has 'never been so scared'. 'The level of trust is lower than in the Cold War, and a false alarm now is more likely to trigger a nuclear launch than it was.'[174] And haunting these years has been the continuing ever-deepening horror of war in Syria. Over seven years, hundreds of thousands were dead or wounded, with millions displaced. The UN High Commissioner for Refugees labelled it a 'colossal human tragedy' in 'this senseless pursuit of a military solution'.[175] Laws of war had been flouted blatantly and disregarded by all sides, including latterly and ominously with the active involvement of Russia and Iran. It became viewed as a mini world war.

What is clear now from our mass of research interviews and conversation is that evidence for what were claimed to be 'unthinkables' had usually been there. But typically, blind eyes were turned. This was either because of a lack of will to believe the signs, or an active preference to deny and not to engage. As a result, for many corporate and public service leaders, the shockwaves from these unthinkable events started prompting legitimate concerns. What were the true calibre and capacities of those in the highest positions of responsibility to first foresee them and then handle the impact?

As we will show, the evidence has not been encouraging. Indeed, it is disturbing and increasingly so. While the phrase 'thinking the unthinkable' has an attractive rhetorical symmetry, a more appropriate and accurate phrase in almost all cases is 'thinking the unpalatable'. The evidence of what was threatening or about to happen was usually there. But it was often not seen or understood. Or worse still, no one believed it because it did not fit their framing of the way things were expected to be.

The West's disbelief at Russia's actions into Eastern Ukraine, then its seizure of Crimea – an integral part of sovereign Ukraine – remains an object lesson in the shocking impact of unthinkables. The West was wrong-footed. It had no eye on the ball and was caught with its diplomatic trousers down.

After Putin's covert invasion of northern and western Georgia in 2008, these were the next salvos for what over four years since 2014 became Putin's 'hard war against Ukraine, and soft war against the West.'[176] What was unthinkable was that such moves into Ukraine were not listed on the West's risk assessments. The Pentagon's Quadrennial Defense Review had been published days before Moscow annexed Crimea. It barely referred to Russia. Instead it prioritised the fight against Islamic militant groups and the risk of war with China.

Western governments had misread Putin's warnings, such as his speech to the 2008 NATO summit in Bucharest.[177] He could not have been clearer about his intentions to restore Russia's spheres of influence. But in the mindset of international geopolitics at that time, dark intentions like invasion to restore ex-Soviet territories to Russian control were viewed as too unlikely or unpalatable to be taken seriously.[178] 'We were victims of our own wishful thinking,' said one former EU Commissioner. Even at the highest EU executive levels they did not even consider the possibility of the dark intentions for Ukraine and Crimea which we now know that Putin was nurturing. In sum, 'Russia was no longer dominating the NATO agenda'[179] when it should have been.

Why did leaderships appear to be not just flailing but in freefall as they tried to respond belatedly to 'unthinkables' like these? Why have corporate and government responses appeared to be so inadequate? Our core conclusion from our high-level interviews and hundreds of conversations, plus thousands of pages of transcripts, is the following.

The conformity that qualifies leaders for the top in many ways disqualifies them from appreciating the enormity of disruption, its implications and the kind of radical new approaches needed.

Think carefully about this finding and reflect. Professional conformity qualified a huge number of leaders to somehow beat off rivals and climb the greasy pole to the top. But in so many ways that same conformity now disqualifies them from embracing the scale, speed and implications of the profound new enormity of change that is underway. There is a 'thud of anxiety that comes from living through, or alongside global upheaval. … We have all been touched by it, the galloping, migraine-inducing pace of events.'[180] Instead of embracing the implications of this seismic challenge to that conformity, the default response tends to be denial.

It is that serious.

End notes

[156] See for example 'The President changed. So has small businesses' confidence' by Landon Thomas, *The New York Times*, 12 March 2017.

[157] 'Tethered to a raging buffoon called Trump' by Roger Cohen, *The New York Times*, 13 April 2018.

[158] Condoleezza Rice, interviewed on *Channel 4 News*, 1 May 2018.

[159] 8 May 2018.

[160] Remarks to The Atlantic Council in Washington DC, 3 April 2018.

[161] See 'How the West got China wrong', cover story and editorial, *The Economist*, 3–9 March 2018.

[162] Following the almost unanimous vote by the National People's Congress on 11 March 2018.

[163] 'PM ignored bombshell "Don't risk poll" memo' by Simon Walters, *Mail On Sunday*, 3 September 2017.

[164] 'Theresa May's vapid vision for a one-party state' by William Davies, *The New York Times*, 12 May 2017.

[165] Editorial comment in the *Evening Standard*, 7 June 2017.

[166] 'Freedom in the world: democracy in crisis' by Michael J Abramowitz, President of Freedom House.

[167] Interview in northern France during coverage of French election, BBC Radio 4, 17 February 2017.

[168] 'The end of liberal international order?' (2018) by G John Ikenberry, *International Affairs* 94 (1) pp. 7–23.

[169] Session title at Munich Security Conference, 17 February 2017.

[170] op cit. John Kerry, 8 July 2017.

[171] 'The man who thinks Europe has been invaded', BBC analysis before the general election on 8 April 2018.

[172] Speech by Air Chief Marshal Sir Stuart Peach, UK Chief of Defence Staff, Royal United Services Institute (RUSI), 14 December 2017.

[173] Evidence by Sir Mark Sedwill to the UK Joint Committee on the National Security Strategy, HC625, 18 December 2017.

[174] 'Face of the cold war: I've never been so scared' by Matthew Campbell, *Sunday Times*, 15 April 2018.

[175] 'Syrian conflict at 7 years: "a colossal human tragedy"', UNHCR, 9 March 2018.

[176] Ivanna Klympush-Tsintsadze, Ukrainian Vice Prime Minister for European and Euro-Atlantic Integration of Ukraine, remarks to the Brussels Forum, 10 March 2018.

[177] President Putin's remarks to Bucharest NATO Summit, 2 April 2008.

[178] Discussion with former US State Department official, 10 March 2018.

[179] Remarks by Torgeir Larsen, director of the private office of the NATO Secretary General until 2017, 1 November 2017.

[180] 'Hungary was right about the migrant crisis' by Roger Boyes, *The Times*, 12 July 2017.

10
THE COST OF CONFORMITY

Conformity is no longer the career booster that most assume. Increasingly it is becoming a killer of careers and reputations.

But how many leaders are willing to recognise that? Are too many trapped by the conformity which got them to where they are? We argue: yes. And we know that from the many hundreds of leaders who have talked candidly to us. To succeed and thrive as a leader in this new normal, they must release themselves from those zombie orthodoxies which got them there. It is a brutally tough conclusion. But remarkably, too, there is no dispute.

Are you nodding agreement? If so, then you are joining the vast majority at the top who have given an almost ubiquitous positive reception to our findings. They don't rave openly about them. Almost none of them show their hands publicly or stand up to be counted. And there are no headlines yet. Indeed many remain understandably coy and discreet, partly because of fears about the cost of being identified. Yet from behind the backs of their hands they confirm: 'Yes! That is me and what I face.'

Why are conformity and compliance such obstacles? Why did so many leaders appear to be struggling as they tried to respond belatedly to 'unthinkables'? Why have corporate and government responses appeared to be so inadequate? It is because they are not prepared to come to terms with the scale and multidimensional nature of the new challenge. It is vast and intimidating.

The failings and this new reality can even be compared to the devastating impact of war on our populations and generations who have never experienced conflict or adversity. Most people and leaders have never experienced the new and growing scale of adversity which will threaten all that they assume will somehow be pretty good or better.

That is why there are many good reasons to compare the scale of threat and challenge to a new state of war. You need to recall that dramatic but practical assessment from Chris Donnelly, a former adviser to three NATO Secretaries General. His contention is that what leaderships face is 'comparable to what happens in wartime ... yet we think we are at peace'.[181] As a result, 'the global pace of change is overcoming the capacity of national and international institutions'.

Yes. Let us repeat. Overcoming the capacity of the institutions which we expect to sort things out! And you did read comparable to what happens in wartime. Both issues have become the source of extreme stress and vulnerability in this period of new ill-defined normals and unthinkables. You may resent or take fright at such an apparently negative message. Yet in this new age of unthinkables there are strong and compelling reasons to accept that such worse case projections need to be taken seriously.

Hence the ongoing red alert.

End notes

[181] op cit. Interview with Chris Donnelly, 6 July 2015. See also op cit. 'Rapid reaction force for Success', Chris Donnelly, *World Today*, June & July 2016.

11
THINKING THE UNTHINKABLE: HOW WE TESTED IT

From the start we set the bar of ambition high. To ensure intellectual weight and impact for the research, only the highest level of current and recently serving public servants or business leaders were interviewed.

A first suggestion was to convene a panel or a bigger conference. We rejected this. There was the practical impossibility of coordinating diaries in order to bring together such busy executives. More importantly, it was vital to hear the frankest possible assessments. This was unlikely to happen if we brought highest-level peers together to listen to each other. Therefore we aimed for one-to-one interviews or conversations, which sometimes lasted up to 90 minutes each. We knew that this would be the most efficient and productive use of their time. They and their experiences would be the sole focus of discussion. We were right.

We took an active decision not to be prescriptive about the emerging direction of travel for the project's findings. The priority in the first 30–40 minutes was always to encourage each leader to unburden themselves. We wanted them to voluntarily reveal the pressures both on them personally, and on leadership more generally. It was important not to lead them on and influence their thoughts. Usually, only in the final third part of each meeting were the project's interim findings shared. This was to gauge the level of agreement, qualification or disagreement. While time-consuming, without exception this methodology and the wealth of one-to-one engagements produced extraordinary frankness and revelations about the new fragilities facing top-level executives, regardless of which segment of leadership experience they came from.

Our invitation was for the meeting to be off-the-record, with no public acknowledgement it had been held. All accepted on that basis. Subsequently some did agree, or ask, to go on the record. That rich process of disclosure and revelation continues as the scale of unthinkables keeps rising. The take-up has been remarkable. So has the candid nature of discussions. Currently the project has records from several hundred top-level conversations and interviews, with 2,500 pages of transcripts. This starkly reflects the private and human levels of executive anxiety. We are most grateful for the extraordinary openness and frankness that each interviewee has shown. As additional corroboration we have added publicly available sources: transcripts of conferences and public events or media interviews that addressed similar themes.

By social science standards this is described as a 'very meaty dataset'.[182] Subsequently, the interview data has been validated and coded using processes recommended by a leading independent academic in the field.[183] You will find fuller details of the data and analysis in the appendix and on our e-platform accompanying this book at www.thinkunthink.org.

In this new state of disruption and 'wartime', we originally identified nine key words and phrases which encapsulate why unthinkables are too often not thought about. They have routinely been repeated time and again during the multitude of conversations and interviews for this project.

Our original interim findings, published in February 2016,[184] were based on our **impressions** from the data. They were:

1. Being overwhelmed by multiple, intense pressures

2. Institutional conformity

3. Wilful blindness

4. Groupthink

5. Risk aversion

6. Fear of career-limiting moves (CLMs)

7. Reactionary mindsets

8. Cognitive overload and dissonance

9. Denial

Two years on, there is no reason to dilute these key findings. Quite the opposite. The realities of the struggles faced by leaders and those serving them have not gone away. Instead the reasons why unthinkables are too often not thought about are now even deeper and broader, and therefore more concerning.

This conclusion no longer derives from our subjective impressions out of thousands of pages of notebooks and transcripts. For this book and update they have been validated painstakingly through detailed data crunching in an intense standalone process that has been subject to peer review.[185] We have checked our original findings by undertaking a detailed deep dive into the data and transcripts. This doesn't just mean transcripts of our own interviews; it also includes transcripts from events or broadcasts relevant to our research.

Firstly, the accuracy of transcripts was re-checked line by line. Then we used qualitative data analysis software to code almost a hundred key words and phrases.

This new process has reconfirmed and substantiated with statistical rigour those original findings from 2016. It has also produced important modifications and additional insights.

Here is the revised list of 11 key words and phrases. These themes not only corroborate the nine key concepts we first identified in 2016. They substantiate our original findings and add important new developments.[186]

The issues most frequently cited by leaders are at the top of the revised list. If grouped together, the first three confirm in an even stronger tone how troubling the challenges are for those at the top.

1. **Short-termism**

2. **Confused**

3. **Fear**

4. Risk aversion

5. Purpose

6. Inclusivity/Diversity

7. Overwhelmed

8. Groupthink

9. Institutional conformity

10. Behaviour

11. Cognitive overload

Without exception, when we put these overarching conclusions about the enormous cost of conformity to top executives and public servants, they nod agreement. Since 2016 there has been zero pushback on the findings. Yes: zero!

Now three important additional issues have been added: the pressures for new **Purpose, Inclusivity/Diversity** (with equal number of mentions), and **Behaviour**. These are an important confirmation of a direction of travel already signalled by **Thinking the Unthinkable**.

But how will **Purpose, Inclusivity/Diversity** and **Behaviour** be addressed? Identifying new issues does not necessarily mean there will be a wide acceptance of the resulting radical recalibration that is needed for **culture, mindset** and **behaviour,** plus an embracing of new **purpose, values, courage** and **humility.** Use of the words and mentioning the issues is fashionable. But does that produce the strategic change and rethinking by leaders that is needed?

Conformity and self-interest from the current leadership cohort mean the reluctance to show flexibility is entrenched. Are a good number of eyes and minds opening? 'If you roll the clock back, probably to 20 or 30 years ago, when I and some of my contemporaries came into the City, the conversation about values, behaviours, culture, was almost non-existent. Now that has shifted and that's what excites me and that's what gives me the hope,' Katherine Garrett-Cox, CEO of the Gulf International (UK) Bank told us. For eight years she was CEO of the £3.3 billion Alliance Investment Trust before activist investors forced changes in the boardroom and she left.

This ongoing challenge remains at the heart of our work and this book, as you will discover. But the top-level resistance to the scale of change needed remains intense. This is confirmed by the unreserved, on-the-record message from Unilever's CEO, Paul Polman, who is arguably the most prominent top executive voice on the scale of change needed. 'Some CEOs are scared stiff, [but] we must be disruptive, taking risks and challenging the status quo. We must be bold in looking at new technologies, and be creative.'[187]

End notes

[182] Dr Christina Silver, Co-founder and Director. Qualitative Data Analysis Services (QDAS). Research Fellow, University of Surrey. Co-author with Nicholas Woolf of *Qualitative analysis using NVivo: the Five-Level QDA method* (2018) Abingdon: Routledge.

[183] ibid.

[184] op cit. *Thinking the unthinkable* (2016) by Nik Gowing and Chris Langdon.

[185] Using NVivo Plus 12, the state-of-the art qualitative data analysis software programme from QSR. Research work carried out February to April 2018 (and ongoing) by Didi Ogede with guidance from Dr Christina Silver, Co-founder and Director of Qualitative Data Analysis Services (QDAS). She is a Research Fellow at the University of Surrey.

[186] Conclusion submitted by our Researcher, Didi Ogede, 2 April 2018.

[187] op cit. Paul Polman, 6 July 2015.

12

'PEOPLE DON'T KNOW WHETHER TO BE EXCITED OR PARANOID'

There continues to be much to learn from 2014, whoever you are in the business of working out how to embrace unthinkables, then how to counter them.

In retrospect, the evidence of probable Russian intent had been identified by some. But at the critical time, no national intelligence agency within NATO's 28 member nations shared actionable evidence which pointed to a probability that Russia would act so dramatically.[188] Russia had not lost its great skill for deception – maskirovka. The 'unthinkable' should have been near the top of political and corporate watch lists through late 2013 and into early 2014. It was not even on them!

Instead NATO and many Western governments found themselves in a state of silent shock. It was not just Russia's surprise. It was the alliance's inability to realise what was unfolding. Officials and military officers 'were immediately outside their comfort zone,' according to one top-level NATO insider. 'They weren't used to thinking, "Bloody hell, we've got a military crisis on hands. What are our tools?" because they're not used to thinking in those ways.'

But some had tried to raise an alarm. One very senior diplomat (whose assessment was well ahead of the curve on what would become a major crisis with Russia) was routinely blocked by officials. 'I was getting a stream of instruction from [redacted] to pipe down, shut up, de-escalate and take a back seat.' Officials in Whitehall were 'dumbing everything down and [ordering] "Don't rock the boat, don't escalate, don't cause problems."' Only when this diplomat eventually managed to hack through the obstructions to get 'contact with ministers' was there 'a very fair hearing'.

A month after Russia's surprise, Professor Michael Ignatieff, then at the Kennedy School of Government at Harvard, put his cold, analytical finger on a stark new reality which is now well into its fifth year. He warned leaders, and those who serve them, of the end to all they assumed professionally about a certain global order and normative political practice.[189]

Within four months, the number of 'unthinkable' events had multiplied while leaderships were still struggling to understand and get a grip on the enormity of what was unfolding. 'We are still arguing about how to react accordingly' said Ignatieff. He described 'the new reality of multiple events making us search for our bearings' with a 're-ordering underway'.[190] Ignatieff was not the only one identifying this new watershed. 'We are experiencing a new normal,' warned the leading democracy policy analyst Thomas Carothers, Vice President of the Carnegie Endowment for International Peace.[191] The trouble is that few on the highest rungs of the leadership ladders were that convinced.

At senior executive levels in government and business, 'unthinkable' events like these leave a widespread sense of astonishment, bewilderment, impotence and anxiety. It usually morphs into fear. 'People don't know whether to be excited or paranoid. They are typically both,' said a prominent risk counsellor. 'They mask their fear. ... They mask their discomfort,' said a former minister. In private, senior officials confirm deep failings. But in public there could not be any suggestion of the possibility of failure. 'I do not think that after the way the world has evolved in the last few years anyone – not just the Foreign Office – is going to be able to predict those things,' said Sir Simon Fraser, the outgoing head of the UK Foreign Office. Asked at a valedictory lecture if he accepted the widespread impression that 'civil servants are too slow and cautious', he conceded 'sometimes that is the case'. He added: 'the realities have changed and continue to change significantly. All the evidence is that power has been hollowed out, and the process is continuing.'[192]

Sir Simon even drew on that rather ugly word which sums up that process: de-responsibilisation. While there is an ever-greater need and urgency to think unthinkables, many of those in the fast track to the top are often 'demotivated' and 'they do not feel empowered' as was once the case. Among those serving the top leadership, there is increasing caution and greater concern about taking responsibility. So they do their best to minimise and offload it. Many have described how what was once inspirational leadership acting on insight and vision has been replaced by a new bureaucratic imperative for 'managerialism'.

This prompts a critical question. Are the unanticipated events really 'unthinkables' which no one identifies or sees coming? Or are they inconvenient truths for which top officials and C-suite executives seek alibis? One of the country's top practitioners in the corridors of government and power told us: 'There's a distinction between "nobody saw it" and the statement that those who would have needed to act didn't hear it, didn't want to hear it. And they're two different things. That "nobody saw it" is a very strong statement. I suspect that for some of these things it would not be true that nobody saw it. They might not have seen or been able to predict the details. But they might have been able to see that something big was coming.'[193]

End notes

[188] Confirmed weeks later publicly by the then NATO Supreme Allied Commander General Philip Breedlove at the Brussels Forum on 23 March 2014, followed soon after by the then NATO Secretary General, Anders Fogh Rasmussen. Both identified significant failures of both intelligence and analysis, which they said must be reversed.

[189] Michael Ignatieff, presentation to Chatham House, London, 19 March 2014.

[190] 'The post-Ukraine world order' by Michael Ignatieff, 50th Ditchley Annual Lecture, 12 July 2014. This was further expanded and developed into 'The new world disorder', *New York Review of Books*, 25 September 2014.

[191] *The new global marketplace of political change* by Thomas Carothers and Oren Samet-Marram, April 20 2015.

[192] Speech on Leadership and Reforms in the Civil Service at the Institute for Government, 15 July 2015.

[193] Remarks by Lord Nicholas Stern, Professor of Economics and Government, London School of Economics; President of the British Academy 2013-17; Chief Economist and Senior Vice President at the World Bank 2000–3; former senior civil servant. Interviews: 5 February 2015 and 7 February 2018.

13
'THE HEAP IS ROTTING'
DO LEADERS GET THAT?

The frankness of many at the highest levels is remarkable. They wonder aloud how to handle this new VUCA world that is Volatile, Uncertain, Complex and Ambiguous. 'The world has changed and so … our leadership has to change. It's not optional,' said one.

They anguish over the deepening affliction of 'short-termism', with 'myopia mounting' about how to handle 'unthinkables'.[194] One prominent retired public servant went so far as to warn that, in his words, 'the heap is rotting' in public life, but 'the people at the top of the heap want no change and want to keep their position'. He believes this could threaten a 'breakdown of society' – even 'anarchy' – as the contract between leaders and the led increasingly fractures. The farsighted alert was often rejected as too extreme. But candid revelations in our interviews suggest it must not be ignored.

One leader immersed in a complex change programme for a major international organisation spoke for many who find the sheer scale and nature of this new VUCA world rather scary. 'You ask, is it a new challenge? Is it serious? Yes, I think so. … I've been now at the executive level for ten years. I've worked in this environment for some decades. It's by far the most challenging time [for the organisation] in modern history.' In 2015 he told us that he was working to break down silos and address vested interests. 'I am trying to see where in my organisation are the places – it could be very small places – where adaptation is happening more quickly,' he said. Interviewed more recently he suggested that there would be no handbrake turn in culture. 'Even over the past eight months, I would argue that I have seen some change in the practice of leadership. I am not saying improvements.'

The profound implications for leadership mean that this must be embraced – not wished away. One very senior public official posed the question that all leaders should ask: 'Is there something radically different, with a new paradigm required for decision making … and a weakening of government power?' After all, 'people do irrational things'.

Behind closed doors, one leading business figure even described an executive fear of being an imposter. 'I know what the board want, I know what the shareholders want, but I know what I can't deliver.' It highlights a deepening tension. Because of the growing conflict of new forces there is an increasing inability to deliver in the ways shareholders or stakeholders expect, despite being highly paid to do it. 'CEOs [are] lavishly paid prisoners of this system that they occupy.' And the perspectives elsewhere at the top are often too narrow as well. 'Even if boards can identify issues and do horizon gazing, they don't have the depth of experienced people at staff level to say: "Go look at that and plan,"' said one Chair.

It is the same with the new threats for nation states. Some who believe they have an unthinkable issue that should be brought to top-level attention find they often face a wall of resistance because their view does not fit the mindset. 'Our leadership is strategically fatigued,' said one very highly placed government official. 'I'm talking about politicians and most of the Whitehall village. And much of British society. The Twitterati for sure. But the world is changing. The world may bring harm to you in ways you cannot imagine and ways you cannot manage. There is a resilience deficit, a lack of understanding of the scale of emerging threat.'

We asked our interviewees: 'Are we right to be staggered how narrow-minded and one-dimensional the corporate sector is, even at chief executive levels, when it comes to understanding things which are going to affect their businesses?' 'Yes,' was frequently the off-the-record answer from C-suites. Alarmingly, this confirms the stark, largely still unlearned lessons from the failures in the banking industry in the years leading up to 2008. The ensuing Global Financial Crisis resulted from unthinkables which were known and could and should have been thought about. Nevertheless, 'it was rather like a nuclear war,' as Alastair Darling, then the Chancellor of the Exchequer, said. 'You know you think it will never happen. Then someone tells you that a missile's been launched. It was very scary. That moment will stick with me for the rest of my days.'[195] Even the Queen expressed the common public concern to leading economists when she met them that year. She famously asked: 'Why did nobody notice it?'[196]

Ten years on, C-suites still raise the burning question of why this unthinkable crisis was apparently not anticipated. Why is more heed not given to the unequivocal message from 2008 that, in the words of one banker, 'a system that appeared relatively robust had, on the flick of a switch, been shown to be fragile'? He added: 'Everyone went over the cliff edge at the same time' because 'the contagion wasn't classically economical or financial; it was sociological'. In other words, a banking crisis revealed something much deeper: denial and wilful blindness, even if during 2007 and early 2008 the looming inevitability was quietly the focus of gossip over champagne, whisky, beer, coffee and the water cooler. Everyone just wanted to make whatever they could, while they could, before the wheels came off.

Events since 2014 have revealed an updated iteration of precisely the same problem. Management systems block farsighted analysis and thinking. Embedded institutional conformity required to qualify for promotion and professional progression can be deeply counterproductive at a moment of rapid change. Time and again this came up in interviews. It is built in from the get-go, from the very moment of getting a job in the system, many said. 'When they get into business, or they get into civil service, there is a huge amount of psychological pressure [on employees] to conform,' said one CEO. It is the same in public service. Managers, officials and military officers 'advance by doing the conventional very well,' according to one senior public servant who said he was keen to change the system which he acknowledged is currently suppressing any instincts and skills needed to identify the unthinkables.

If leadership does not change, then the next generation is watching, learning, impatient, and does not like much of what it sees. 'I was mostly with people in their 30s, and one of the things they kept kind of pushing me on was when is it okay to speak out and will anyone listen?' said one CEO.[197] We have made significant efforts to sample their concerns and ideas too. We have witnessed the unequivocal sentiments of millennials by attending an enormous number of gatherings, both large and more modest. Listening to the experiences of one gathering of leaders of the future just before this book went to press confirmed how little is changing. Their mood is one of even greater impatience and frustration, which now verges on anger.[198]

We heard a veteran former leader echo passionately precisely these NextGen emotions. Mohamed ElBaradei is a Nobel Peace Prize winner and former Vice President of Egypt. In a tour de force presentation to leaders about the deep dangers from the current levels of disruption he issued a passionate appeal for the Next Generation to be listened to.[199] It is 'vital to listen and move fast', he said. This would help dilute the growing existential threats. Dr ElBaradei said the next generation is 'refreshingly different. It is time to listen to them, share their wisdom and empower them.' He even cited his seven-year-old grand daughter from the generation beyond that. When he could not give an answer to a touchy question during a family walk, she said in an insistent voice: 'I want an answer right now!'

The NextGen mood was encapsulated in one remarkable interview. 'The emperor [leadership] has no clothes,' was the blunt view of Aniket Shah. At the time he was already one super talented 28-year-old representative of the next generation. He had the top-flight career CV of someone double his age. A graduate of Yale, he already had a career in banking and asset management and was working with Professor Jeffrey Sachs on the UN Sustainable Development Goals.

Aniket went for the jugular: 'I have come to the conclusion that all of these organisations or institutions that we once held in high esteem and sort of revered tremendously are actually dying a very slow but painful death. Because they are having to deal with fact that we have a highly educated, highly transparent younger generation that has grown up and come to age in times of financial distress. [It was] caused, by the way, by the generation above us in a world that is going through huge environmental crises caused – of course – by the generation above us. Now we find ourselves … slightly stunted, slightly stultified. … We look up and we know exactly what these people do, as we live in a transparent world. And we say, "You know what? The emperor has no clothes. We can do this a lot better."'[200]

That means challenging the leaders who are at the top now, or ignoring them and the organisations they run, then heading in a different direction.

This justifies a profoundly important finding. The next generation have great insights and instincts about what is going wrong and why, and what is needed to counter the often merciless new pressures from disruption. 'Far too many people are probably sitting in a job that they actually hate, with people that they probably don't respect, and they're just sitting there and biding their time.'[201]

Millennials should not be dismissed as irritations who will eventually conform. They must not be marginalised as too inexperienced or too new in their jobs. That is their strength.

Instead the NextGen need to be regarded as a major new source of vision and enlightenment. Leaders must actively engage millennials, listen to them, take their energy and views seriously, and give them a far greater voice in the running of organisations.

This is not about idealism or a new form of political correctness. The evidence is there. Engaging the NextGen goes a long way down the track to understanding then embracing disruption.

We have already showed how Safaricom in Kenya became blinded to how they were alienating the next generation of both customers and employees. They confronted potentially existential threats by swiftly giving new influence to the next generation.

Here is another important example of where voices of scepticism and anger were calmed, and waverers were convinced.

The breakthroughs at OCP in Morocco because of a new NextGen energy have been remarkable. But they can't be taken for granted.

End notes

[194] op cit. 'The short long', Andrew Haldane and Richard Davies, May 2011.

[195] 'Britain was two hours away from total social collapse' by Simon Watkins, *Financial Mail on Sunday*, 8 September 2013.

[196] HM the Queen quoted in the *Daily Telegraph*, 5 November 2008.

[197] Katherine Garrett-Cox, interview, 26 February 2018.

[198] Youth Climate Summit 2018, organised by the 2050 Youth Climate Group in the Royal Concert Halls, Glasgow, 28 April 2018. #YCS2018

[199] Keynote speech to the Horasis Global Meeting in Estoril, Portugal, 6 May 2018.

[200] op cit. *Thinking the unthinkable* (2016) by Nik Gowing and Chris Langdon, p.11. Also op cit. *'Want to lead? Then tear up the rule book'*, Nik Gowing and Chris Langdon.

[201] op cit. Katherine Garrett-Cox, 26 February 2018.

14
LE MOUVEMENT: MOVING CORPORATE MOUNTAINS AND CULTURE

What kind of initiatives and determination will secure the right mindsets, behaviours and culture changes for configuring and energising leaderships to handle the new reality? We found an important example headquartered in Casablanca, Morocco. The company is the giant phosphate producer OCP and the initiative is called 'Le Mouvement'. Its impact so far has been extraordinary and far greater than even insiders expected.

Encouraged personally by OCP's chairman and CEO Mostafa Terrab, the next generation has been driving change and attitudes since 2016. They have become the company's own internally created cohort of consultants. They are breaking down ageist walls, shredding cobwebbed work patterns and building new bridges of positive engagement between people and departments which have never existed – ideas which never got traction as managers defended their departmental power and fiefdoms are now generating new innovation and human energy.

'All the initiatives were really talked down. So, the impact that Le Mouvement has ... is actually creating a space for experimentation,' 35-year-old Hasna Ziraoui told us. She joined Le Mouvement in late 2017 after five years in OCP doing routine commercial work managing and chartering ships. 'In the beginning, honestly, I was not convinced. I have to say that ... I stayed in my work [having watched it from the start], and I didn't give it a chance. But now that I embarked on this journey, I'm really convinced. Every day you see many initiatives and improvements.'[202] Jbili Abdenour, also 35, has no doubts: 'I'm 100%

convinced that if we didn't have Le Mouvement, for sure, we wouldn't develop that. We'd just continue like what you did before.'

Remarkably the success of Le Mouvement has generated a handbrake turn against the value of consultants. OCP have discovered they can get much of the insight and vision they need from inside their hitherto repressed human resource capabilities. 'We don't want basic consultancy who work, who come and bring you the solution, and tell you "This is the solution. Take it or leave it. And pay us,"' said Jihane Sadiq, facilitator for Le Mouvement.

What is OCP? It is the easier title for Office Cherifien des Phosphates. The corporation is a giant agricultural and minerals business. It is the world's leading producer of phosphate rock and phosphoric acid, plus animal feed supplements. OCP is also a major global producer of fertilisers and high-value products. The phosphates are extracted by gigantic diggers from enormous open cast mines in many parts of Morocco. The reserves are so vast that they are predicted to last for hundreds of years at current rates of consumption. OCP is the fifth largest investor in Africa.[203] Employing 23,000 people, OCP therefore has a core and arguably irreplaceable role in Morocco's economy.

OCP's revenues confirm that. In 2016 they were estimated at $4.4 billion, despite what its management commentary described as 'softer market conditions and a contraction of total revenues for the whole fertiliser industry'.[204] Prices fell by up to 34% due to factors like competition, subsidy policy changes, crop prices and weather conditions. Nevertheless 'profitability improved substantially' which was 'notably driven by lower input costs, improvements in our operating efficiency, market and product diversification and higher fertiliser sales in high growth markets'. By late 2017 revenues were up 13% despite 'challenging market conditions.'[205]

But in 2016, OCP faced a potential existential crisis. It was a scale of challenge, described internally as the 'old game'[206] versus the 'new game'. 'Most of the problems are in culture, in the processes, organisational procedures, and habits of people,' Badr El Amrani told us. He is aged 35 and one of many leading lights in Le Mouvement.

OCP realised that everyone in the company had to 'embrace the new game in this new world'. Those who work for OCP must go 'from Good to Great'.[207] There had to be an end to 'conformism, de-responsibilisation, silence and predictable events'. There had to be a new 'motivation, pleasure, trust, open-mindedness, listening, sharing, contributing, transparency, interdependency and connection between departments, but above all between collaborators'.

Above all, there was no doubting the new corporate mantra from chairman and CEO Dr Terrab. 'To prepare OCP's leaders, let's push them to think the unthinkable.' Those at the top had to ask how to make this uncertainty the new norm. One leading way would be 'to take out the millennial generation from the conformism and the silence'. Additionally, 'to face this unstable and uncertain environment, agility must be in the heart of the managerial practices'.

The audit of progress so far is that this is what is happening. Le Mouvement was designed as a new internal staff feedback network. Its unusually freewheeling mandate was to overturn conventional thinking and conformity. There must a new corporate determination to break down walls and turn company thinking on its head if necessary. There had to be 'utter openness' with 'free imagination'.

The principle was that 'every employee can dedicate time, be empowered and become accountable for the group's development'.[208] The intention was that 'people shared opinions, ideas and thinking without any hierarchical boundaries with the whole top management'.[209] Its values would be 'pleasure, motivation, trust, openness and listening'. It would recognise OCP's own failing and inability to grip in any adequate way the scale of change on multiple fronts.

A key driver was demographics. There is a much younger age profile in OCP: ten years earlier, the average age was 45; in 2016 it was 35. So the challenge of the company finding itself out of touch was clear and real. Employees in their mid-thirties would become the drivers for Le Mouvement and change.

Mid-level, fast-track staff and executives had also realised for themselves that there needed to be new ways to help recalibrate internal minds and attitudes to the new reality of unthinkables. From the start Dr Terrab offered them a 'blank cheque' for disruption. 'You have carte blanche' he told them. 'Come up with three big ideas, and at least one can go ahead without any question.'

How did staff receive the proposal? It 'shocked and surprised them. They weren't expecting that,' one senior executive told our project. But many then rapidly embraced the opportunity. From the start, Le Mouvement's working principles have been that nothing is excluded from consideration, even the darkest scenarios for the company and the nation. Employees have debated openly the likely impact on the economy of Morocco if there is a crash in both prices and demand for phosphates. There are also new European Union health and environmental concerns about levels of cadmium found in phosphates from North Africa.[210]

Above all, any innovation could be proposed and debated. 'It's really giving us that space to experiment. Worst case is we fail, and best case is we do something great,' said Hasna. What happens if they fail? 'Well, we learn from it, and then we do better next time. It's like babies. ... In this space, everyone understands that it's okay to fail, you know? ... I think there's a common understanding that we learn from failures and that's an opportunity, whereas before, it was not the case. ... It's a safe space where we can all fail. And if we don't fail, we don't succeed, anyway. So, that's the understanding from everyone. I think everyone knows that. ... Thank you for trying.'

Discussions happen by way of a new collaboration process. 'If someone has an idea and thinks it is a good one which can bring an added value (not necessarily a financial one) to themselves and/or for the group, they have to consult enough stakeholders to ensure it is realisable. Next the person has to convince others to join to realise the idea, and this is what we call a "situation". It is not a project. There is no deadline, no hierarchy, no control structure, no methodology. It is a free constitution of groups from any facility, department, subsidy, representative office or partner.'[211]

Remarkably for such a massive corporate, in 2016/17 OCP's processes had done little to embrace digital. The smart new generation at OCP in their twenties and thirties could not believe it. We spoke to Badr El Amani about how he joined Le Mouvement's challenge to this laggardly reality. He is now a leading figure in OCP's groundbreaking #Switchtodigital initiative, which is a product of Le Mouvement.

The first target was to provide everyone in OCP with a personal 'digital passport' by way of a series of conferences called 'Digital Talk'. Badr and his colleagues confronted a simple contradiction. 'Before this initiative, everybody heard about digital outside of OCP. But when they go in their offices into OCP, digital disappears. We only have a lot of paper, a lot of classical applications. We have smartphones. But we have no professional applications on our smartphones.'

That in itself was unthinkable: increasingly most OCP employees took digital for granted outside work, but they had little or no access inside OCP.

Le Mouvement created new 'social enterprise networks' right across OCP. They set out to 'explain in simple ways, simple words, what digital is, what the benefits of going digital are, what can change in our ways of working through this training, and everyone had access to this platform to do his training,' Badr explained. And then: 'We invited a lot of digital influencers from all over the world to talk and present experiences for other companies who came [through] the digital transformation in the last years.'

But the core deficits in mindset and culture were profound. 'The biggest challenge for us was to move from a technical discussion to a mindset discussion and put digital in the heart of business transformation of OCP. [We had to] convince our top management that digital is ... not about technology; it's about ways of working; it's about new business models; it's about a new mindset, new ways of collaboration etc. And the technology comes at the end to support these digital initiatives and make them possible.'[212]

Members of working groups still had to keep their usual jobs going. But they had to adapt them in order to commit time to Le Mouvement and grip the enormity of change needed. 'We were about ten people within the group. I was the only guy with an IT background. ... All the others came from other business units. They didn't have any technical skills or previous knowledge of digital or IT experience. But all of them, and me with them, believe that digital is a key business enabler for the next transformation that OCP is about to perform.'

Le Mouvement soon flattened OCP's usual hierarchies 'with a real mix of profiles and backgrounds inside one team'. Changing culture, mindset and behaviour was at the heart of their way forward. We heard the reasons for creating it and the progress in a brainstorming[213] which brought together not just senior OCP figures, but executives from other organisations too. Together they openly volunteered the need for a 'culture of courage, humility and daring'. The **Thinking the Unthinkable** project also led one of Le Mouvement's thought leadership Café Culture sessions for more than a hundred engineers and staff from all levels at OCP's Polytechnic University in Ben Guerir, north of Marrakesh.[214]

Has Le Mouvement brought big new perspectives and breakthroughs? Very much so, according to the signs so far which include improved financial performance in a tough new market. 'It is gradually transforming the company, and especially the mindset. ... It has given space to the next generation,' Karim El Aynaoui, Managing Director of the OCP Policy Centre,[215] told our project.[216] 'Le Mouvement is a change of culture. What made it successful is the very explicit expression of humility from the chairman [at the start],' said another senior executive. It is an 'ongoing effort and will take time. People are smart enough and can see change and will adapt. But they do not know where it is going.'

Another said: 'The opportunity to propose solutions was the leverage [with staff] for success.' As a result, 'we have realised that change is part of our life. What is difficult is the rate of change. We have to recognise that,' said one of the mid-level executives who is helping to drive Le Mouvement and its principles. What is the choice? 'It's up to every individual to choose whether they want to embark on this adventure and try something great, or just keep on doing their work the way they did,' said Hasna Ziraoui. 'Everywhere there is the resistance of people not understanding it. But like everywhere you can have a force against, and a force for. But it's spread out among all the sites. And it's based on the will of the people to work in the movement or applying the movement methods.'

But progress has been uphill. 'I can't pretend that the mindsets inside have changed in one year. This is long-term work,' said Badr from #Switchtodigital. 'But we already see some minor changes, and in some areas, some major changes in the way we are doing at least [the] IT project.

Because now we have introduced the concept of agility in working. We established a digital factory. This is a new achievement. ... We have a digital factory to deliver digital products. And this digital factory is not only technical guys. We have business experts. We have agile coaches. We have developers. We have at least seven or eight different profiles working together in a team to achieve a business objective. This is really a new way of working, of doing things.'

There are other projects too, like #OCPMaintenanceSolutions and how to turn the vast, old mining wastelands into growing quinoa, the wheat-free alternative to starchy grains. Critical to the new upside-down approach was realising that departments often could not rise to the challenge of a supply request. They were neither cooperating nor knitting their functions together in innovative ways. They either had the product or they did not. If they did not, then OCP colleagues had to go searching elsewhere – and probably outside the company – for skills that such a corporate giant should have for itself.

Here's Jihane, aged 31, facilitator for Le Mouvement: 'We're working [up to now] like provider and customer. It means, for example, I'm a customer in the business team. I need some new application, I'm going to see my provider, which is IT department. I ask them, 'What can you do for me? If you cannot do it, I am looking for someone else outside to do that.' But, today, like the business team, we are involved with the IT department to think together for the real [sic]. It's like the design-thinking way of working'.

What is the oil that lubricates Le Mouvement? For a start, a change to meetings. In the past at OCP they have long been formulaic and a process with a top-down command spirit from managers. 'Before, we did like lots of meetings, and we have not really seen a lot of results ... not good results after the end of meetings,' said Jihane. 'People will be more comfortable because their work [is] not depending on one manager, because before ... if you have trouble with your manager he will put you in difficulties, and you will not have a bonus at the end of the year.' Hasna added: 'In order to have a good grade from your manager you had to be visible. So you had to show yourself. But some people are not like that. Some people are shy and they do great work. Except they are less visible. ... It's important to be evaluated by your peers, because they know how you work. And you are not the same with your manager as with your peers.'

Now managers have to make time at least once a month to say to those who work for them: 'What are your needs? 'And there is an even more fundamental message of change. 'We are here to help, not to give you orders or something like that.' The new reality was described as a 'flattening experience' – or it was described with the neologism 'de-hierarchy-isation'! Instead of working in 'blocks' or with a 'unit' running the initiative there is a self-organised network of contacts and clusters seeking 'solutions without a hierarchy'. The network changes dynamically and 'frees people' in ways that can 'adapt inside and outside the corporation'.

The freeing-up is about 'creating spaces for people to work together: to listen and speak on big ideas'. It is about stimulating insights and alternative ideas that don't ever make it through the system, because that system discourages such ventilation from all levels. 'We ask anyone who has information with value added to share opinions, and for it to be taken into account.'

Has OCP embraced these responses to the new unthinkables? Has Le Mouvement worked for everyone inside OCP? The view in 2017 was: no – at least not fully yet. In 2018, things have picked up momentum and OCP is changing fast. It was 'not easy for everyone to accept this'. It is also 'very uncomfortable for managers'. Badr said: 'We bring a lot of transparency, and for some people, this transparency is not welcome. ... This minority can show some resistance.' Some at the higher levels say Le Mouvement gets in the way of their main responsibilities. 'There are some people who are still not convinced, because they don't have really time,' said Hasna. Which creates the question, 'What is the new role' for them? Is there an age or generational split? Are younger OCP employees more willing to accept the new spirit and opportunity? No. It is 'common to all ages'.

One core discovery at OCP is that they don't need to hire outside consultants on anything like the previous scale. This is because of the previously suppressed talent inside the company. 'You give them ideas to consultants and they give the ideas back!' said Dr El Aynaoui. Remarkably OCP has discovered from within new self-confident ways to generate OCP's own solutions. 'It was really, really important ... to not go back [to] the past way of consulting. Our site were fed up about the way of consulting, and they don't want to receive more consultancy,' said Jihane.

OCP discovered it can generate its own 'consultancy' from hitherto undervalued internal insights and wisdom. 'Yes, it's all generated internally. ... It should become an internal capability at the end, and this is the spirit of Le Mouvement. Capability building. We are exploring new ways of working, new businesses. We are having consultancy to do that, but ... we are building capabilities to be able to do this again by ourselves,' said Badr.

Led from the top by Dr Terrab, OCP's Le Mouvement certainly identifies with the overarching problem of how to think unthinkables. 'The risk for companies and governments is that anything can happen; anything rough and sharp and sudden. I do not think we are systematically embedding these processes. I do not think we are prepared,' said Dr El Aynaoui. Everyone and every institution must recognise that there are Black Elephants in the room. 'But we don't want to see them because they are too uncomfortable.' And all too often there is an offloading of issues – that de-responsibilisation highlighted earlier in this book: 'If there is a crisis, it is not my responsibility.'

So what is the fundamental principle behind Le Mouvement? 'Nations must be prepared and must organise themselves.' But the capacity of those at the top to handle this is limited. 'Why do we not get the best leaders through the democratic system? It is a weakness.' A core reason is that fewer want to have to endure the inevitable 'cycle of purges' against leaderships. 'This must be managed in the most efficient way and at the lowest cost to society.'

Can staff and executives like them cope and adapt? 'There is an end to conformity. We were struggling. People who don't believe it, they are destabilised,' said one senior voice, a chief executive. 'We are past the time when a leader knows exactly how to do it [to lead]. If we are able to share with the people and the staff [then we will know] all that we need to know but do not address. We [must] make sure we cover the issue.' There is no point in prevaricating or playing for time. 'It is not "what if" it happens; it is happening! They are facing what they have not faced before. You have to pick one or two with the courage to succeed. You build one success and hope that seeing is believing. But it is not easy; not easy!'

This CEO urges his staff to read the British author Rudyard Kipling regularly because they 'must not be afraid to be foolish when they propose something different'. What about a new courage and humility, and the creation of a safe space? 'It is not about telling them you are courageous. You have to show it, by taking risks for your job.' How do the board and shareholders react? 'They are not aware.' So should they be told? 'They see the results.' We ask again: should they be told? There is laughter in the room. 'No! No. Don't scare them.'

But this is not just about how OCP and these other companies are having to try to reconfigure themselves to think unthinkables. Le Mouvement has exposed the failings of the education system. 'It is where we learn conformity,' said one senior executive. In the education system, 'we learn to be afraid of change and how to protect ourselves'. The education system is 'one of the most conformist and has not changed for centuries'.

What are the takeaways so far? 'We do not expect something precise, but we ask people to find a new way of working together so it has impact in two or three years,' said one of the younger executives organising Le Mouvement. 'We long for our managers to lead this experience.' The attitude of top managers is described as 'encouraging'.

'We have a real change in the sharing habits. ... Honestly, for most wide initiatives, there was very little resistance,' said Badr. 'If you take, for example, the social network, almost three months after launching this network, we have 3000 people connected to the network, which is a very good number. And people are publishing information. They are sharing stories. They are discussing topics. They are creating work groups on this network. And we have very little resistance regarding this aspect.' Hasna said: 'I've been in OCP for five years, and we did notice a change, and a quick change. At first, the way I saw it, is like we basically had to comply with everything, even if sometimes we saw opportunities to improve our daily work, we didn't have the support or the means to improve what we saw was wrong.'

Le Mouvement is an inspiring initiative that is opening doors to new solutions. 'It is something we have to nurture and protect. [It is] not a guarantee. We have to take care of it. ... You must have courage and humility at the top,' says Karim El Aynaoui.

This is an achievement which many others could learn from OCP. In the end the 'risk' taken by the CEO was not a risk. The initiative has worked. It has borne corporate fruit. Our Thinking the Unthinkable project will continue monitoring progress for lessons to be shared with others. So stay tuned to our web platform for more developments.

End notes

[202] Skype interview with two men and two women from Le Mouvement, 20 March 2018. Three of them, (Hasna Ziraoui, Jbili Abdenour and Badr El Amrani), are aged 35; Jihane Sadiq is aged 31.

[203] *African Economic Outlook 2017.*

[204] OCP management update bulletin, 8 December 2016. See www.ocpgroup.ma

[205] OCP Press Release, 30 November 2017.

[206] Internal document provided to TTU by Jihane Sadiq, Direction Controle de Gestion & Business Steering, OCP, April 2017.

[207] *Good to great: why some companies make the leap...and others don't* (2001) by Jim Collins. London: Random House.

[208] Café Culture hand-out.

[209] Email from Jihane Sadiq, Direction Controle de Gestion & Business Steering, OCP, 8 May 2017.

[210] 'Toxic dispute erupts over "safer" fertilisers' by Rochelle Toplensky and Henry Foy, *Financial Times*, 13 July 2017. Also 'Fertiliser mines row leaves EU between a rock and a hard place' by Rochelle Toplensky and Henry Foy, *Financial Times*, 21 July 2017.

[211] op cit. Email from Jihane Sadiq, 8 May 2017.

[212] Group discussion, 20 March 2018.

[213] 11 December 2016.

[214] 10 May 2017. To watch the video of the event, go to www.thinkunthink.org/digital-footnotes.

[215] Dr Aynaoui is also Dean of the Faculty of Economics and Social Sciences at the Mohammed VI Polytechnic University, Ben Guerir, Morocco.

[216] Interview, 14 March 2018.

15

'IF YOU ARE NOT PREPARED AND YOUR PANTS ARE DOWN, YOU ARE REALLY GOING TO GET WHACKED'

So, we are travelling through an uncharted, catalytic stage in a dramatic new process of breathtaking realignment. There is retreat from previously widely accepted norms, and even retrenchment that shows no signs of ever going away. Instead it is generating often-panicked handbrake turns to left and right, plus surprises at every junction or road sign.

Brexit? President Trump? Did you believe these would happen and that a majority of voters would chose them in a free, democratic process? Did such possibilities even have a place on your risk assessments? If not, then you are afflicted by the inadequacies of leadership that this book is about.

Such disruption hangs like an ever-heavier cloud over all of us and all we do, regardless of career, status, or global location. Since 1945 and the end of the Cold War in 1989, there has been an assumed overarching trend towards stability, growth, greater prosperity and a new international order of respect and wealth. This is now being undermined and arguably overturned. The effectiveness and relevance of global institutions like the World Bank and International Monetary Fund (IMF) is being questioned. This is due to new forces of disruption that have shattered expert assumptions and shaken the conformist thinking of leaders. The US President's decision to unpick decades of hard won economic agreements led to a warning letter from 1140 economists, including 14 Nobel Laureates. They warned that Trump's policies were the same kind of 'flat earth economics' that unbalanced the global economy in the 1930s and led to the Great Depression.[217]

The dominating mood is 'nothing if not gloomy', with a 'pervading sense of powerlessness'.[218] It is 'very difficult for traditional institutions to cope with this'.[219] 'At a very deep level we are at a moment … where the crisis of leadership is greater than it has been at any time, certainly in the lifetime of the IMF.'[220] NATO nations were bluntly warned: 'If you are not prepared and your pants are down, you are really going to get whacked.'[221] New thinking is having to search for new ideas by returning to old thinking which had long assumed to be redundant. 'We have to figure out how to adapt to this new environment,' was how one US Colonel characterised how to handle matters now. 'I don't think we are there yet.'[222]

The new reality is even more intimidating because of the multiplicity of simultaneous threats. 'It is more unpredictable, and it's more difficult because we have so many challenges at the same time.'[223] There are 'a great deal of transdisciplinary thinkers who are deeply bothered'.[224] But overall, missing globally is 'anything much in the way of solutions'. The world continues to travel 'to the brink' and shows no signs of pulling back from it.[225]

Through 2017 and into early 2018, business leaders told the PwC Annual CEO Survey and others that their confidence levels were by far the highest in recent memory. But while market valuations seemed unstoppable, the fundamentals of geopolitics were shifting dramatically and rapidly in dark directions. Despite the new cash-driven buoyancy of market optimism, 'CEOs fear wider social threats that they can't control … in a fractured world'.[226] PwC Global Chairman Bob Moritz reported that CEOs who are claiming unprecedented levels of confidence don't know how to handle 'threats the business world is not used to tackling directly by itself'.[227]

Significantly, that includes geopolitics, which many business leaders say has never really occupied their attentions. Now it has to. On each day of writing for this book there has been a new and ominous reason to underscore that new imperative about the new unthinkables of geopolitics. An increasing number are not even merely unpalatables. They could not have been foreseen, despite prolific efforts to facilitate foresight and convene new thinking.[228] 'The world is much more uncertain and volatile than it has ever been before. And that is because of some factors coming together now that have never come together before. And they amplify each other. You have a totally different world order and we struggle with that enormously,' said Paul Polman, CEO of Unilever, reflecting the view of many who requested not to be quoted by name.[229]

Twelve days after multinational expressions of despair at the Munich Security Conference in early February 2018, President Putin reinforced the reasons for such gloom. He unveiled a new unthinkable: the scale of Russia's massive military modernisation well beyond a level of development which was already surprising the West.[230] It was the opposite to the sudden parallel rays of optimism appearing suddenly around the Korean peninsula. It further justified the widely held view that Putin was now determined not just to be 'in the disruption business' but also be 'disruptor-in-chief'.[231] Russia had entered 'a revanchist, dangerous mode'.[232] In believing that Russia would want to become like the West, the USA 'ignored 400 years of Russian history and tendency'.[233] There is a pattern where a 'modern nation state has chosen to step outside the rules that govern behaviour of civilised countries'.[234] A leading Russian opposition figure has compared Kremlin strategy to a 'geopolitical casino' where 'Putin's strategic goal is chaos. Then he can dominate. He grabs when opportunities present themselves.'[235]

It made no difference. Putin then announced to a joint session of parliament in Moscow that Russia has developed 'invincible nuclear weapons'. One is hypersonic and can reach anywhere in the world. Putin said of the West: 'They do not take account of a new reality and understand ... [this] is not a bluff.'[236] It was bleaker than even the most expert of experts on Russia had signalled was coming. 'No one imagined so much happening in such a short time [with] increased uncertainty and unpredictability.'[237] After a gloomy prediction of no better US/Russia relations in the next 15 years, one leading Russian analyst regarded as an independent voice quipped: 'I just hope we don't blow up the world.' The International Campaign to Abolish Nuclear Weapons, which won the Nobel Peace Prize in 2017, warned that mankind's destruction is potentially one 'impulsive tantrum away'.[238]

Progress towards disarmament and greater stability was being rolled back. NATO and European nations had to confront the reborn necessity to prepare again for nuclear war. German public opinion was already leading the disbelief that this option had returned. 'In that context, thinking the unthinkable becomes more imaginable,'[239] even though Berlin urged restraint. To most in the international community, Russia's use of a rare military nerve agent to try to kill a former double agent in the UK[240] confirmed what they were silently fearing. Europe and NATO united swiftly against an apparent act of war and a new existential threat on European soil. Russia was now 'a strategic enemy, not a strategic partner'.[241] After President Putin's re-election for another six years, extraordinarily he was likened by the British Foreign Secretary, Boris Johnson, to Adolf Hitler at the 1936 Olympics.[242] Putin would use the 2018 World Cup for the same kind of propaganda aims, alleged Johnson. Russian officials expressed outrage. But there seems to be increasing vindication of those who even very recently were marginalised professionally for raising the likelihood of this kind of dark scenario that could threaten us all. 'We may have to fight for the preservation of prosperity and the world order ... to stiffen ourselves for wars of necessity, not wars of discretion.'[243]

After the nerve agent attack in the UK, even the hitherto-wavering Trump administration decided to issue a presidential condemnation of Putin's Moscow. The nerve agent attack had been the first chemical weapons attack on the territories of Western nations since World War Two. The White House recognised Russia's outright challenge to global rules of stability which had taken decades to create. Their statement in parallel to a robust meeting of the UN Security Council said: 'This latest action by Russia fits into a pattern of behaviour in which Russia disregards the international rules-based order, undermines the sovereignty and security of countries worldwide, and attempts to subvert and discredit Western democratic institutions and processes.'[244]

This statement and its phraseology, then the mass expulsions of Russian diplomats – 'undeclared intelligence officers' – from more than 20 countries[245] would have been unthinkable even a few weeks earlier.[246] It was a 'moment of reckoning'.[247] Western nations united in an unprecedented way to condemn 'a brazen attack ... on all of us' and the 'sovereignty of our partners'.[248] Together, they then 'crippled Russia's spy web'.[249] The new geopolitical atmosphere was being described as worse than the Cold War – at least then 'both sides knew the rules of the game'.[250] Now there would be an 'increased risk of miscalculation, inadvertent escalation or even war'. The nerve agent attack on a sovereign territory had confirmed the unthinkable direction of travel. Now 'there are no rules'.[251]

Yet there are also extraordinary geopolitical surprises. The shrewd and totally unexpected North Korean agreement for its athletes to perform in the Winter Olympics 2018 under a single flag representing a united Korean peninsula confirmed how there can be true unthinkables. It seemed a lone atoll of hope in a sea of tempestuous geopolitical waters.

Then remarkably a few days later came the sudden North Korean offer (transmitted to President Trump via South Korea two weeks later) for a meeting between Kim Jong-un and President Trump. The announcement gobsmacked longstanding Korea watchers and those regarded as 'experts'. Our project tweeted: 'We confirmed with a top Korea expert a few hours ago: unthinkable development. So hands up any official, public servant or corporate insider who shared this possibility with their bosses!'[252] No one responded! President Trump had apparently taken the impetuous risk to say yes to Pyongyang via Seoul, without even consulting any of those experts, or even his Secretary of State who was travelling abroad. Policy-making resided in the US President's finger tapping on the keyboard of his mobile phone. Even his National Security Adviser at the time had no role. History may show this unthinkable moment to have been visionary. Many feared it carried huge risks and will be exploited by Kim Jong-un to ultimately embarrass Trump and the US. What unthinkable might follow then – especially after the presidential demeaning of National Security Adviser Lieutenant General H R McMaster and his replacement by the conservative hawk-of-hawks,[253] John Bolton?[254]

Are you still holding tight? Are you gripping even tighter?

The big and growing message for increasingly anxious leaders is this: the dramatic upscaling of these new, ill-charted complexities and uncertainties means that assumptions of great wisdom and insight are – or have been – turned on their head. New forces of disaffection have harnessed disillusionment, resentment, grudges and an overall sense of being both misled and wronged by political and corporate leaders. Most, if not all, have been unwilling to even consider thinking the unthinkable, let alone encouraging those they work with to do so. Those leaders have largely tuned out as a reaction to deepening anxiety. This is despite the fast-accumulating evidence that should impose an urgent imperative for change.

End notes

[217] 'Don't replay 1930s, Nobel economists tell Trump' by Dominic Rushe, *The Guardian*, 4 May 2018.

[218] 'A distracted Trump makes room for Putin' by Philip Stephens, *Financial Times*, 23 February 2018.

[219] Anne Applebaum, Professor of Practice and Director of LSE Arena. Presentation on 6 February 2018.

[220] James Boughton, former IMF historian, quoted in 'Spring breaks through the storm' by Shawn Donnan, Gemma Tetlow and Sam Fleming, *Financial Times*, 22/23 April 2017.

[221] Presentation to NATO Defence College in Rome by Matthew Fisher, Foreign Affairs and Security analyst for the *National Post*, Canada, 20 October 2017.

[222] 'US army dusts off Cold War playbook' by Eric Schmitt, *The New York Times*, 9 August 2017.

[223] NATO Secretary General Jens Stoltenberg speaking during a NATO exercise in the Baltics, quoted in 'NATO chief: world at its most dangerous' by Daniel Martin, *Daily Mail*, 9 September 2017.

[224] Conversation with Richard Hames, strategic futurist and editor, *The Hames Report*, Melbourne, 30 October 2017.

[225] Closing remarks of Wolfgang Ischinger, Chair of the Munich Security Conference, following three days of deliberations by many of the world's most senior leaders, 18 February 2018. To watch the video of the event, go to www.thinkunthink.org/digital-footnotes.

[226] PwC Global Chairman Bob Moritz, 22 January 2018. They are 'extremely concerned' about geopolitical uncertainty (40%), cyber threats (40%), terrorism (41%), availability of key skills (38%) and populism (35%). Most tellingly, these threats outpace familiar concerns about business growth prospects such as exchange rate volatility (29%) and changing consumer behaviour (26%).

[227] ibid.

[228] See for example: *Shaping the future of geopolitics: foresight and strategic game changers: hard and soft power in a changing world*, papers for the conference convened by ESPAS, Brussels, 22–23 November 2017.

[229] op cit. Paul Polman, 6 July 2015.

[230] Remarks during the Anglo-German Königswinter Defence Conference, 17–18 November 2017.

[231] Both phrases from Al Cardenas, US Republican Party strategist and lobbyist, appearing on NBC's *Meet the Press*, 5 March 2018.

[232] David Miliband, President of the International Rescue Committee, UK Foreign Secretary (2007–2010), *Today*, BBC Radio 4, 14 March 2018.

[233] Lt Gen Ben Hodges, Commander of US Forces in Europe, 1 November 2017 – just before his retirement.

[234] Robert Hannigan, Director of GCHQ (2014–17), speaking on *Today*, BBC Radio 4, 14 March 2018.

[235] Anti-Putin opposition activist and chess grandmaster Gary Kasparov in *Putin: the new tsar*, transmitted on BBC 2, 9 March 2018.

[236] State of the union speech in Moscow by President Putin, 2 March 2018.

[237] Remarks by Torgeir Larsen, director of the private office of the NATO Secretary General until 2017, 1 November 2017.

[238] 10 December 2017.

[239] 'Germans think the unthinkable on going nuclear' by Frederick Studemann, *Financial Times*, 7 February 2017.

[240] On 4 March 2018 in Salisbury, Wiltshire.

[241] UK Prime Minister Theresa May to the 28-nation European Council in Brussels, 22 March 2018.

[242] Remarks by UK Foreign Secretary Boris Johnson to the Parliamentary Foreign Affairs Select Committee, 21 March 2018.

[243] Remarks by General Sir Richard Barrons (retd), Head of UK Joint Forces Command to 2016, 1 November 2017.

[244] White House statement, 14 March 2018.

[245] 'More than 100 Russian diplomats expelled from the West in response to Salisbury nerve agent attack' by Sara C Nelson and Graeme Demianyk, *Huffington Post*, 26 March 2018.

[246] Announcements made on 26 and 27 March 2018.

[247] Nikki Haley, US Ambassador to the United Nations, press briefing, 26 March 2018.

[248] Australian Prime Minister Malcolm Turnbull, 27 March 2018.

[249] UK Prime Minister Theresa May, 26 March 2018.

[250] Dr Andrei Kortunov, Director General, Russian International Affairs Council, interviewed on *Today*, BBC Radio 4, 27 March 2018.

[251] Estonian President Kersti Kaljulaid, *Today*, BBC Radio 4, 27 March 2018

[252] 9 March 2018.

[253] 'Don't get distracted: John Bolton is a huge threat' by Simon Kuper, *Financial Times*, 5 April 2018.

[254] 22 March 2018. Even John Bolton was reportedly surprised by the unthinkable of a sudden call from President Trump. 'I didn't really expect an announcement this afternoon,' John Bolton told *Fox News* on 22 March 2018.

16
PESSIMISM? REALISM? OPPORTUNISM?

You might be tempted to label and even dismiss the analysis as pessimistic. You should not. <u>Thinking the Unthinkable</u> is about being realistic.

It is loaded with positives and new opportunities. It is about accepting the new unthinkables and realities, however unpalatable they are. Then you must be courageous enough to recalibrate leadership skills smartly and at high speed. 'There is a need for a new way of learning,' says Lord Nicholas Stern as he has led and continues to lead efforts to achieve that.[255] On thinking the unthinkable: 'There is nowhere near enough yet.'

This requires new awareness, flexibility, receptiveness, breadth of perceptions and above all willingness to modify what you do and how you do it. And the public expect it. Building trust is the number one job for CEOs, ahead of high-quality products and services, according to the Edelman Trust Barometer for 2018. There is a 'fast-recovering belief in CEOs rewarded for speaking out on issues'. 'Nearly two-thirds [of survey respondents] say they want CEOs to take the lead on policy change.'[256]

But for too many leaders, the risk and mental barriers are too great. 'The problem for business leaders and CEOs, and the problem for politicians, is that courage normally means losing your job. Parochial self-interest takes over,' says the former corporate deputy chairman and ex British Minister Lord Mark Price.[257] 'The reality is that we need the courage to tell people that the world is changing at a rate of knots. And that within that they will need to change the way they do things and think.'

Does that happen? 'Unpalatables are what I face all the time,' one very senior official confided. 'Very reactionary mindsets. ... Political leaders do not want to know. ... I gave them long lists. But few want to believe it, let alone take on board and prepare.' The official gave more details but writing them here would point to their source!

So this book should already be opening eyes. Then it should reassure, because our overall intentions are positive. The changes underway are not an ephemeral freak. The system is under ever-greater strain from complex, interconnected risks. Leaders must not delude themselves. There can be no turning back. To expect or plan for anything else is a deeply flawed assumption.

There is even now the danger of 'runaway collapse.'[258] This grave warning from the World Economic Forum (WEF) was in early 2018. Yet 12 months earlier the WEF issued a similar warning. It had highlighted a risk from 'failure of leadership' which is an 'existential issue for companies.'[259] At the start of 2017, political processes had already been identified as under threat. 'There are clear reasons to worry about the health of democracy. ... This could be a pivotal moment in political history, and it requires courageous new thinking about how best to manage the relationship between citizens and their representatives.'[260] Voices investing hope in the future of democracy were struggling to gain traction.[261] Instead there were ever-darker warnings like The people vs tech: how the internet is killing democracy (and how we save it).[262]

So are there signs of progress and productive engagement?

In January 2017, one hundred corporate leaders did sign up to a new WEF commitment to 'responsive and responsible leadership'. The words were brave and suggested forward movement. But where was the new courage and new thinking by leaders? Over the next 12 months, an apparent inertia, complacency or fear about what to do exposed the blindness and instinctive caution of leaders and their institutions. If leadership was failing, where were the signs of new engagement? There were few, if any. Somehow the required handbrake turns were regarded as for others only. This became a sombre confirmation of the scale of both the threat from unthinkables and the level of denial.

A red alert in early 2018 from Larry Fink, Chairman and CEO of BlackRock, the global investment giant, was a remarkable indictment from a top insider of leadership attitudes.[263] He seemed to be saying: 'What the hell are you doing, my fellow chief executives? What planet of denial are you on?' He shocked his corporate peers. 'Public expectations of your company have never been greater,' Fink wrote in his annual letter. 'To prosper over time, every company must not only deliver financial performance, but also show how it makes a positive contribution to society,' he warned. He did not spare his criticism. 'We also see many governments failing to prepare for the future.'

Some accused Fink of a shameless commercial opportunism and a marketing stunt to get more business. Were they genuine deniers, or just jealous competitors who had been wrong-footed? In our view, the brutal directness of Fink's alert was correct. It was long overdue. In so many ways it was encouraging, and for the right reasons. It struck the precise chord of concern that has been at the heart of the red alerts from **Thinking the Unthinkable** since the shock events of early 2014 sparked our process. Yet during that time few took any notice. It was not politically expedient to do so. Few wanted to listen to us, let alone publicly acknowledge the inevitability of the new upside-down anxiety and direction of travel that was unfolding. Despite what many were confiding privately to us, in public they were either conveniently blind, in denial or suggesting they had too much to lose by being as forthright as Fink.

But one of the toughest global business leaders was emphasising the need for leaders of companies in particular to define their purpose. This was reinforced by the findings of our updated data analysis in April 2018.[264]

End notes

[255] op cit. Lord Nicholas Stern interviews: 5 February 2015, 13 November 2016 and 7 February 2018.

[256] 2018 Edelman Trust Barometer, 22 January 2018.

[257] op cit. Lord Price interview, 25 July 2017.

[258] *Global risks report 2018*, World Economic Forum, 17 January 2018.

[259] Additional remarks at the *Global risks report 2017* launch by Rick Samans, Member of the WEF Managing Board, 11 January 2017.

[260] *Global risks report 2017*, World Economic Forum, p. 33.

[261] See for example *Democracy: stories from the long road to freedom (2017)* by Condoleezza Rice. New York: Twelve Books.

[262] *The people vs tech: how the internet is killing democracy (and how we save it)'* (2018) by Jamie Bartlett. London: Ebury Press.

[263] Larry Fink, 16 January 2018.

[264] op cit. Data analysis is detailed in the Appendix.

17
PURPOSE...WHAT PURPOSE, AND WHY?

Remarkably, many reading this will have no clue as to why identifying purpose has become so critical in the search to address unthinkables.

'Companies don't know what their purpose is. ... Many companies simply don't do it. ... They need the tools to be able to conceptualise and implement what their purpose is,' says Professor Colin Mayer, a leading figure in the search to reinvent the corporation which is fast gaining traction.[265] Despite the ignorance of most leaders about the massive value of purpose, embracing a new attitude to it is vital and urgent, as we will show later. 'Purpose is not about profit. Purpose is about how to create business benefits to us as customers and communities. And in the process, it produces profit. But profits are not, per se, the purpose of business.'

So there is a brutal message: grip the concept of purpose and redefine yours. Alternatively, continue to head deeper into the underworld of ever-gloomier anxieties about unthinkables.

Yet leaders continue to be blindsided, like the men and women executives wearing dark suits and blindfolds on this book's cover. In too many ways they promote an inexcusable level of denial.

'The feeling is explicable, but it does not make it any nicer. A feeling that the old elites in all these countries have somehow failed. They have also been self-interested. They have not served the public good which they claim to serve. ... It is not something we should dismiss and say, "These stupid idiots – what are they talking about?" ... You have to find an alternative way to appeal to a public which is disillusioned and feels disenfranchised.'[266] Additionally, democracy is increasingly seen as a myth that reinforces the elites, who then make the decisions in the name of the public. 'The old system has failed the people, and the people realise it. ... Governments have lost authority. It does not matter how you vote. It does not make a difference.'[267]

So current assumptions and attitudes are not just inappropriate. They are irrelevant, flawed and downright counterproductive for identifying then embracing the new unthinkables.

How can those at the top be convinced to choose to change this, and define a new purpose? The early adopters were pioneers who pushed back institutional reluctance. 'I actually think people are thinking and caring more about purpose, and I think that's both personal purpose and corporate purpose,' said Katherine Garrett-Cox.[268] 'I think ... if you can find that connection and you find yourself working in an organisation where you genuinely feel you're making a difference, where people care about it and value it, and you're working with likeminded individuals, that is a very unique thing.'

Here's how one of the world's biggest corporations tried to do just that. The CEO of PepsiCo, Indra Nooyi, pushed hard for better performance, and with it a new sense of purpose. But achieving this depended on changing the company culture in order to react to a fast-moving and disrupted market.

Easy to come up with a catchy new ambition. Harder to make the transformation.

End notes

[265] Remarks to the British Academy event on the Future of the Corporation by Colin Mayer, Peter Moores Professor of Management Studies at the Saïd Business School, University of Oxford, 8 February 2018.

[266] Professor David Marquand, *The World at One*, BBC Radio 4, 24 December 2017.

[267] Professor Robert Tombs, *The World at One*, BBC Radio 4, 24 December 2017.

[268] op cit. Katherine Garrett-Cox, 26 February 2018.

18
PEPSICO: 'PERFORMANCE WITH PURPOSE'; HOW CULTURE EATS STRATEGY

A big majority of top leaders are still hesitating. While the most candid go as far as to confide that they are scared or overwhelmed by the scale of disruption, few have yet to mobilise in ways that end the default to conformity across their company or government department. This is due to two factors. First is their anxiety about leading a revolutionary attack on the status quo. Second is active resistance to seismic changes in the ranks below the C-suite.

This is indicative of what has been variously described to us as the 'frozen middle' or that 'permafrost' which 'lacks muscle'. We have examples – which we cannot name – where those at the top have had the courage and humility to lead a move against conformity. They have communicated their determination to those who work for them. But then they have been thwarted either by indifference or by active resistance and dragging of the anchor chains.

More broadly, there are first corporate fears – even from CEOs themselves – that capitalism is at risk. There are also signs of first moves towards greater joined-up recognition of the nature and true scale of the threats, then the imperative for coordinated action. The voices are not yet large in number. But they are more public and starting to urge the need to act with a degree of togetherness to warn that the way leadership is currently is not the way it should be. And the need is urgent.

Indra Nooyi has been President and CEO of PepsiCo since 2006. In 2014, she was ranked number 13 in Forbes's list of the world's 100 most powerful women. She was second on the 2015 Fortune list. These awards recognise more than the corporate performance in financial numbers. She is one of the few CEOs who have long positioned themselves publicly out front for changing corporate culture, mindsets and behaviour. A decade of concerted action began in 2009. For much of the time she struggled uphill against a general corporate spine of resistance. 'We had to change the culture of this company. When people say "culture eats strategy", I lived it first-hand. I saw how many people sort of said, why should we change our company that's been so successful, for a future we don't quite understand?'[269]

Had she experienced automatic buy-in to her ideas? 'When we become CEOs, they give us CEO pills, and that allows us to remain strong in the face of all this criticism,' she has often been quoted as saying. 'People talk about a honeymoon period, but there really isn't a honeymoon period, because from day one you are the CEO.' The challenge is both attractive and daunting. 'When you become CEO, overnight, you are the person calling all the shots. You're responsible for making sure you get all the information from the company, crystallise it down to simple ideas, and then tell the organisation what to do. It's a very daunting job to be a CEO.' In harsh times like the 2008 financial collapse, 'one had to learn in a hurry how to run this company through extreme periods of adversity. There's no book you can read.'

In 2006 Indra Nooyi's new driver for the world's second-largest food and beverage business became the slogan 'Performance with Purpose'.[270] The company's aim would be to deliver 'sustainable long-term growth while leaving a positive imprint on society and the environment'. The portfolio of products had to be changed at the same high speed that consumer tastes and demand were changing. PepsiCo had to be must be 'transformed to offer healthier options while making the food system more sustainable and communities more prosperous'. She was determined that this would not be dismissed as window-dressing. 'As we looked at consumer trends, and we looked at where we thought the markets were going, we knew we had to retool our portfolio. That was not even a question. We knew that if we didn't do it, our future was in jeopardy.'

Nooyi defined it as 'a great opportunity for us to change our portfolio, go where the consumer's going, and gain market share. But I was not stupid enough to say this can be done overnight. I knew the journey was going to be long, arduous, and was going to be filled with pitfalls. [That's] because it's not just the desire to change the portfolio, but to line up the entire company's innovation and marketing execution and budgets to go where this marketplace was going.

For ten years Indra Nooyi had driven the company realising that scarcity and climate change meant PepsiCo could not 'continue with business as usual'. If it did then PepsiCo was likely to discredit much of what had been achieved and could still be done. Sugar, salt and saturated fat levels had already been reduced. The number of nutritious products and beverages was up. Since 2015, she had been driven by the fear that corporates were losing touch with the new and more values-based expectations of customers. And that was not value by money. It was a whole new and different type of social value. The voices were getting louder. Yet generally the reactions in corporates and the public sector remained cautious and muted.

The public mood was suddenly changing unthinkably fast. Corporate complacency carried a new cost. Consumers were no longer just consuming indiscriminately in the ways they, their families and those around them had always done. Producers like PepsiCo could no longer benefit from consumer ignorance or indifference. It could not take convenient refuge behind its own slogans which suggested products were initially 'fun-for-you' and then 'better for you' and finally 'good-for-you'. Consumers were developing more than just different tastes. Driven by the NextGen they had different values born of a new sense of social responsibility, both for themselves and the world around them. As a result, increasing numbers were deep-diving into the nature and details of products so they could be sure they met new consumption criteria. They boycotted and did not buy products which represented anything they did not like.

But Pepsi had a culture that did not really want to embrace the fast-changing realities. 'I think this culture change is what took so long. Through that process, obviously people were impatient. Because the way our whole investing works, it's, yeah, you need to make the strategic changes. . . [But] once you start to change the culture of the company, everything else happens fast.'

The next generation were fast becoming very particular and demanding on this issue. But far too many big companies and governments were either blind or downright dismissive. 'We are in danger of creating angry customers and angry consumers,' we heard Indira Nooyi warn several large gatherings of fellow CEOs. Many nodded quietly. But how many really agreed? How many still conformed to the executive driver that 'value' meant the highest financial returns and the best quarterly earnings?

'Trust in institutions is near all-time lows as consumers increasingly expect companies to make money in a way that does not burden society,' Nooyi told LinkedIn.[271] In PepsiCo there had to be a 'galvanising of our entire company to embrace a deeper sense of meaning in our work. From the start we knew this wouldn't be easy. We knew it wouldn't happen overnight. We knew it would take a willingness to overcome the doubts of those who said it couldn't or shouldn't be done.' She talked of how, in PepsiCo, the old guard and old attitudes were being retired out.

It would be tough. But so what? That should be the new driver. Customers and consumers were demanding new attitudes and new ways. 'We also knew something else. We knew that being a good global citizen wasn't just the right thing to do. It was the right thing to do for our business.'[272]

Big demographic and generational changes were creating other new realities. The next generation did not naturally default to want to work in big corporations. Their different values extended to where they work, how they work, and what kind of organisation they will not work for. Loyalty to a brand means less. Attachment to new principles and values means more.

'They [millennials] no longer look at it [work] as just another paycheck. They look at it as "How can I go to work and make a difference in society?"' she told the Fortune CEO Initiative in New York City, attended by one hundred of the more enlightened CEOs.[273] She said it sitting alongside Mark Bertolini, CEO of Aetna. Mindful of that deep push back from the next generation, he had told the same chief executives that 'the capitalistic model no longer works. ... We are in danger of losing our operating licence.' It was Nooyi's alert expressed differently.

The Nooyi principles for deepening Performance with Purpose inside PepsiCo through to 2025 were unambiguous. The official line is that there is great excitement and engagement in almost every market. There is significant evidence that this is the achievement. 'Needed: systemic change' is the bold headline in PepsiCo's own public audit of Performance with Purpose so far.[274] 'The global food system is at an inflection point. Intensifying, interrelated challenges – in public health and nutrition, climate change, resource scarcity, human rights and other areas – require us to act. The vast network of farmers, traders, suppliers, processors, manufacturers and retailers that field our world must embrace change to create a healthier future for people and our planet.'

But what comes next is an example of how these bold and admirable principles can easily appear to stumble or be sidelined internally. Despite the clear message from the top, a giant corporate like PepsiCo, which is deeply sensitive to the dangers and the cost of unthinkables, can still be caught out in an all-too-public way by occasional internal failings.

On 10 April 2017 PepsiCo posted a video promotion for the Pepsi drink in cans. The title was 'Living Bolder'. It featured the highly paid model and reality TV star Kendall Jenner. The advertisement starts with a photo shoot in a US street. She steps out of it to join a heavily policed demonstration. The mood is good but potentially tense. Jenner is seen walking to the police line, apparently trying to defuse the tension. She does so by handing a can of Pepsi to a police officer, who is equipped with riot gear at the ready. He half smiles as if calmed by the Pepsi. It appears that, single-handedly, Jenner has calmed the police. This prompts cheers from the demonstrators.

The timing of the use of a can of Pepsi to calm a police officer who might soon be under orders to bang heads could not have been more ineptly timed. Police officers in various parts of the US were facing charges for killing scores of black Americans or disproportionate use of force. Many were acquitted. The Black Lives Matter movement, set up to reflect anger at the police targeting of black people, had significant momentum nationwide.

PepsiCo was widely accused of making an 'insensitive' video. An NBC News report described in sarcastic tones the hole PepsiCo had dug for itself. 'If the Black Lives Matter movement were led by a 21-year-old white supermodel armed with a can of fizzy soda, then maybe everyone would just get along. That's the vision presented in Pepsi's new ad featuring reality TV star Kendall Jenner.'[275]

The PR disaster was potentially an existential backlash of the very kind Indra Nooyi knew was there, and had warned about. Those 'angry consumers and citizens' had pushed back hard and very fast. Even her own massive corporate structure – which she believed she had sensitised to the issue under the Performance with Purpose – had been caught out.

On this occasion the internal systems failed. The global corporate policy had somehow been lost for a national marketing team in the enormous US market. This was missed in the pre-launch review process. As a result, additional checks and balances had to be introduced.

The promo ad was axed after less than one day to avoid reputational damage. In a statement on its website, PepsiCo said of the video, 'Clearly, we missed the mark.' They did not intend to make light of serious issues. 'Pepsi was trying to project a global message of unity, peace and understanding.' In 24 hours the advert had vaporised without trace.

It was a vivid example of how even the most sensitised of corporate structures does not automatically have the depth and breadth of internal behaviour, culture and mindset to think unthinkables. Well-established and ingrained top-down processes and attitudes are just not enough anymore.

This is even under a CEO like Indra Nooyi who more than any other CEO is fully seized of the disproportionate damage that can be done by such an unthinkable error. Nooyi revealed later that she had not been aware of the ad which caused such "consternation". She told Fortune:

'This has pained me a lot because this company is known for diversity, and the fact that everybody who produced the commercial and approved the commercial did not link it to Black Lives Matter made me scratch my head. . . I take everything personally. The minute I saw people upset, I pulled it. . . at the end of the day, our goal is not to offend anybody.'[276]

But from such a mistake can come a new precision and determination to ensure Performance with Purpose will not just work but succeed, both within PepsiCo and beyond. Is Indra Nooyi unbalanced at times by disruption? 'You can look at it with pessimism, that, "Oh, my God, all of this is changing," or optimism, to say perhaps this is the time to rewrite some of the rules and rebalance the competitive equation in the industry. I'm in the latter camp. And I'm looking at the world and saying, "Interesting times." I just hope I have the energy to help us through it. Right now, I do."[277]

So what principles will make that possible?

'All that we want to do is to make sure that this entity called PepsiCo, in whatever shape or form, on our own and in combination with others, remains a vibrant company that is growing; that's creating shareholder value, for the short and the long term. That's what we're singularly focused on. If it means changing our business model, but doing it in a way that doesn't take us way off our core competence so we don't fall flat on our face, absolutely we'll do it. But we have to do whatever transformation, keeping in mind that there are things that we're good at.'[278]

End notes

[269] This and subsequent remarks are from an interview with Indra Nooyi on the *Freakonomics Radio* podcast, 31 January 2018.

[270] *Performance with purpose*, PepsiCo, 17 October 2016.

[271] 'Indra Nooyi just issued a major challenge to the world's CEOs' by Daniel Roth, LinkedIn, 19 October 2016.

[272] '10 years ago, I said PepsiCo had to be about more than making money. Here's what's in store for the next 10' by Indra Nooyi, LinkedIn, 17 October 2016.

[273] 25 September 2017.

[274] op cit. *Performance with purpose.*

[275] 'Pepsi pulls controversial Kendall Jenner ad after outcry, *NBC News* website, 5 April 2017.

[276] 21 September 2017.

[277] ibid.

[278] op cit. Indra Nooyi interview for Freakonomics Radio.

19

'YOU FUCKED UP THE WORLD' LET'S TALK ABOUT FIXING IT

So where has this book taken you so far? Why should you keep reading it then devote time to working through the implications?

It is not written to scare. It is designed above all to reassure, then to share positive new possibilities and routes for leaders to explore. They – like you – are not alone, even though many probably feel they are.

If there are problems, then it is natural to assume that there must be solutions. Do they exist? If so, what are they? After all, identifying a problem must mean there is a solution. **Thinking the Unthinkable** has set out to find them. We have found that such an ambitious assumption of once-and-for-all solutions is too grand for the moment. There is no single solution yet. We echo a consensus view here. 'We face a host of significant problems, many of which can spiral out of control very quickly, and not a lot of solutions,' wrote Ivo Daalder, President of the Chicago Council on Global Affairs after the three-day Munich Security Conference in February 2018.[279]

But we signal that there are ways to face up to – then deal with – the scary stuff. From our hundreds of interviews and conversations with those at the top, there are certainly new ideas and options. 'We are slowly thinking the fact that the world is now more fragile,' confirmed Kristalina Georgieva, CEO of the World Bank.[280] 'Changing institutions like mine to be leaders in providing solutions. That is the hope.' Yet so far there are nothing like as many new ideas or solutions as the scale of disruption to conformity suggests or requires. So do please help us identify and track them down.

With an imperative to find positives, our research work has discovered first-mover examples of solutions. As you will see later, we report them as a valuable contribution to finding that new and far broader common ground. All are experiments. Some work. Many are well-intentioned stabs into the unknown. Each in their own way at least recognises the immense new scale of unthinkables. Some actively seize the opportunity from disruption. Rania Nashar, the new CEO of the Saudi Commercial Bank, sets an important benchmark ambition. She took the executive reins in 2017. She has communicated a new core principle to those working for her. It is: 'disrupt to grow'.[281]

By way of this book and the ongoing **Thinking the Unthinkable** community and research process, those stabs into the unknown can be shared actively with the vast number of leaders and organisations. They know they need to find new models. But most are not sure where to look. Our work is designed to provide the periscope that scans the horizon and provides new reassurance on what there is out there. We urge that you become part of that ongoing process too.

One next step is to bring together many of the anxious top leaders we have met confidentially to share experiences. The aim would be to build reassurance in a time of often-acute anxiety. We have already witnessed a small number of examples of how positively that works. But how to do more and broaden awareness? How to introduce them to each other and then create a movement or process of mutual concern which gives new confidence and helps redefine leadership for the new normal – frailties and all?

This is the urgent challenge. But time is short. It is not just us at the **Thinking the Unthinkable** project who say that. It is the leaders themselves, when in their most frank mode.

Leaders – even the most competitive and self-assured – privately talk of wanting to find that reassurance from disruption. They realise the scale of new realities, and especially the intensifying questions about the purpose of corporates and governments. They also realise this needs a new courage, humility and above all way of working.

But they need new space and confidences to achieve it. This would help release them from the tyranny of quarterly reporting because 'every CEO hates quarterly reporting: it's like running up a down escalator.'[282] It would also lighten the burden of constraints that limit their space to respond effectively to the apparently unstoppable waves of new public scepticism.

There are also the new pressures from the millennial generation, especially with their demands for greater social values and responsibility. Corporates can make money, but they must do so with a different set of those values. 'Boards: how much do they put value to values?' asked a more radical CEO from the next generation.[283] 'What if they are not aligned? ... Boards tend to just want conformity.' For so many reasons these pressures have been core to creating the backlash and turbulence from Young Leaders 3.0.[284] They need to be attracted, engaged and taken notice of. Instead many are alienated by the fast-changing institutional realities of corporate and government life. They are shunning it.[285] Remember what we saw Indra Nooyi tell one hundred fellow CEOs who are at the enlightened end of the spectrum: 'They [millennials] no longer look at it as just a paycheck. They look at it as "How can I go to work and make a difference in society?"'[286]

The disillusionment of new generations is more than just irritation. The attitudes and life views of those in their forties and younger are a quantum difference from the way many top leaders in the fifties and sixties assume they should still run things. In summary, one headline before Italy's constitutional referendum in 2016 shouted 'Generation X tires of gerontocracy'.[287] 'The next generation want to share, especially the millennials in their twenties and thirties. They are not obsessed with ownership,' says Jean Liu, President of Didi Chuxing, the phenomenally successful Chinese startup rival to the ridesharing apps Uber and Lyft.[288] 'Creating a flexible lifestyle is natural to the next generation, especially flexible hours. ... There is a disruption of the mindset powered by technology.' Additionally, there is 'no patience for poor internal values in an organisation,' says a senior IBM executive quoting her 25-year-old daughter's work experiences.[289]

Jason Blackstock stepped down in early 2018 as head of STEaPP, the Department of Science, Technology, Engineering and Public Policy at University College London (UCL). It provides 'current and future decision makers with the skills and experience to navigate a rapidly changing world'[290]. He told us: 'When I'm giving lectures to my students in this millennial generation, when you're talking about the problems, the response goes something like, "Yeah, yeah. We get [that] you fucked up the world. But let's start talking about what we can do to fix it." In other words, they get that things aren't where they should be or where they would like them to be.'[291] Conforming to the way leadership has been is no longer the intention of the vast majority who make it to graduation. Now the intention is to make a difference and not just to fall in step with the system that in their view has left so many legacies of dysfunctionality and division.

Instead of further alienating them, there are enormous opportunities to engage this next generation in the ways they are looking for. As we show later, there are examples of Generations Y and 3.0 reverse-mentoring those who are older and more set in their ways. It works. It reenergises conformist minds who until now have pushed back and found reassurance in disruption by not changing.

If that does not happen, those in NextGen that do not like the purpose that they see or experience in corporates or governments – an ever-larger number – routinely decide to up sticks. With no compunction or sense of loyalty, they leave and move on. As a result, there is an ever-tighter market for skills and labour. There is also a 'disastrous mismatch between the skills that schools currently provide and those that young people will need to thrive in the workplaces of the future'.[292] So the new trend of upping and going if dissatisfied is itself a new disruptor. Retention is 'an expensive problem. People are moving around more than ever.'[293] '44% of millennials will move jobs in two years. Organisations aren't set up for that high a turnover.'[294]

This is confirmation of the growing existential threat: will there be enough new leaders in the next generational cohort? 'Companies are increasingly run by average and mediocre people. ... People coming out of business schools and universities don't want to join big corporations anymore,' said one top C-suiter.[295] 'The next generation is absolutely switched off,' said another concerned CEO.[296] They 'do not want to go to the top levels'. Have executive search firms accepted this and bitten this bullet of change? It appears not. They are 'dog lazy' because they will not recognise this, one leading CEO told us dismissively.

As well as the determination to force a new sense of purpose on corporates, there is one other new positive. Mobility is increasingly a talent asset as opposed to liability. Money is no longer enough to lure talent and keep it. 'These days, we don't discount talent for moving after three years. Often it is a sign of curiosity,' says Damien O'Brien, Chairman of the executive search partnership Egon Zehnder.[297] 'The ability to adapt and learn is more important than sectoral experience.'

But there remains a tortured and unresolved question. How willing to release the shackles and let go are the chairmen, CEOs or C-suiters who have qualified for the top through conformity? The leadership guru John R Childress wrote with optimism and good reason that the new ambition must be that 'the role of the CEO is one of influence, not control: the leader [must be] an agent of change, not the sole source of wisdom and decisions'.[298] But as 2017 and now 2018 have continued to prove, that is easy to write and conceive of. It is much harder to confront and deliver.

Indeed, it is difficult to achieve when the existential and career threats are so great. Control remains a core instinct of leaders, and even more so it appears to be the default setting. As we discovered, on balance most consider it easier to perform like the executive they have always been. 'If you only work in your own echo chamber and find criticism to be totally illegitimate' then understanding the new realities is unlikely. Instead you 'must have views heard and challenged [and ask] what can I learn from this ... and from criticism'.[299]

The unfortunate reality is that it is usually too difficult to offload embedded constraints and attitudes. Worse still, they then stifle the ability to think the unthinkable. Too many at the top, and those who work for them, are forced down this narrow avenue of conformity when the need is the opposite. And it is hard to escape those shackles.

Micah Zenko discovered this inevitable default instinct too when investigating the effectiveness of red teaming simulations. A Red Team is an expert group which role-plays how an adversary tries to counter all that you do.[300] He asked: do they really help leaders make better-informed decisions in moments of crisis? Zenko concluded: 'Senior leaders will introduce limitations or artificialities ... to ensure that their preferred strategies or ideas are validated during the simulation' with those at the top 'going through the motions, but refusing to learn and improve'.[301]

Leaders cannot evade what is now expected of them. And they have to accept alternative views, however out of sync they might appear to the conformist minds at the top.

Here is the message after what many viewed as the disastrous British government decision to engage in war in Iraq to remove Saddam Hussein in 2003. Did questioning voices with legitimate alternative views from every level get heard in the ways that were needed? 'The readiness to take dissent ... has to come from the top. You need that worry, that still-small voice that tells you that maybe not everything I am being told is correct,' says Professor Sir Lawrence Freedman, a member of the Chilcot enquiry in the UK who endured the gruelling seven-year process which dissected the failures of government and governance that led to the Iraq war.[302] 'At the higher levels of government there is far too much going along with something because this is where the country seems to be, or where the Prime Minister of the day seems to be.'

In other words, resistances and conformity run deep even when the new scale of threats and challenges is enormous and at odds with institutional culture, mindsets or behaviour. That is the time when leaders need to near every view, however alternative. This is a core base line issue for thinking unthinkables.

End notes

[279] 'This week's reads – missing in Munich' by Ivo H Daalder, Chicago Council on Global Relations, 22 February 2018.

[280] Kristalina Georgieva, remarks to the Brussels Forum, 9 March 2018.

[281] Rania Nashar, remarks at the Future Investment Initiative, Riyadh, 25 October 2017.

[282] Private remarks from a former Deputy CEO, 13 March 2018.

[283] Private remarks, 26 February 2018.

[284] To sample the pressures, see *Young leaders 3.0: stories, insights and tips for next-generation achievers* (2014) by Jason Ma. USA: Young Leaders 3.0 Press.

[285] 'More graduates reject careers in the city' by Nicola Woodcock, *The Times*, 12 July 2017.

[286] Remarks to the Fortune CEO Initiative at the Ritz Carlton Hotel, New York, 25 September 2017.

[287] 'Generation X tires of gerontocracy' by Rachel Sanderson, *Financial Times*, 3 December 2016.

[288] Remarks at the Future Investment Initiative in Riyadh, 25 October 2017.

[289] Presentation by Anita Karlsson-Dion, Vice President of Cognitive Process Services at IBM, Melbourne Big Ideas Summit, 30 October 2017.

[290] STEaPP, the Department of Science, Technology, Engineering and Public Policy at University College London (UCL).

[291] Interview on 27 February 2018. Some 3000 students have been through STEaPP's 'How to change the world' course.

[292] Sir Michael Barber, quoted in 'Stakes rise for a system threatened by skills crisis' by Miranda Green, *Financial Times*, 15 November 2017.

[293] Patrick King, Head of Insights Team for Learning Solutions at LinkedIn, OEB conference in Berlin, 8 December 2017.

[294] See for example 'Find yourself a reverse mentor fast – millennials are taking over the workplace' by Phoebe Luckhurst, *Evening Standard*, 13 September 2016.

[295] Private remarks, 13 March 2018.

[296] Private remarks, 26 February 2018.

[297] Quoted in 'In the old days you could buy talent with money: Damien O'Brien' by Manu Balachandran, *Forbes India*, 21 February 2018.

[298] *A time for leadership: global perspectives from an accelerated European market place* (2000) by John R Childress. The Leadership Press: Los Angeles/New York.

[299] Remarks by Hillary Clinton on leadership at the World Knowledge Forum, Seoul, 18 October 2017.

[300] The principle of Red Teams was conceived during the Cold War to try to understand and anticipate Soviet (Red) thinking. They have since become fashionable in business and government circles.

[301] *Red team: how to succeed by thinking like the enemy* (2015) by Micah Zenko. New York: Basic Books, pp. 19–20.

[302] Sir Lawrence Freedman speaking at the Institute for Government for the launch of his book, *The future of war: a history* (2017; London: Allen Lane), 9 October 2017.

20
'YOU AIN'T HEARD NOTHING YET'

How to bring leaders together and create that new ever-growing, always-sharing critical community of lily pads for action? How to converge their anxieties in order to create a few giant lily pads, or even one massive lily pad, with their executive navigation systems set for progress? The coming-together would symbolise a new community of concerned leaders that could have traction for a significant change of perceptions and actions.

The ambition is achievable if the default veneers of executive self-protection and self-justification can be stripped off. The new vulnerabilities and anxieties can be shared by way of the new process. This is not in order to point a finger of blame. It is designed to highlight firstly the challenge from unthinkables, then what is not working and where work is needed.

It is a massive ask. In many ways it goes against the executive grain to share so much. That grain will fight – and is fighting – against the inexorable forces of gravity. Yet at the same time, towards the end of 2017 and in the first months of 2018 we have seen how the momentum of anxiety is there and growing. There are signs that there is at last a greater will at the highest levels to share. This is even though the instinct is to default to traditional responses. But they are responses that are now out of sync with the dramatic scale of the radical new culture and behaviour that leaders need to adopt.

Indeed, those default responses are not only inappropriate. They are downright destructive.

In response it is tempting for boards, or those who make the highest-level appointments, to believe they must be seen to act decisively. It is assumed that high-profile sackings, a change of name, face and image are the required response for apparent 'failure' or at least failings. It is presumed that a clear out will automatically remove 'the problem'. Sending instant signals can reassure those who need to receive them. But in reality, such a new broom or clean sweep betrays the scale of misunderstanding. Are board members even mentally calibrated to handle the scale of disruption to all they assume and are conditioned for?[303] Is it far more profound than most are prepared to even nod towards, let alone embrace with the vigour that is needed?

The figureheads at the top will inevitably be assumed to be the core problem. Mostly they are not. Indeed, as you will see, some of our examples of qualified success are from CEOs who have been in their jobs for a decade or more. It appears longevity often has greater value than many board members or impatient investors might assume. When there is an apparent failure to handle new instability or disruption, wielding the corporate axe can tend to be the default strategy.

It is evidence of how attitudes and the system itself are under acute stress. They are just not calibrated for the scale and intensity of change that has shocked corporates and governments since 2014. Above all, the human capacity to cope with increasingly unforgiving cultures and systems has been exposed as inadequate to handle the scale and intensity of change. This is not just an assertion. Critically, it is what large numbers of leaders themselves told us. That human capacity has become super stressed and increasingly ineffectual. But somehow the existing ways of doing things are allowed to muddle along, without the issues being either accepted or embraced.

Overall, the scale of issues that leaders face is modest compared to what lies ahead. As Al Jolson memorably told the orchestra for his new movie *The Jazz Singer* which premiered in the Warner Theatre on Broadway in 1927: 'I tell yer: you ain't heard nothing yet.' New talkie films would now have their own recorded music, so live musicians like them would no longer be needed.

Jolson was the first of many singers who had to tell their musicians that the days of the silent movie were over, and they had yet to accept it.

Most, though, hoped that the new reality would be a passing irritation rather than the seismic disruption for them and their skills which Jolson warned lay ahead.

Jolson was right; the musicians were wrong, even if for understandable reasons of fear.

Disruption is how it turned out, however unpalatable Jolson's warning sounded.

End notes

[303] See a typical letter of anxiety from Susie Cummings, Founder and Chief Executive of Nurole: 'We cannot fill boards using old recruitment practices', *Financial Times*, 12 January 2018.

21

A 'NEW WARTIME' THAT NEEDS NEW WEAPONS

By now you must be recognising yourself or a leader you work for.

Leaders who made their way to the top in a period equivalent to 'peace' now find themselves wrong-footed and flat-footed by this existential 'war'. The weapons in this 'war' do not explode and kill people. They are new ideas and ambitions which have high impact, then detonate and destroy assumptions of stability.

The scale and nature of these new 'weapons' exposes narrow-mindedness and blinkered assumptions. Top leaders find themselves unprepared and even ill-suited to the pressures and demands of the new 'wartime'. Our interviews and conversations confirm their private struggle to cope. Leaders frequently volunteered the descriptions 'scared' and 'overwhelmed', and occasionally they even admitted this willingly in public.[304]

Here is how one very senior executive recounted a visit to a colleague who never wants to leave the impression he is overwhelmed. All issues are still on his desk – just! All that was missing was a frog sitting in boiling water. 'I think you talk to most CEOs, they hate their lives because they are purely reacting to whatever is coming. I went to see [redacted]. ... Five times in the meeting he said: "This sits at the edge of my desk" [pointing to documents he would prefer not to deal with, but has to keep in play], and I said, "OK. You've said it five times now. I want to make sure I understand what you're saying." I said, "Let me guess: are you saying that you have so much shit coming your way every day that you don't have time to focus on this? It's not because you don't want to.

It's [because] you just don't have time? But equally you can't say it's off your desk, because that's equally unacceptable. Hence your phrase: "It's at the edge of my desk"? He said, "Absolutely right."'[305]

Some we met candidly admitted they were no longer sure they could do the job any more. One senior figure at a leading business school speculated that many top executives were realising their time was up. It was 'time to cash in their chips while they have value.'

Leaders at the highest levels are not meant to feel that way, of course. And if they do, they should never show it. Yet without exception, in our closed-door meetings, chairmen, chief executives and top-level public servants nodded (often aggressively) with agreement and relief that the new frailties they themselves are feeling are being identified and recognised at last. Former UK Prime Minister Tony Blair publicly captured the strains: 'Making sense of it is very hard. I feel like a student of politics again. I spent most of my political life in a state of reasonable certainty.'[306]

If you are surprised by this depth of gloom, then so are we as co-authors. In many ways surprise has now morphed ominously into shock.

But why has this happened? Even experts who have made their careers and livelihoods from consulting, teaching and writing about leadership confirm how they find the scale and depth of unthinkables scarily overtaking the capacity to respond and adapt. Those who have made a career from examining and advising on leadership realise that the framing which has made their reputations may increasingly no longer be appropriate.

Although the comparison is rather unfortunate and dramatic, their predicament can be likened to the secret and usually lonely personal trauma of being an alcoholic. Just like those with a drink problem, these leaders know they have big difficulties like feeling overwhelmed by the new intensity of non-normal events. But for reasons of career, reputation and pride they stay largely silent, even among their close confidants. As we have witnessed, only when in the same room as a handful of their peers, and after a polite but increasingly frank dance around the issue for an hour or two, do they all express relief.

At last their predicament is now being recognised and talked about. At last, as with alcoholics, they can acknowledge their own struggle, start to identify the triggers and deal with them. It is then that the floodgates of revelation and self-doubt can open with a new confidence, thereby confirming the very human scale and recognition of the new vulnerability.

We believe that opening to the new unthinkables will become a new strength too. Such openness will lead eventually to solutions. Then those lily pads in that infinite ocean of uncertainty can begin to approach each other and merge. This pooling of experiences should then offer new insights and benefits to those leaders who come out and reveal that they too are searching for new ways.

Some will feel this is an exaggeration of the mood and what was said. But it is certainly the way it frequently seemed during our hundreds of contacts. That is a major first stage achievement. But as with alcoholism, identifying a 'problem' does not in any way guarantee that there is a quick, ready-made or achievable 'solution'. It is the same for unthinkables. So far, there are a few disparate, partially tested ideas and experiences out there which need to be shared. There is not yet any heartening evidence that they work universally in the decisive ways that are required by such enormous challenges to leaderships.

And they are not just the same old challenges being recycled and given a re-tread. No! Many leaders have confided that they consider them existential not just for them personally but more importantly for the organisation or company they lead.

Such frankness is remarkable, especially given the likely professional cost to any leader of revealing possible weaknesses or failings to voters, shareholders, investors, regulators or those who recruit him or her. Routinely such apparent weakness is punished by being sacked or voted out. But is it really a weakness to admit that disruption is upending so much of the relative state of stability that has comfortably been assumed until now?

Far from it. Admitting the new existential threat represents precisely the courage and humility that is needed. We argue that both of these are strengths. Neither of them is a weakness. Indeed, one solution is not to sack or force out those at the top. It is to keep those who have been there for years, know the system inside out, and have been bloodied by leading through not just the ups, but the downs of other crises as well.

The record and achievements of a CEO like Indra Nooyi show that at PespsiCo.

What follows is the similar, upbeat experiences of two banks: DBS in Singapore and DNB in Norway. The risks taken by their CEOs hold important lessons of the kind of positives that come from longevity and continuity.

End notes

[304] For example, Fortune CEO Initiative at the Ritz Carlton Hotel, New York on 25 September 2017; or Session 2 at the Future Investment Initiative conference in Riyadh, 25 October 2017.

[305] Private remarks, 13 March 2018.

[306] 'The boys of Brexit: Tony Blair and Nigel Farage' by Maureen Dowd, *The New York Times*, 18 September 2017.

22

THE NEW GANDALF: 'HOW TO ENSURE THE SWITCH GOES ON'

In the search for solutions to think the unthinkable we have only found a few successes. We are looking for more. Singapore's DBS is one. It is South East Asia's biggest bank, with 22,000 employees in six main operating countries. During 2018 its plan is to expand to 25,000.

The bank's board and top executives can feel confident now. But after DBS took the risk of starting a transformation process in 2009, it has taken nine years of experimentation to get to this point. The route ahead and the options were never clear or proven. Success never came fast. It was never assured or guaranteed. Even now, the process is not over. But an initial determination for 'fixing stuff' in a helter-skelter banking environment of digital change is now embedded in the bank's operating DNA.

Indeed, there were times in the early years after 2009 when understanding the nature of unthinkables facing the bank and then confronting them never really achieved traction, let alone breakthroughs. And the challenges kept changing. So uniquely, DBS realised it had to re-invent and evolve its transformation ideas at least each year. This was especially true as the profound impact of digitisation drilled ever deeper into the basic foundations of how banks assumed they would operate and function. In 2014 DBS was forced to ask itself, 'Is our traditional revenue going to be eaten away?'

Yet in confronting the implications of digital it achieved a sustained breakthrough. Several years of quarterly growth reassured the board and any sceptics that new returns can flow from transformation. Now DBS is a model which others should learn from and try to emulate. And that model for change is not just for banking. It could be for every corporate and institution. The important lessons come from how they confronted change and then achieved it.

The CEO, Piyush Gupta, became the driving force when he arrived at DBS in 2009. He had worked in Citigroup for 27 years. He joined what was the Development Bank of Singapore. It had been set up 40 years earlier to fund the small, young, island state's industrial development. It was highly bureaucratic with a very public sector way of working.

Piyush Gupta confronted a culture of complacency, innovation inertia and myopia towards global realities. The roadblocks and anchor chains he faced came from that. Ultimately the bank's survival would be threatened by an embedded DBS culture which was not calibrated to confront the unthinkable that banking had no options but to change fundamentally. Why? 'The world was changing around us.' But the bank was not changing. Any thought of re-modelling culture to respond to change was viewed as 'fuzzy'.

How did Gupta handle what he faced? 'Don't assume the word "disruption" means you can't do anything about it. "Disruption" is not the word you should be thinking about: it is "transformation". "Transformation" assumes that the technologies are happening in a way to benefit you. ... You must not be stubborn. I spent seven years then working to turn my company into a world-class multinational. Now I try to convert it into a startup! It can be done. But you have to make a lot of effort in experimentation. Incubation, ideation, hand-holding – trying a bunch of different things.'[307]

DBS had to become 'customer obsessed, data driven, take risks and experiment, be agile, and be a learning organisation'.[308] In 2009 DBS was none of those, despite the early seismic changes and unthinkables that were already evolving around it. The DBS way forward was reinforced when Singapore's PAP government experienced a shock push back by voters in the 2011 election. A Deputy Prime Minister told Piyush Gupta: 'The world is changing. We need to recalibrate, with reskilling, retooling, refocusing the entire economy. ... If we are not smart and [do not] do it right ourselves, then someone will come and do it for us.'[309]

Now it has a culture of active engagement being expected from all employee levels and ages. As far as possible there is no discrimination by hierarchy. The new inspiration is the culture of the super successful GANDALF corporations – Google, Amazon, Netflix, Apple, LinkedIn and Facebook. These new 'non-bankers are the ones that push boundaries'.[310] DBS sees itself as potentially the missing D in GANDALF.

It is some change! The transformation process is not driven as a convenient 'nice to talk about' by a couple of irritating has-beens in a forgotten corner of a distant office. It is driven personally from the very top by the CEO through a Chief Transformation Officer, Paul Cobban. His Transformation Team is a high-profile engine room of the bank with a dedicated staff of 50. Much of the DBS success story for seeking solutions can be told by the Transformation Team, warts and all.[311] Their core role is to implement what has become an intense, ongoing dynamic culture of change which embraces the scale of disruption, and which no one in the bank can be allowed to avoid.

Is that enough after nine years? 'Clearly not, as we still feel like we have quite a long way to go to get to the stage where we feel we are ready to take that level of challenge on,' Paul Cobban told us. Even with success there is no room for complacency. So led by the Transformation Team the bank has been committed to a process without end for routinely reviewing all options for constant change and self-assessment. Solutions don't just happen. New options and ideas are tested. Many work, but many don't.

How wacky and maverick can DBS employees be with suggestions and new ideas? 'One of the big challenges we are facing is to create this psychological safety net. Importantly we don't penalise anyone who suggests ideas which fail to mature or deliver as expected.' Instead it is becoming like the culture of Silicon Valley in the US, where failure is a badge of honour, although 'we are not quite there' yet. 'We still have a culture of still wanting our idea to work and putting our own personal brand on those ideas.'

DBS has adopted the principles of design thinking and the concepts of human-centred design.[312] The aim is to work out where the blockages are and who are the blockers. 'We realised that we were not great at meetings. They often had low attendances, poorly planned agendas, bad punctuality and a lack of equal share of voice,' explained Paul Cobban. They created a new 'meeting MoJo' ('based on a Google concept of the psychological safety net').

It would ensure 'psychological safety in a meeting for everyone, however junior. MO is a "Meeting Owner" who makes sure everyone in the room gets an equal share of voice. He or she clarifies the purpose of the meeting, then summarises it. JO is the "Joyful Observer" who spends 30 seconds giving a verdict on how well MO did what was expected.'

DBS believes it has got itself to a smart, agile commercial position that puts it way ahead of its competitors. That is confirmed by the international awards it has received. But today DBS has a new, unexpected threat 'The most real, near-term existential threat is the attack from the big tech companies. Especially in this part of the world with what's happening in China, we feel very much that they are knocking on our door. We can see our revenues under threat etc,' was how Paul Cobban described the new challenge.

While concerned, the official DBS tone is one of admiration for new competitors and what is regarded as their incredible success journeys. 'When we started our journey, we didn't know. None of us anticipated how the Alibabas and the Tencents of the world would expand into banking and finance. Seeing how they can scale into the financial services is astonishing. Even the Chinese regulators have had a tough time regulating them because they grew so quickly.' One unconnected leading top-level executive based in China for many years described this huge new threat to global corporates like his own. It comes from Chinese 'companies on steroids' with a message 'move over, it is us [who are] coming now'. It means 'we can't compete'.

The threat was massive and immediate. As a result, Piyush Gupta realised that DBS should no longer allow itself to be regarded as a bank. It had to become a tech company which happened to handle people's increasingly digital money. Therefore he had to convince investors. He had to 'put a dollar value on our digital strategy'. He told them 'don't value us like a bank; value us like a tech company'. Creating this and selling a new, attractive investment jacket was seen as a tough challenge on a 'really intellectual path'.[313] But it has been working.

Securing board understanding for the scale and nature of the new disruption – then their support for radical action – has been vital. Bank analysts say that Piyush Gupta deserves praise for seeing what was coming over the horizon after 2009 well before his peers and competitors. It may have been unthinkable and unpalatable to many. But it could not have been denied or evaded in the way many top conformist minds usually defaulted to. It had to be confronted.

But nothing was guaranteed. There were big risks. Would the bank's business benefit from change? Would the staff push back and make Gupta's life hell? Would the board lose confidence and patience?

The new CEO had to build his credibility. Nothing happened as quickly, conveniently or smoothly as things might seem now. Investors wanted improved quarterly numbers every three months. Transformation would take several years. The cycles of outsiders expecting swift delivery of business results and the realities of transformation were dramatically out of sync.

In the first five years 'we were just fixing stuff. When we got to 2014, we pivoted. [We said]: "Right, we are now going to go full-on digital." And by then we'd already had a good set of both financial and non-financial outcomes that fed that credibility. ... Had we not had the financial results we have had, I think it would have been a whole different story!' Paul Cobban told us.

A key learning from DBS is that Gupta realised the urgent need to be sure that the board understood both the threats from unthinkables and digital disruption as well as the new business opportunities. He took them on a site visit to South Korea, regarded as arguably the most advanced country both for developing digital technology and embracing the implications at the time. Gupta 'spent time with the board recognising the digital strategy that we've now embarked upon was imperative. As a result we have an incredibly supportive board, who are advocating what we have done to the other boards they are sitting on,' said Cobban. 'You can argue that we could have done it sooner. [Nevertheless] it has given us this incredible advantage over our industry peers in where we are right now.'

Another key learning from DBS is the doubtful value of consultants who arrive with their precisely calibrated models and tick boxes for change. This did not fit with the Gupta vision that the best chance for DBS to secure change would be through ideas generated internally by those who work in the bank. One consultant contract was ended early as responsibility for creating new ideas shifted dramatically to DBS employees at all levels.

'Piyush is very reluctant to seek help and execution. He believes we should do that ourselves generally, but using his guidelines.' One insider described how when he suggested 'Let me try some stuff out,' Piyush said 'Go ahead. Do it!' In his previous workplace the response would have been 'No. No. I want to do it. That is my job.' This is an acceptance of the principle of a new humility. Unlike the culture in most institutions and corporates, it should no longer be expected that those at the top know the answers. It is likely that – even if they don't have the executive status – others working for him or her are likely to have great suggestions for innovations which must be thought about.

A central element of the DBS way of transformation has been deep engagement by employees at all levels. Piyush Gupta kept asking: 'How do you create an environment where people learn new things?'[314] He was determined to move any permafrost and treacle in the middle and upper layers. 'Some employees had suggested implementing hackathons.[315] He took up the idea and spread them more widely right across the organisation. DBS stopped spending money on 'fancy business school training for our top senior talents'. They were put through the hackathon experience instead.

'We run all kinds of hackathons,' Piyush Gupta explained. 'We run 20 or 25 of them. We have 40- and 50-year-olds who work with kids in their twenties to spend five days in a warehouse and come up with an app. The excitement people have when they come up with an app to solve a trivial problem is massive. But is all about changing people's mindsets. And the confidence to know they can actually do things that make an impact and the way work progresses.'[316]

For those locked away for five days, how does the mindset change, both for that next generation and those at the top? 'We started with 20-year-olds in the first hackathon. In the third one I said I did not want anyone under 40 in the room other than the people we got from the startup. So we created teams of ten: two people from the startup and eight people in their forties. We gave them a problem. They spent 72 hours. ... Solutions they came up with were presented by the 40-year olds. The confidence it gave them to know that they can do WhatsApp and bring it to the work environment and work...' He clicked his fingers for emphasis. 'That's a switch. The switch goes on!'[317]

The impact on staff and their attitudes has been seismic. 'A lot of guys ... tell me that was the most profound thing they ever went through in their career. For the first time they realised they could actually work quickly and get things done. It was the first time they experienced this startup culture, which was the intent,' said Paul Cobban. DBS also started using hackathons to hire staff for a new technology and innovation centre in India. 'We attracted 20,000 applicants, of which we hired about 50.'

The strategy has gone a long way into breaking down the generational walls. 'Millennials get an intentionally disproportionate share of voice when it comes to feedback about the way we work.' At a company conference, one session was run and designed by millennials on 'This is what we think about how we should work at DBS.' They generated data which showed the divide of thinking between the baby boomers and the Gen X people and the millennials.

Has it worked throughout DBS? 'Definitely. DBS has transformed. As I sit amongst the rest of the team and look around the workspace, it's full of trees and open plan. ... The energy in the room is just completely different. The dress code is different. Everything. The vibe is just completely transformed. Our strategy has been applied bank-wide. But like any transformation it is uneven and you get some areas where they have embraced it more than others.'

So after eight years, why has the DBS transformation initiative worked so far? 'We have made a very deliberate approach of trying to change the culture of the whole organisation towards a more adaptable, innovative and agile approach. Other companies typically start in one area or have a separate team called the Innovation Team that does all the innovation work. And then these teams have difficulty selling what they have done into other parts of these companies,' is Paul Cobban's conclusion.

At DBS, employees often share their experience with two or three companies each week. But the DBS view is that the far greater size of many corporates makes it harder for them to replicate and implement the model successfully. Others are also way behind. 'We are very open because it is our people who have helped make it happen. And we are ahead in the game. And it is because we've got eight years of foundational culture training.' But inevitably there is a flattering downside: the increasing number of DBS staff being targeted to be poached by other companies.

What about the business of implementing transformation and taking employees on what for many could be a rough journey? 'In the first couple of years … I came across people who said "The new guy is here: I'm just going to keep my head down and he will be gone soon." But after four years and after six years people don't say that anymore. They see that over that period of time the people who have progressed in the company are those that have embraced a new paradigm of thinking,' said Paul Cobban. 'DBS does not "hire and fire"; it works for some companies but not for us. However we have a rigorous performance management process and talent program to evaluate our people. What we've found is that the leaders who have embraced the digital transition have found that their careers have accelerated compared to those who have been less supportive. The latter have found it harder to stand out.'

Can this dramatic transformation process and culture work for other sectors? Piyush Gupta is cautious. 'No, it is not easy.' We witnessed him being asked, for example, if DBS's transformation could work for shipping and especially the struggling container business. Both are viewed as needing urgent rejuvenation. 'In banking we deal in bits and bytes, so it is easier to transform. … You can completely change the role of players right along the banking chain. … Shipping must move their physical oil and physical iron ore – something you can't get away from. It is the core of the business. But at some level I do think you can transform and make progress.'[318]

Hence the caution of this ongoing **Thinking the Unthinkable** work: a problem does not necessarily mean there are automatic solutions. Instead there are likely to be options that can be assessed and experimented with. But there are no guarantees.

End notes

[307] Piyush Gupta, remarks during a discussion on leadership at the Sea Asia conference in the Marina Bay Sands Hotel, Singapore, 25 April 2017.

[308] Presentation by Piyush Gupta, 17 November 2017.

[309] op cit. Piyush Gupta, 25 April 2017.

[310] 'Banking so smooth that it is almost invisible' by Abhishek Raval, *Express Computer*, 7 October 2016.

[311] Interview on 28 February 2018.

[312] Human centred design has been developed by the Stanford d.school at Stanford University, famous for its work on design thinking, and ideo.org. The methods have been adopted widely.

[313] op cit. Piyush Gupta, 17 November 2017.

[314] op cit. Piyush Gupta, 25 April 2017.

[315] A design-sprint event. See wikipedia.org/wiki/Hackathon.

[316] op cit. Piyush Gupta, 25 April 2017.

[317] ibid.

[318] ibid.

23
CONSORTING WITH THE FRENEMY TO SURVIVE

DNB ASA describes itself as Norway's leading investment bank, and the country's largest financial services group. It focuses especially on the shipping, energy, retail and seafood sectors. But is it still a bank?

Remarkably, in 2018 Rune Bjerke, the CEO, was still in post after 11 years in the job. It is far longer than almost all of his banking contemporaries. Why does he believe he remains the best top executive for DNB? 'You have to renew yourself, be curious and listen. You have to ask questions all the time and bring in young people. You have to recruit people in data science.'

Above all he believes you have to be a first mover and make friends with your enemy. In this new disruptive environment those you fear have to be viewed as 'frenemies'. 'Banks are being transformed into a tech company and developers,' says Bjerke. 'A bank is no longer an important concept. It must work like a tech company.'

In May 2015, DNB secured first mover advantage by launching its VIPPS mobile payment app for smartphones. The move was revolutionary at that time. 'VIPPS is a disruptor. It may one day become the bank.' Within four months the bank was market leader. One million account holders had signed up. DNB was ahead of the market with a fundamental change to what DNB was about.

But Bjerke knew that predatory global competitors like Amazon and Facebook would soon be snapping at DNB's heels. Their aim would be at first to wound, then to dominate. 'We feared new players were coming into the market with a new app.' He was much concerned that their message to customers would be 'forget the banks'.

Instead of circling the DNB wagons to protect VIPPS against any powerful hostile attackers who would try to overcome and destroy it, Bjerke went on the offensive. 'We will not surrender: how will we cooperate with our enemies?' was his line. He identified the likely 'friendly enemies' and worked to first engage then embrace them. 'We make common interest,' was the approach. They would be viewed as frenemies. 'We invited the competition into our own mobile wallet company' and 'we disrupted our bank.'

That scale of disruption illustrated how Bjerke realised that his bank had to be kept at the cutting edge, however uncomfortable the internal disruption might be for those working inside it.

The new reality of a bank becoming a tech company would require a vital transition for staff. Even if they believed they had a secure job handling financial issues, they have all needed to ask themselves if their skills are still relevant. Must they be retrained? Do they have the capacity to adopt the new skills needed? These questions have an even-sharper new relevance as algorithms and Artificial Intelligence rapidly replace human functions.

For similar reasons, the scale of digitisation means customers no longer expect to have eyeball contact to discuss their financial issues. Bank branches are irrelevant to most customers who have accounts. Statements are checked online via the apps. Many more transactions are contactless or completed by digital transfer: there are 20 million log-ins per month in 2018. The need for hard cash in the hand is diminishing. Mortgages can be applied for and granted online in a matter of minutes. The need for a meeting then paperwork over several weeks has all but vanished. The mortgage book has increased by 5%.

As a result DNB has reduced the number of walk-in branches from 520 in 2007 to just 57 in 2018. 'You cannot get cash in any of our branches,' says Bjerke. They keep no cash under the carpet or in a safe. 'We just need showrooms like for car sales.'

But the strategic shift goes much deeper. DNB is no longer persuaded by the 'master's degree disease' of well-qualified MBA graduates with skills that are no longer appropriate for the new direction in which the bank is heading. They want to 'open up to new people'. The new recruitment figures tell the story. '50% of our recruitment is now from technical universities. We are not just looking for business school students as in the past.' A constantly self-disrupting bank like DNB wants digital engineers with people and gaming skills more than financial wizards.

And critically, one enlightened CEO has remained in charge throughout. It shows that achieving change amidst such disruption does not necessarily require a change of top names. Old dogs can be taught new tricks. Indeed, they want to learn new tricks. Age and experience can continue to have not just significant value, but enhanced value too.

There is an enormous cost to denial and unwillingness to embrace the new reality of the multitude of unthinkables. There is a 'singular lack of crisis about the new world, and the role business should play'.[319] As a leader, you are expected to know everything and always ooze self-confidence. Why could there ever be a need to admit to frailties? It could damage your professional reputation, career and employability. After all, your board, shareholders, staff and employees expect nothing less. That is why you were appointed. On the way up, you displayed all the right skills, attitudes and strengths. You were expected to inspire, then guarantee success in moving forward and sorting out problems.

It is important to accept the scale of frailties and not be ashamed. It helps justify the imperative to find a new culture, mindset and behaviour, with new courage and humility.

Before we gave a **Thinking the Unthinkable** presentation to 80 senior executives at the top of the Westfield Tower in Sydney, Australia,[320] a professional specialising in leadership and succession sent an email to us. 'I am watching a good number of business and state leaders managing clear symptoms of distress, stress, depression etc – a sinister and mostly invisible issue for performance out there.' Such pressures add extra stress, which in turn creates additional reluctance to be bold about gripping the scale of challenge.[321]

At around the same time in late May 2017, the wife of John Brogden, CEO of the Australian Institute of Company Directors had shocked a conference on mental illness by revealing publicly that he was in hospital with depression. Brogden had been due to address a breakfast for 200 top executives on why mental health must be 'top of every CEO's agenda'. He had survived a suicide attempt a decade previously. He had recently attended three funerals of top executives. John Brogden chose to resign.[322]

Putting the workplace health crisis on the agenda of every leader is the ambition of Professor Jeffrey Pfeffer, who is Professor of Organisational Behaviour at Stanford University Business Graduate School. In a new book, *Dying for a Paycheck*, he examines in chilling detail how modern management harms employee health. His conclusion is: 'The workplace profoundly affects human health and mortality, and too many workplaces are harmful to people's health ... affecting people in numerous occupations, industries, and geographies, and cutting across people of various ages and levels of education.' His goal is for the book to 'wake people up'. He says: 'This is a serious issue that has serious consequences for corporate performance and for people's well-being. We should care about people's psychological and physical health, not just about profits.'

End notes

[319] op cit. Norman Pickavance, 6 February 2018.

[320] 17 May 2017.

[321] 'Stress and the city: bankers feel the pressure but fear admitting it to bosses' by Hayley Kirton and William Turvill, *City A.M.*, 17 October 2016.

[322] 'John Brogden steps aside as he fights depression', *The Australian*, 18 May 2017.

24

'Toasted, roasted and grilled: a dark future?'

None of this should be a surprise or shock. There have been plenty of warnings. But they were framed by a time of relative predictability and respect for norms before Trump, Brexit and the new adversarial approaches of Russia's President Putin and China's President Xi. The UK vote for Brexit then the election of President Trump must be viewed as just the overture for even more seismic unthinkable events to be reckoned with. But are leaders willing to recalibrate as they should? Are they equipped practically and emotionally for the nature and scale of what is already with us and still to come?

In 2015 there was a powerful call for what was labelled an Intuition Reset.[323] Understanding the past and recent present does not really help explain what is now looming. 'However we identify it, there is a powerful human tendency to want the future to look like the recent past. On these shoals, huge corporate vessels have repeatedly foundered,' wrote Richard Dobbs, James Manyika and Jonathan Woetzel, directors of the McKinsey Global Institute which tracks leadership issues. 'It's especially difficult when ... everything you thought you knew about the world seems to be ... wrong. Or at least a little off. Dramatic changes come from nowhere, and then from everywhere, Major shifts can blindside even the most circumspect among us – first slowly and then all at once.'

While most leaders believe that ex officio they have power, in reality they no longer have it in the unchallenged way they assume. It is just as Moises Naim warned so perceptively in 2013 in The End of Power. He wrote: 'The reactions to my probing always pointed in the same direction: power is becoming more feeble, transient and constrained.'[324] That trend has been sharpened by the populist and nationalist push back seen in many places during 2017 and 2018. 'Old power – top down, jealously guarded, held by the few – is giving way to "new power" – bottom-up, participatory, peer-driven' argue Henry Timms and Jeremy Heimans.[325] Power is being disrupted. The future is becoming mighty different. Who will the future leaders be? 'Those best able to channel the participatory energy of those around them – for the good, for the bad, and for the trivial.'

That is what Trump and Macron have achieved in the US and France during 2017 and into 2018. Others who are not in the power mainstream of politics or business – at least yet – have similar ambitions for disruption'

So the question again: which leaders or aspiring leaders have bothered to take note? And how much did they realise the imperative to recalibrate their skills and embrace all that is now unfolding? How many leaders do anything more than just politely take note before consigning such books to oblivion on a shelf or pile on the floor somewhere? Did they even notice or log the alerts? Or were they largely in a mindset of complacency and denial? Did they say to themselves: 'That does not mean me or us'? Quite probably.

We ask: will you consign this book of red alerts to oblivion too, rather than considering the new options and taking action? The predicament is just like an aircraft where the engines have been cut by volcanic dust and the plane keeps gliding smoothly assisted by gravity and optimum use of air currents. But it cannot do so indefinitely. Eventually forward momentum expires. Then what?

That is where we are now with leadership. Evidence of denial by top leaders proliferates, at least publicly. The plane is gliding, but at ever-higher speeds. But increasingly there is less control. Where or how will it land safely? Or will it crash after all control has been lost? Distractions keep persuading the C-suite waverers and naysayers. They believe that the plane will keep flying just fine as if the volcanic dust had not damaged the engines. They are on a superhuman roll of complacency and convenient deaf ears, despite the evidence pointing to a horror that looms.

The reasons are understandable. After all, why be pessimistic when the stock market bulls have been running so fast and profitably in late 2017 and into 2018? This was despite the contradictions, 'the paradox of high returns and high anxiety'.[326] A sudden loss of nerve was inevitable. But few dared to predict it, at least out loud. The departing head of Eurozone Finance Ministers did dare to break the silence. 'If there were to be an economic shock this year, many of our countries and the monetary union as a whole are not prepared,' warned Jeroen Dijsselbloem at the start of 2018.[327] He was right. But with global markets gyrating around their highest valuations for a decade, and the high-speed train of market exuberance powering forward, who was going to take the risk of jumping off before any such crash?

Experts and economists conceded they were no longer in control of narratives because there was no precedent for what was happening.[328] President Trump even gloated that he had a hand in the 50% rise in market values in his first 12 months in office. It was down to him and – oddly for a businessman – he seemed to believe it could never end.[329] But it did, ten days after he made that boast.

The wild ride started on Wall Street on 5 February 2018.[330] Markets were unnerved by new data on US wage growth. Inflation was starting to replace stagnation, and loose monetary policy was coming to an end.[331] Fears instantly went global. Irrationally high commercial optimism had suggested that all was well and unthinkables had no place. One Chief Investment Officer wrote in 2017 that 'the gap between confidence and activity has rarely been as wide'.[332] 'Wide' should probably have been reinforced by the description 'illogical'. And what comes next? 'The stock market could be smashed if certain variables change,' warned one distinguished analyst.[333] 'Expect the unexpected!'

President Trump then provided it. He signed a series of orders for the US to impose trade tariffs. China reciprocated. The markets panicked and started slumping again.[334]

Two extraordinary highs had already corrupted any ideas that huge unthinkables might threaten the record bull run. The first was the highest-ever stock market valuations. Second came evidence like the 2018 PwC CEO Survey (which we highlighted earlier), confirming that CEO confidence levels were the most bullish ever.[335]

In late January 2018 the number of CEOs expecting higher growth in the following 12 months had doubled to 57%. Faced with a tick box and record returns, why would any C-suiter dampen expectations that the bulls would just keep running? Within days, the market unthinkables of complacency were suddenly being talked about openly. 'A much bigger shakeout' was coming. 'We don't think it will be over in a matter of days,' warned Bob Prince, Co-Chief Investment Officer at the world's biggest hedge fund, Bridgewater.[336] Was he signalling what many feared behind the backs of their hands: the long expected but long delayed 'end of an era of tranquillity?'[337]

Why is this part of the red alert?

The optimism captured by the likes of PwC was blinding many at the top to what were also identified as significant 'existential threats.'[338] The contradiction was captured starkly by *The Wall Street Journal* headline in a commentary at the end of the Davos 2018 in late January: 'The Global Economy is Great. Be Afraid.'[339]

The Managing Director of the IMF, Christine Lagarde, reinforced the reasons to be fearful. Using unusually stark language – even for her – she painted a binary choice for leaders between utopia and dystopia. The acute pressures of growing global inequality and climate change are fast increasing the risks that our world will be 'toasted, roasted and grilled' and faces a 'dark future'.[340] While signalling that 'all signs point to a further strengthening' of global economic performance, in the days before the crash she also warned that the executive enemy is complacency. 'Use this time [of growth and high returns] to find lasting solutions to the challenges facing the global economy.'[341]

Why so?

Fundamentally there were reasons to fear a deep and fast-growing strategic gloom. The 87-year-old financier George Soros has made enormous amounts of money from being right. At Davos 2018 he even went so far as to warn that 'the survival of our entire civilisation is at stake'.[342] He described a 'revolutionary period' comparable to the fall of the Soviet empire. He listed the fast-growing risks from nuclear war, nationalism, a collapse of values and climate change. Even the insurance industry, which believes it is best equipped to read risk, was haemorrhaging money from the new scale of catastrophes. 'Losses have been extensive across reinsurance, commercial insurance and personal lines,' reported Swiss Re.[343]

The head of the British Army went public at the same time to warn that Russia is the biggest state-based threat to the UK. General Sir Nick Carter warned that the nation is not prepared for hostilities which could be provoked 'sooner than we expect'.[344][345] The warnings were then reinforced, first by the Vice Chief of Defence, General Sir Gordon Messenger, and then by the Head of Joint Forces Command, General Sir Chris Deverell just after the nerve agent attack on the Russian double agent Sergei Skripal in the English cathedral city of Salisbury.[346][347]

Simultaneously, The Economist was reporting shifts in geopolitics and technology which are renewing the threat of great power conflict.[348] It published a major analysis of why 'the world is not prepared' for 'the next war'. This at a time when 'in this fragile world we are facing a protection crisis: the inability to fundamentally change the behaviour of belligerents'.[349] At the same time the US Defense Secretary was warning of 'greater volatility' with the new challenge of 'Great Power competition'. General James Mattis said that the US's 'competitive edge has eroded in every domain of warfare' faced with the 'revisionist powers' of Russia or China.[350] China's investment in global maritime investment and influence was now of special concern to the US.[351] Six weeks later President Putin confirmed such US fears during his dramatic and chilling video presentation of new Russian military power to members of parliament in Moscow.[352]

Putin's Russia was preparing for a scale of conflict which he and they seemed determined to provoke

Unthinkable? Not any more.

End notes

[323] *No ordinary disruption – the four global forces breaking all the trends* (2015) by Richard Dobbs, James Manyika, Jonathan Woetzel. New York: Public Affairs, pp. 1, 12

[324] *The end of power: from boardrooms to battlefields and churches to states, why being in charge isn't what it used to be* (2013) by Moises Naim. New York: Basic Books, p. xii.

[325] *New power: how it's changing the 21st century – and why you need to know* (2018) by Henry Timms and Jeremy Heimans. London: Macmillan.

[326] op cit. Larry Fink, 16 January 2018.

[327] 'Eurozone unprepared for shock, fears economic chief' by Jim Brunsden, *Financial Times*, 12 January 2018.

[328] 'Delegates cautious despite economic upswing' by Chris Giles, *Financial Times*, 26 January 2018. See the remarks of Ragu Rajan, recently governor of the Reserve Bank of India, now at the Booth Business School, University of Chicago.

[329] Remarks to the World Economic Forum in Davos, Switzerland, 26 January 2018.

[330] 'US stocks suffer one of worst weeks since financial crisis' by Robin Wigglesworth, Michael Hunter and Emma Dunkley, *Financial Times*, 10 February 2018.

[331] 'Running hot', *The Economist*, 10 February 2018.

[332] Tom Becket, Chief Investment Officer, Psigma Investment Management Limited, analysis for Q2 2017.

[333] Private briefing on 14 February 2018.

[334] Around 22 and 23 March 2018.

[335] 22 January 2018.

[336] 'Bridgewater investment chief sees new era of volatility' by Robin Wigglesworth, *Financial Times*, 12 February 2018.

[337] 'The end of an era of tranquility' by FT Reporters, *Financial Times*, 10/11 February 2018.

[338] Confirmed verbally by PwC Global Chairman Bob Moritz, 22 January 2018.

[339] 'The global economy is great. Be afraid' by James Mackintosh, *The Wall Street Journal*, 26 January 2018, p. B2.

[340] Remarks to the Future Investment Initiative in Riyadh, 25 October 2017.

[341] Remarks to the World Economic Forum in Davos, Switzerland, 23 January 2018.

[342] 'The current moment in history' by George Soros. Remarks on 25 January 2018 at World Economic Forum.

[343] 'Catastrophes wipe $35bn from insurance group's profits' by Oliver Ralph and Alistair Gray, *Financial Times*, 13 November 2017.

[344] General Carter was appointed Chief of the Defence Staff on 28 March 2018.

[345] Speech by General Sir Nick Carter, Chief of the General Staff, to Royal United Services Institute (RUSI) in London, 22 January 2018. To watch the video of the event, go to www.thinkunthink.org/digital-footnotes.

[346] 'Russian cyber attacks "could cripple UK"' by Larisa Brown and Chris Greenwood, *Daily Mail*, 8 March 2018.

[347] 'Military must wake up to information war' by Deborah Haynes, *The Times*, 1 March 2018.

[348] *The Economist*, January 27–February 2 2018, pp. 9–10 and after p. 40.

[349] Warning by Peter Maurer, President of the International Committee of the Red Cross, to the UN High Level Meeting on Peace Building and Sustaining Peace, UN Headquarters, New York, 25 April 2018.

[350] Remarks by James N Mattis on the new US National Defense Strategy, 19 January 2018.

[351] 'How China rules the waves' by James Kynge, Amy Kazmin and Farhan Bokhari, *Financial Times*, 13 January 2017.

[352] 2 March 2018.

25

EAT AN ELEPHANT IN ONE MOUTHFUL - WITH HUMILITy

Since 2014, the debate about reforming attitudes in the British Army has been catapulted into the open. That is when General Sir Nick Carter took over as Chief of the General Staff (CGS). As the new head of the army he faced what he described to us as 'the difficulties of the army's ability to be able to adapt to change and to challenge.'[353] Attitudes and behaviour were way behind what new realities expected. He described the professional environment as 'much more constraining and restrictive than it's ever been before.'[354]

The four-star general embarked on what turned into a four-year reform programme. He would challenge the status quo. It was a calculated risk of the type honed by commanders on battlefields under fire. This time the enemy was inside the system itself. He viewed its culture as out of date, out of tune and obstructive.

The scale of 'the challenge' which he identified meant that he could have no idea if he would pull off the scale of reform needed. Would taking it on result in him being eased out early for being too radical? Or would he be taking a huge personal and professional risk to confront questionable issues and practices that had long been embedded in army life? In March 2018 it was recognised. General Carter was promoted to Chief of Defence (CDS). He would be the most senior military officer running all of the UK's armed forces.

Carter had taken on the unthinkable of making big reforms. He had largely won through. His achievements in the face of a host of sceptics were regarded as impressive. In many ways he made progress well beyond what many viewed as possible. 'Old think' was largely seen off. For that reason, the risks he took to change the Army's embedded mentality and attitudes to disruption are worth reporting. They hold lessons for other leaders.

How did Carter do it? In 2014 he realised that minds and attitudes had to change dramatically. Talent had to be maximised, not oppressed by conformity and tradition. 'We were going to have to play catch up. Maximising talent became my epithet for this change programme,' he told this project four years on.

At the start he made a remarkable discovery. It was fashionable in the army to talk change. But little was really achieved. He discovered there were a total of 375 initiatives underway. Then he asked: 'Well, how many of these are resourced?' He discovered it was just 6%! As he put it: 'The appetite for change in our army is simply glorious, as it was at the Battle of Balaclava. But the reality is that our capacity to deliver it is very limited.'

Carter viewed the scale and nature of the challenge as essentially existential for the relevance and fighting effectiveness of the UK military. The context was 'much more constraining and restrictive than it's ever been before.'[355] He made clear that the existing leadership model was not fit for purpose. Old thinking and thinkers would have to go if necessary. This was not about ageism. It was about open minds to embrace new realities. 'Good quality leadership unlocks everything else' the general impressed routinely on those he commanded. Leaders must be 'downward looking' with a constant aim. It must be 'tirelessly to really know our soldiers'. This should include the core new reality that 'Generation Y (and Z) are different'. They often have bold ideas of how the military can function. They needed to be heard and listened to.

Why the urgency and imperative? 'For nearly 15 years we were focused entirely on trying to win the fight in Iraq and Afghanistan. And the world had changed around us.' The intensity of focus on fighting those two conflicts meant the army had to play catch-up to deal with new realities. The new nature and scale of global disruption which had already been identified by **Thinking the Unthinkable** in 2014 meant there were massive new strategic challenges of a wholly different order.[356]

The world and the nature of warfare had become a newly unthinkable place for which planning and mindsets were not configured. Indeed, they were way behind. This was much more than a debate over reducing significant personnel numbers or the quality of equipment. Instead it had to be about the perceptions and capacity to change fast the officers who lead, and those who serve them, especially from the next generation.

The big issues went well beyond war fighting or taking on insurgencies and terrorism in far off countries. On almost his first day Carter was confronted with the scale of the army's unacceptable culture. The hangover from decades of tolerated, unaddressed but inappropriate behaviour came in the results of a sexual harassment survey that landed on his desk. 'I discovered that our attitude as an institution to bullying, harassment, discrimination, and diversity was, to put it mildly, overly laddish. We had a cultural problem. It had to change if we were going to become an employer that could embrace the change in demography in our country and maximise the talent that we needed.'

Rather than a culture of just obeying top down orders, Carter believed there had to be a new inclusivity. He set out 'to cascade the idea of empowerment down into the bowels of the institution'. The revitalised system had to 'set sensible constraints and then we allow our soldiers to learn from honest mistakes'. Views from all levels must find not just a voice but a hearing. 'What I was determined to do was to create a culture and institution in which people would argue and debate until the decision was made, and then obey orders. So fundamental.' New safe spaces were created for young officers to debate and brainstorm under the banners of the digital Wavell Room blog site for feedback contributions,[357] BrAIN which is the British Army Intrapreneurs Network,[358] and the Royal Artillery's Dragon Portal to promote innovative ideas and thinking.[359] New ideas, however off the wall, could now mean important credits and recognition in a soldier's personnel record. This in turn could hasten chances for promotion.

What were the Carter principles? 'You need innovators. You need people with imagination. You need people who are prepared to challenge received wisdom. And you need people who are prepared to take a risk with their careers in order to go outside, develop themselves, come back in and generally add to the dynamic of thought that you need to be able to do this. ... With experimentation comes the opportunity to move to another horizon.'[360]

Where did he focus reform? At the lower levels from where the army is 'bottom-fed'. 'We've focused a lot of attention on the sergeants' Mess and the corporals' Mess. Where I think we have definitely resonated is in the low levels.'

As he reflected before taking up promotion in June 2018 to lead the UK's military, General Carter summed up the big lesson for all leaders in one take away. 'The most important characteristic of a strategic leader is humility. And it's the humility to listen. And therefore with that is the humility to invite challenge. That's so important, and particularly for an hierarchical institution like an army.'[361]

Carter had created big expectations. In turn this drew frank broadsides about why achieving change would be so difficult. Here are some of the alerts he heard at his RUSI Land Warfare Conference in 2017.[362] 'Trying to implement change is like trying to move a cemetery: the people there are not much help,' said the head of the US Army in Europe, quoting a frustrated NATO Secretary General. One very senior officer said that the new competition means 'we have to get ahead of the bang' because it is a different kind of bang: because of cyber, subversion, the weaponising of information. 'We must think on a different timescale and in different ways – different conflicts require different kinds of people,' said another. 'There must be [new] innovation and adaptability. . . We must be open to challenge from the younger generation: when they say there are smarter ways to communicate then we must listen . . .The assumption of technological superiority can no longer be taken for granted. . . it is one of the most intellectually challenging times for officers.'

As a result we must 'get the right talent and educate commanders' including recruiting from outside the traditional pool. We must 'unlock the potential' and that talent 'must be empowered'. This is because 'much is beyond the current range of capabilities', yet there is a 'fixation with the status quo'. 'We are totally unprepared for the new realities.' And when they confront officers 'under stress, you [often] default into habitual behaviour and human levels'. Above all: 'commanders must allow those who work for them to fail' because fear of failure suppresses the kind of 'cunning, curious, clever' risk taking and maverick thinking soldiers who are needed to think unthinkables. The traditional career structure is too rigid. Without any possibility of new career benefits, mavericks would never find a place. 'If ... they don't profit from it, you will never, ever encourage able people to go and test the envelope. And you'll never encourage people who've got maverick, or imaginative, or innovative tendencies to go and do this.'[363]

A reassuring first catalyst for General Carter had been when Christopher Elliott, a retired major general and an ex-Whitehall insider, published what was described as a 'Diplomatically couched bombshell.'[364] After scores of interviews with senior military insiders, Elliott described an 'entrenched MoD [Ministry of Defence] system whose default settings were set to strangle enterprise, discourage initiative and work to lowest common denominator of all the parties involved', where 'the system was allowed to run the individuals, rather than the other way round'.[365] He then asked 'how good people and capable public servants could find themselves making perverse decisions – despite their talents'.[366] Elliott's analysis swiftly divided commanders and civil servants at all levels. Some who could be said to be from the conventional, 'flat earth' cohort in defence and across Whitehall scathingly dismissed the Elliott analysis because it was written by a 'two star who never really made it'. Others praised him for 'saying what finally had to be said about what's wrong with our leadership'.

Was the challenge for the British Army unique? No. Far from it, even if many of those serving claim that to be the case. As our **Thinking the Unthinkable** work confirms, the army's predicament is similar to that faced by most of the corporate world. 'He's trying to change the military structure because he realises that in modern warfare it's not like Waterloo where you've got your square and everybody just follows orders. It's very different, much more similar to the speed of digital change,' said Lord Mark Price. 'You're in a battlefield: it's not [that] you are there and [the] enemy is here. You have to respond and react. And you can't just wait for HQ to send down another order to say attack in this direction. So he's trying to change their culture, ironically for the military to become less like the military.'[367]

But how to achieve the kind of massive change in military behaviour, culture and mindset that was needed? After all, 'You can't eat the elephant in one mouthful,' the general told this project.[368]

Carter knew he did not have time. He would have to make significant impact and progress as quickly as possible. He recognised that change needed to be led from the top and driven from the bottom and he started an active search across the generations at all levels of army commanders. He wanted to identify those with new thinking on the leadership price of traditional mind-sets and what must swiftly replace them. He knew some with smart, visionary ideas might not yet have revealed them for fear of being marginalised as non-conformists. He had to find them too, and reassure them.

An early start, six months into his tenure, was when he brought together around 800 people, including all the commanding officers and regimental sergeant majors 'in a socking great marquee at tables of 12. And we asked a big question: how do we make this great institution greater? Very important question, that, because it means that we don't think we're bad; we think we're great, but we want to become greater.'

Reassuringly for an army, they identified combat ethos and fighting spirit, hard earned in Iraq and Afghanistan, as a fundamental first issue plus historic legacy (which he described as 'sort of a half point, not as big as the [other] three'). But even more important for achieving reform were two other key issues. First was that the empowerment and decentralisation soldiers expect in conflict should also be embraced by the army culture in peace time. Second came the fast-growing issue which is dominating our **Thinking the Unthinkable** work: the imperative for a leadership culture based on values.

Throughout, General Carter viewed the scale of change needed to reconfigure for the new unthinkables as not just an 'era of change' but more profoundly as a 'change of era'.[369] That required far more than just tinkering. Those serving him had to be 'valued' and 'less inward looking'. There had to be 'talent development' not just career development. That talent should be drawn from a 'much wider base than before', with 'greater diversity and culture'. Empowerment must be encouraged, not blocked by 'over centralisation, a suffocating assurance and safety regime. . . . a convoluted chain of command, risk aversion . . . .unfriendly frictions'.[370]

From the get-go the general had confronted at significant speed the inevitable costs of taking on a system and trying to push through change. But early progress was recognised. In 2016 as part of the reassigning of military jobs at the highest levels of command across the three services his posting as Chief of the General Staff was extended by two years in line with Lord Levene's reforms designed to produce greater continuity and effectiveness.[371] That gave him more time to see off the waverers and foot draggers, then consolidate achievements.

Even the Head of the Army revealed how much that he too had realised that he had to learn and change. In the spirit of humility which he urged on his officers, General Carter told them that in late 2016 he subjected himself to a 360-degree personal assessment tool. As a result, he resolved that he had 'to be more accessible, recognise I don't have to win every argument, and give people more space and time to deliver'.

Had he been an adaptive leader? 'You can't be an adaptive leader if you don't listen and you're not prepared to change your mind.' General Carter even quoted to us the view of a senior partner in McKinsey, David Chinn. 'He often 360s me and he says "The one characteristic always stands out is that you are prepared to change and adjust your approach because you're prepared to listen and then you're prepared to adjust." I learned a lot from this observation.'

This was an important discovery. From the start there had been loud mutterings of resentment among those serving him. While some were welcoming, one very senior former insider told this study that the general had alienated many of those serving him by being seen as pushing too hard and too fast. 'It is a pity. He was too bossy, not inclusive enough and is not taking enough officers with him, except his favourites,' said one very senior insider. As the months passed, the spirit of inclusiveness seemed to be supplemented by an iron will to force through what he wanted. Waverers or non-deliverers who were regarded as having been given their chance were sidelined and substituted with others. As a result, 'a lot of people [who were ready to be persuaded] are wavering,' confided one insider. Another said: 'The trouble is that when this happens too many officers just sit on their hands and wait.'

In the limited time available, did General Carter succeed in changing the British army command leadership culture in the way he believed was so necessary? 'It remains patchy,' he told his generals in early 2017. The Army is 'attired differently, is career-managed differently and is beginning to think differently'. To encourage the sceptics, he said, 'we have made significant progress. I have been impressed how [all levels from] commanding officers and regimental sergeant majors have grappled with the challenge.'

Core principles had emerged. By 2017 Carter was urging his generals to:

- take the initiative: don't accept the status quo.
- shape events rather than being shaped by them.
- work tirelessly to know our soldiers.
- set a clear direction, and make sure it is clearly understood by those you lead.
- know, care for and motivate those you lead.
- have empathy and the humility to listen, as well as the humility to adjust a plan when it is going wrong.
- take time to lead, to train [with] less process.
- make sure those you lead are valued.
- set standards and have the moral courage to enforce them.
- promote the phrase 'be exceptional every day'.

Had General Carter found ways to embrace mavericks and less than orthodox thinking within the hierarchy of a command structure? 'Well, they need nurturing. But you also need to recognise that there's still conventionality about our career structure. The trick is how you give meaning to what it is that they're trying to contribute without in a sense upsetting the apple cart. ... War has a catalysing effect to give place and position to mavericks. Lawrence of Arabia, Orde Wingate. You know, the people who are in charge at peacetime invariably are not necessarily the people in charge at wartime.'

In April 2018 Carter told us that on the four areas that had been identified early in 2015, 'I have done better at some than others'. Overall 'certainly inside the army, nobody is in any doubt as to how the strategic context now requires a very different set of approaches.' Anything more would have been remarkable. As the Unilever CEO Paul Polman told this study separately, when it comes to achieving the profound change that is necessary, 'It's very, very difficult to get that kind of level of change that is necessary internally, even if you're the chief executive, and even if you're the chairman.'

One Whitehall observer summed up General Carter's dilemma: 'everyone calls for more flexible, more adaptive thinking. Well you can call for it, but it won't necessarily happen. And strategic leadership is often deciding not to do things.' But General Carter's view is that there is no other option: he had to keep pushing forward to improve the agility, smartness and relevance of the next leadership generation, especially in this new era of unthinkables and unpredictables.

The gradient to overcome was steep. An important principle that worked was 'to cascade the idea of empowerment down into the bowels of the institution. I've done that by doing it from the bottom up. I've identified two or three places where we can run pilots.'

With his view that change must be driven from the bottom, Carter highlighted for us how he believed those pilot schemes had achieved significant change. One of the 'most effective' pilots was at the Royal School of Artillery which 'traditionally for several hundred years had regularly measured its performance on its ability to train the best gunners it could. The problem was that it wasn't always done in the most productive way. They cost me nearly £100 million a year. When we started the pilot we only delegated £1.7 million pounds to them, to the commandant there, for his travel and subsistence [budget]. What we did was to say: "Right! Imagine that you are now the king and that you own all of the resource levers that make up the £100 million that you cost me. So, all of your vehicles, all of your ammunition, all of the manpower, the infrastructure, the electricity bill, the whole lot. You own this! What we want you to do now is to think about how you can deliver your output in a more productive way, with you utilising all of these different commodities and resources to achieve the best and most productive effect."'

The challenge of course was about culture change. So much of the army has accepted centralisation as a given. What was needed was a culture that enabled de-centralisation and empowerment. How was this achieved? 'We gave him [the commandant] clever people to help him do this – McKinsey [the consulting firm]. And the upshot was that in year one of the ten-year forward programme he saved £13 million. ... We gave him back £5.7 million pounds ... as a gain share, for him to invest in his institution.'

This was the application of the battlefield principles of mission command (devolving responsibility) to peace time work that Carter's soldiers had specifically asked for at the brainstorming in the 'socking great marquee'. 'If an opportunity presents itself on the battlefield, they don't have to refer to their commander or to the one above. They avail themselves of that opportunity because they can understand the context in which they're operating – the sense of purpose.' What does the empowerment achieve? 'By being more productive they're contributing to the overall purpose of the British Army. [They realise] that saving some money [means] we can invest, for example, in additional improvements to the Challenger tank, or whatever the capability enhancement is that we want to have, or better accommodation, whatever else it might be. ... That's a work in progress. But it is resonating with the Commanding Officers. And they're very excited about it.'

Many principles and ways of working had to be turned on their heads. Carter confronted the fact that the army was bad at doing the basics of business, especially how it ran itself. 'We are traditionally useless at it because we don't like to use data to make decisions. Equally, we're not good at programme management. We're not good at commercial skills. We're not good at contract management. We're not good at writing requirements.' McKinsey were brought in 'to educate ourselves in how to do those things.' They were 'integrated' into army processes and 'upskilled us'. They were 'embedded into our teams. And we have joint teams with them that do joint work to jointly upskill.'

And the outcome? 'We have built a programme to upskill a large part of the army headquarters to be good at this stuff. That has changed completely the way we discuss things at the board table. The conversations around the board... are totally different to the ones that we had when I started three years ago.'

Were consultants just an expensive luxury? Or were they fundamental to the process of catalysing transformation of what in essence much always remains a war fighting machine? 'You have to make yourself match fit to run a business as well and McKinsey helped us do that. I think that consultants are good if you use them in the right way for the right things. What you don't want to do is to turn up, write a lovely report, and then [disappear] off again.' And the outsiders have picked up new insights from being inside the army machine. 'They've learned a shedload from us as an institution!' said the general.

So why couldn't army insiders learn in a similar way by going outside, collecting new experiences, then bringing them back inside? Carter was surprised, for example, that his new encouragement to get far broader experience outside the army – say in business – was being actively shunned. 'I wanted to try and create a sort of brains-based approach to the way that we educate people and develop people. I thought to begin with it'd be relatively straightforward just to give them opportunities in academia or placements or whatever. What I pretty quickly realised was that the individuals were not coming forward as much as I would like. And the reason for that was: for them it was a career risk. Because of course it meant them taking a year out and not necessarily having the same quality of report on them [which influences promotion prospects] as their peer who is still inside the army.'

'So, what I did was to change the incentivisation. I made it important that anybody who did this would be reported on by the right sort of report writer who could make a comparison across the rest of his reporting field so that people profited in career terms from the experience.'

Did this work? 'Yeah. Fundamentally, now we've got a completely different set of volunteers coming forward to do this now.' Are they fast trackers? 'Not necessarily. They're people whose potential might be maximised in this certain area. Some of them are faster than others, because what's then happening is that people are seeing career reward that comes from that personal development.'

So overall has Carter managed to eat the whole elephant of reform in one mouthful? He believes the signs are as positive as he hoped.

'I think time will tell whether everything has stuck. … What you've got to do is you want to describe the journey to consume the whole elephant, and then work out in strategic terms which bite you take at which time. For us, we've been relatively systematic about picking some things that really matter, and working back like running pilots to achieve things – how you then energise the change in culture. Because culture trumps strategy every time.'

Did he have to turn hard left or hard right at any points because of unexpected developments or approaches not working out? 'I have adjusted the direction of travel, but I haven't done any, as you would describe it, handbrake turns. I haven't had to do that. I've had to refine. I've had to say, "Well, that will have to wait until that's been done." I've had to limit my appetite for change in certain areas in order to be able to reinforce something and not something else, as one would do. So, adjustments, but not handbrake turns.'

Somehow an iron determination must be balanced with flexibility. Were there moments when this was threatened? 'You're probably never quite doing a U-turn but you are adjusting. So yes and no. I suspect there have been times when one's had to bite one's lip a bit and be a little bit more reasonable in one's view. But ultimately it is about being prepared to make those adjustments.'

What were General Sir Nick's main takeaways as he headed for the top job in the UK military? He was doing so at a time when the appropriateness of the armed forces mindset and configuration was never closer to being tested because of the new Russian threat on multiple fronts.

There must be a 'compelling rationale for why you want something to occur'.

He reiterated his conviction that 'culture trumps strategy. And in the army the way we've built all that is about leadership.'

Above all, to sell new principles of leadership you need to tell a story. It is more important than the strategy. 'You're almost better to have written the story before you write the strategy.'

General Carter believes that 'the genie is out of the bottle' on empowerment. How many top leaders are prepared to take what they view as this same big risk in order to handle the scale of new disruption?

End notes

[353] Conversation with General Sir Nick Carter, 11 April 2018.

[354] Update assessment of the reform process, interview at Army Headquarters in Andover, 2 August 2016.

[355] Interview with General Sir Nick Carter, 2 August 2016.

[356] ibid. He went on to crystallise them in a speech to the RUSI (op cit. General Sir Nick Carter, 22 January 2018.)

[357] wavellroom.com. 'The Wavell Room is a blog site . . .to stimulate discussion and deviate from the norms of extant thinking and doctrine.'

[358] BrAIN 'aims to: (1) Inspire people to question the status quo in order to ensure the British Army continues to evolve and be the best it can be. (2) Connect people inside and outside of the organisation who are passionate about the future of UK Defence and connect people with ideas with those able to change policy. (3) Empower individuals to make a difference; rank does not dictate your ability to create change.'

[359] Dragon Troop from the Royal Artillery runs a Twitter account to encourage discussion on conceptual development, leadership and innovation.

[360] op cit. General Sir Nick Carter, 2 August 2016.

[361] op cit. General Sir Nick Carter, 11 April 2018.

[362] RUSI Land Warfare Conference. 27–28 June 2017.

[363] op cit. General Sir Nick Carter, 2 August 2016.

[364] Professor Beatrice Heuser, University of Reading, quoted on the back cover of *High command: British military leadership in the Iraq and Afghanistan wars* (2015) by Christopher Elliott. London: Hurst & Company.

[365] op cit. High command, Christopher Elliott, p. 2.

[366] ibid. p. 6.

[367] Interview with Lord Mark Price, Minister for Trade and Investment, 25 July 2017.

[368] op cit. Interview with General Sir Nick Carter, 2 August 2016.

[369] CGS notes for his General Staff conference, 12 January 2017.

[370] op cit. Interview with General Sir Nick Carter, 2 August 2016.

[371] Lord Levene of Portsoken, a former Chief of Defence Procurement, was appointed in July 2010 by the Secretary of Defence to chair the Defence Reform Group, to make proposals for major changes in the Ministry of Defence. One reform was to extend duration of senior appointments.

26

'MONUMENTAL, COLLECTIVE, INTELLECTUAL ERRORS'

Increasingly the locker of ideas and self-assurance is almost bare. The hinges and bolts are rusted. The doors are swinging wildly in ever-more erratic winds. Missing are 'the kind of strong statements of vision, powerful calls to action, and new ideas for addressing common challenges that have been the hallmark of years past,' wrote former US Ambassador Ivo Daalder after the Munich Security Conference in February. 'This year, leaders came to complain, even threaten each other, not to offer a positive vision for the future.'[372]

The very existence of such discomfiting alarms confirms the scale of unthinkables at the heart of our **Thinking the Unthinkable** work. But how far are leaders prepared to accept such turbulent new implications for the way they lead? They may be unreal, but they are the new reality.

Looking back, Hillary Clinton makes clear the cost to her US presidential election bid of not even being willing to believe that 'democracy was under attack', or that President Putin would carry out the unthinkable of electoral interference in the way the Russians did.[373] 'I never imagined that he would have the audacity to launch a massive covert attack against our own democracy, right under our noses – and that he'd get away with it,' wrote Hillary Clinton.[374] But he did. Then followed the extraordinary revelations 17 months later[375] of how Cambridge Analytica (CA) created for the Trump campaign false allegations of 'lying', 'stealing' or 'criminal behaviour' against 'crooked Hillary'. Using personal data harvested from up to 87 million Facebook users via a third-party app, CA was able to micro-target US voters in key states with false claims about Clinton.

They inserted 'lies into the bloodstream' of the election.[376] They thereby apparently persuaded a critical number of voters to vote for Trump.

Unthinkable? It also suddenly became unbelievable. This unprecedented electoral manipulation left renewed shockwaves in the US and globally. It raised questions about whether democracy in many countries can ever be considered credible again. Then in late April 2018 came first evidence of massive attacks by 6500 Russia-inspired bots with English female names which had allegedly been used in the 2017 UK general election to build support for Labour's Jeremy Corbyn and discredit Theresa May's government.[377]

Violation of norms had become normal. Geopolitical interference and subversion – by way of digital manipulations of the election process, or proxy armed action in places like eastern Ukraine – went unpunished. Putin led this assault on international norms. President Xi of China did the same, with Beijing deploying different methods. This then extended to targeting those 'enemies' who had betrayed Russia or China, like the Russian double agent Sergei Skripal in the UK.

The reasons for failing to confront such unthinkables only tend to be revealed candidly after those leaders at the highest levels have moved on. Yet when they are revealed, they confirm the cost of clinging to conformist thinking and those zombie orthodoxies.

For ten years until 2016 Sir Nick (now Lord) Macpherson was the most senior civil servant at the UK Treasury. He had to lead the government's handling of the 2008 stock market crash. Historians and memoirs of those involved have subsequently shown how there was plenty of evidence about the apparent unthinkables that threatened the global financial system in 2007/8, then took it to the brink of a disastrous meltdown. The unthinkables were piling up in full view. But at the time few believed a near-catastrophe would happen, and by his own belated admission even Macpherson was not among them.

Everyone playing the global financial roulette wheel remained optimistic. The expert spectacles were blurring, not sharpening, the vision. Together the combination of wine-bar encouragement and water-cooler gossip meant they all had to believe that for no reason the music would never stop.

When Macpherson retired from the Treasury he bared his professional soul about the preventable errors that he and others had made in the build-up to 2008. 'I see myself as one of a number of people in finance ministries, central bank regulators in the UK and US who failed to see the crisis coming, who failed to spot the build-up of risk. This was a monumental, collective, intellectual error,' he said. 'The fact is, we didn't spot it. We didn't ask the right questions and that was a failure.'[378]

We need to repeat that extraordinary confession to a 'monumental, collective, intellectual error'. Monumental? Collective? Intellectual? We all have to ask: how can such monumental, collective errors be prevented in future so that unthinkables are spotted and the right questions are asked?

After what she described as her post-election months nursing despair and shock, Hillary Clinton was equally frank about what she got wrong in her 2016 campaign. She believes a large part of her defeat was because 'I was running a traditional presidential campaign with carefully thought-out policies and painstakingly built coalitions, while Trump was running a reality TV show that expertly and relentlessly stoked Americans' anger and resentment. I was giving speeches laying out how to solve the country's problems. He was ranting on Twitter.'[379] Others went further, writing of the 'petty bickering, foolish reasoning and sheer arrogance of a campaign that was never the sure thing that its leader and top staffers assumed.'[380]

This was the price of traditional thinking and framing. In the new disrupted world of unthinkables and a new normal there is not just the threat of even-greater similar errors of judgement on a much more seismic scale. They are inevitable. Democrats in 2017 still could not dent what to many were Trump's extraordinary policies and ways of governing. They failed to unseat the Republican candidate in Georgia's special congressional election. 'We still have a terrible brand... In people's minds we are coastal, elitist and out of touch... We're a party in denial and we're being delusional to think we lost by less than we thought we would lose. You either win or lose. You don't get a trophy for participation.'[381]

But do leadership cultures and structures promote a willingness to listen to all ideas, however wacky or unorthodox? We must ask: had the nature and scale of the manipulation being masterminded by Cambridge

Analytica been detected during the US election campaign, would they have been viewed as non-credible? It is unlikely that during the rhetorical intensity of an election campaign the full scale and methods used could have been revealed in a way that would fireproof them against Trump's uncompromising election machine. The Trump campaign would have brutally discredited the accusations as 'fake' or 'lies', thereby probably fuelling an even-greater voter backlash against Clinton.

The effectiveness and relevance of the very structures of political and economic stability which have been nurtured since World War Two are fragmenting.[382] International rules and norms which have been assumed to buttress that stability are either under siege, being abused and shredded, or rendered ineffective.

How will you cope? Or will you push your head deeper into the sands of denial?

End notes

[372] op cit. 'This week's reads', Ivo Daalder, 22 February 2018.

[373] op cit. *What happened?* by Hillary Clinton, p. 356.

[374] ibid. p. 333.

[375] On *Channel 4 News*, transmissions on 19/20 March 2018 and subsequent days.

[376] Conversation involving Cambridge Analytica CEO Alexander Nix and Managing Director Mark Turnbull recorded in undercover filming, *Channel 4 News*, transmitted 20 March 2018.

[377] 'Revealed: how Russians tried to fix the election for Corbyn' by the INSIGHT team, *Sunday Times*, 29 April 2018. But the nature of the data and methodology used were quickly questioned in 'There are some major issues with claims Russian bots swayed the election in Jeremy Corbyn's favour' by Chris Stokel-Walker, *Wired*, 1 May 2018.

[378] 'Veteran of Treasury battle tots up a decade's wins and losses' by George Parker, Political Editor, *Financial Times*, 14 April 2016.

[379] op cit. *What happened?* by Hillary Clinton, p. 76.

[380] Review by Jonathan Swain of *Shattered: inside Hillary Clinton's doomed campaign* (2017) by Jonathan Allen and Amie Parnes. New York: Crown. Review in *The Wall Street Journal*, 21–23 April 2017.

[381] Congressman Tim Ryan (Democrat – Ohio) quoted in 'Georgia defeat sparks Democratic soul searching' by Courtney Weaver, *Financial Times*, 22 June 2017.

[382] Recognised, for example, in June 2017 by the creation of the G20 Eminent Persons Group on Global Financial Governance. It is reviewing the effectiveness and relevance of global institutions like the IMF and World Bank, especially after China created the rival Asian Infrastructure Investment Bank.

27
A 'CATASTROPHIC SETBACK TO CIVILISATION'?

New instruments of stability which have taken years to negotiate and put in place can be gone in days or even hours at the stroke of a pen.

And all of this is before the likely social earthquakes created by the sinister impact on human activity from Artificial Intelligence (AI) and algorithms. Is there clarity on direction of travel, its scope and its timings for areas like the impact on democracy?

No. 'The ultimate impact of AI on democracy is uncertain and unknown, perhaps unknowable.'[383] The rapid evolution of often-human-looking robots is already here. It confirms the blurring of the line between man and machine. Unthinkable? No! 'Sophia' is just one proof of how it is here and coming faster than most will even dare to think.[384] 'Capable of smiling, frowning, scowling, winking, Sophia was exceptional at mimicking human expressions thanks to some clever nanotechnology and artificial connective tissue.'[385] There is even a new reality of humans behaving more like machines. Will 'singularity' – a super AI which matches human intelligence and can catalyse runaway technological growth – lead to 'runaway changes to human civilisation'?[386]

There is no unity of views. Indeed many of those views are diametrically opposed.[387] Yet there are many good reasons to trumpet the truly amazing new human frontiers being opened up by AI for the next generation.[388] It will be the 'ultimate liberation from our current shackles'.[389] It could even mean there will be 'a change to the definition of what it means to be human'.[390] On the pace of development, there are some who say the progression to AI is 'still many decades away' and will lead to more jobs, not less.[391] One reason for the longer development period is that there needs to be a step change in computing power.[392]

We heard one top executive in a C-suite brainstorming session declare to colleagues with a mixture of admiration and apprehension: 'Artificial Intelligence is invading our existence.' He could clearly see the impacts. But he was at a loss on how to handle what comes next.

Whatever the timeline for likely progress, already the alarms are being sounded loudly on three fronts.

Firstly, almost half of us are already losing the 'race against the machines'.[393] AI and algorithms are outsmarting human competence levels. Humans must now work out how to maximise their skills in a fast-changing work environment. They need to confront the complex question of whether they should compete with robots or accommodate them.[394] Secondly, 'designers have difficulty decoding the behaviour of their own robots simply by observing them'.[395] Thirdly is the dark question of how AI faces up to the implications of multiple, potential, malicious uses. A new and ominous 'clarion call' report by 26 leading research institutes has urged 'governments and corporations worldwide to address the clear and present danger inherent in the myriad applications of AI'.[396]

The pace of development is breathtaking. So are the implications for leaders and those who serve them. 'What struck a lot of us was the amount that has happened in the last five years – if that continues, you see the chance of creating dangerous things,' warns that report.[397] The alert says that while there will be many positives from AI, the dual use for many applications will open new, dark doors of societal vulnerability and therefore instability. It identifies, for example, the fast-growing risk of an 'unprecedented rise in the use of "bots"' to manipulate everything from elections to the news agenda and social media. AI will create new 'tools for harm'. These will include 'fake images, video and audio' which suggest (in an unchallengeable, lifelike way) that leaders have said something they did not say.[398]

This new risk and challenge to the credibility of those at the top and the institutions they lead will be immense and unquantifiable. Once again, the quest for solutions requires a shedding of that conformity. Mindsets are not deep, flexible or broad enough to match the enormity of the new digital train that is hurtling down the tracks and picking up speed. Probably, being overawed and intimidated by the scale of unthinkables will shake leaders from their steady-state comfort blanket of increasingly flawed reassurance. But will that happen in time, or in the slipstream of that train which passed long ago?

AI, machine learning and quantum computing are together weakening the grip leaders have long assumed they have on events and how the public trust them. 'The greatest transformation in human society... the greatest change to our way of living' is how the writer and activist Stephen Fry has encapsulated it all.[399] Lord Martin Rees, Astronomer Royal and co-founder of the Centre for the Study of Existential Risk at Cambridge University, highlights the big worry of a new 'big challenge to governance' because of 'the new tension between liberty, security and privacy' created by AI and algorithms.[400] Overall 'the stakes are very high. There is a new kind of risk that is certainly going to be global and involve some kind of catastrophic setback to civilisation.'[401]

This profound upheaval between leaders and those they believe they still lead has even been detected by the masterly BBC radio presenter Jeremy Vine. After airing 25,000 phone calls in 15 years for his weekday chat and music show on BBC Radio 2 in the UK, it is clear to him that 'you [the listeners] are in control... Politicians obsessed with control are losing it... Elites are being upended... Experts are becoming peripheral.'[402] His wealth of anecdotal impressions on air – many of them logged and archived – confirm precisely our own conclusions from our hundreds of meetings and the resulting **Thinking the Unthinkable** data set.

All this before Artificial Intelligence dramatically scales up these trends with more unthinkables that will further disrupt our confidence in the way things are and who is in charge.

One major concern is who will be making money and how. Business's immediate attractions to AI are prosaic. They are essentially financial. 'Although chief executives publicly extol the broad benefits of AI, their main interest lies in cutting costs,' was the conclusion of The Economist's survey 'AI in Business.'[403] This captured the fast-growing disconnect between leaders and the public who fear losing livelihoods, privacy and accountability. Managing this impact of transformative technology on society is fast becoming one of the most pressing issues of our time.

The French president, Emmanuel Macron, appears to be one of very few world leaders with a truly 'big picture' perspective. He grasps the deep implications of AI for those who voted for him and those he represents. 'This huge technological revolution is in fact a political revolution.'[404] So far, it is in a prerevolutionary state in which the tech titans have most of the power and the knowledge. But he says there is an ever-decreasing trust. This is a sure recipe for conflict which a new breed of political leaders must accept – then work hard and fast to prevent.

One tech titan, the co-founder of Google Deep Mind, Mustafa Suleyman, shares the pragmatic anxiety. He said 'it's clear that technology is losing society's trust.' So far he is one of the few technologists willing to speak openly about ethics.[405] His warning in November 2017 was then confirmed by the outrage in 2018 over the revelations of harvesting by an outside company of the data from 87 million Facebook accounts. They sparked within hours a global fury, plus a new and long overdue debate. There was suddenly heated public anxiety about data privacy, the power of tech monopolies, and the lack of information and accountability. There was also the paucity of scope and a will for public debate.

'We are struggling to innovate within the confines of a political and economic system that grew out of a different age and, I would argue, needs radically rethinking,' said President Macron. He was acutely aware that France and Europe could be left well behind in the race of the two AI superpowers, China and the USA. So he announced a $1.5 billion investment in AI. 'If you want to manage your own choice of society, your choice of civilisation, you have to be able to be an acting part of this AI revolution. I want to frame the discussion at a global scale.'

Macron-level conversations on new economic systems and governance of AI have started. But they are mostly confined to a few open-minded companies like Google Deep Mind, and groups of highly motivated academic researchers. One leading figure is AI researcher Max Tegmark from MIT, author of Life 3.0. Dr Tegmark was a leading figure at the interdisciplinary conference in January 2017 which developed the Asilomar Principles on the safe use of AI.[406] The gathering engaged both ethicists and tech people. 'Just because you know how to program computers doesn't make you any more qualified to talk about humans flourishing on the planet,' said Dr Tegmark.[407]

So who is qualified to talk about the implications for society of the plethora of technology-related issues exploding into our daily consciousness? It is a key question which is highlighted by hot issues like Facebook's potentially existential crisis over a massive data leak, the investigation by US Special Counsel Robert Mueller into Russia's involvement in the US 2016 election, and the fast-growing issue of the alleged abuse of power by the tech monopoly giants.

There are even bigger question coming over the horizon. They include questions about the future nature of society, social inequality, and the ethical dimensions behind many of the extraordinary innovations emerging. These are not just in AI, but also quantum computing, biomedicine and gene editing. If we are on the cusp of an extraordinary era of innovation, how will human involvement be able to shape it? The anxieties are so profound that addressing them cannot be left to the IT specialists, although their understanding of the complexity will be a vital contribution.

There is new hope because of the number of interdisciplinary centres now starting to address the ethical and societal issues. One innovation is the Partnership on AI, which links tech companies and civil society organisations. In the UK there are the Future of Humanity Institute at Oxford and the Leverhulme Centre for the Future of Intelligence at Cambridge. Professor Huw Price is a leading figure in establishing the Cambridge Centre. What drives him is the issue of 'mindful optimism'. He says, 'You make your own luck. It's up to society and policy makers and business to make the decisions,' rather than allow technology to rule the roost.[408]

The fast-rising temperature of this already hot topic is shown by the packed room for sessions of the All-Party Group on AI at the Houses of Parliament in London. It is now a go-to event for those interested in AI and society. Its stated goal is 'to understand how AI will impact the lives of UK citizens and organisations, and subsequently, whether and how it should be regulated'.[409] This confirms the gap that now needs to be filled for informed public debate on the technological revolution. Yet there is a disconnect between leaders' attention spans and the complex questions at stake. In Britain, parliamentarians are overloaded by the Brexit 'bandwidth' problem. Few other issues beyond the UK's exit from the EU can command the attention needed. But very soon they and lawmakers around the world cannot avoid addressing big questions on how society will cope with the expected human negatives of AI and automation, especially the likely devastating impact on jobs and the need for a new skilling-up.

Who will reap the rewards? The RSA[410] argues that 'While for most of human history our problems have revolved around issues of material scarcity, the new machine age promises to bring about an era of unprecedented abundance – more than enough to meet everyone's needs. The question is whether we have the political courage and conviction to share the wealth wisely.'[411] In the UK, for example, there is excellent academic work on AI. There have been major start up successes like Deep Mind. But there is a national productivity problem which many attribute to poor, risk averse and complacent management. Innovation is not the core ambition it should be of many managers and executives.

So at the root of most core challenges is to recognise the scale of disruption and upheaval, their speed and then the options for recalibrating both the thinking of those in charge and the system they oversee. It requires changes on multiple levels. It also demands an appetite for risk, especially if the business seems to be ticking over just fine.

Cue the example of Aviva, the huge insurance company.

End notes

[383] Director's report on the conference 'Machine learning and artificial intelligence: how we make sure technology serves the open society', the Ditchley Foundation, 8–10 December 2017.

[384] See Sophia in action for yourself at the Future Investment Initiative in Riyadh: visit www.thinkunthink.org/digital-footnotes to watch the video.

[385] 'The robot revolution blurs the line between man and machine' by John Thornhill, *Financial Times*, 11 July 2017.

[386] 'Algorithms are more valued than empathy', letter from Eric Stryson in the *Financial Times*, 13 July 2018, p. 8.

[387] See for example 'Will robots destroy us?' by Tom Leonard, *Daily Mail*, 29 July 2017.

[388] See for example the Microsoft booklet *The pocket guide to AI* produced 'in collaboration with the robots'. More can be found at microsoft.com/AI.

[389] See for example: *Life 3.0: being human in the age of artificial intelligence* (2017) by Max Tegmark. New York: Random House.

[390] Seán Ó hÉigeartaigh, Executive Director at Centre for the Study of Existential Risk, in the video *Managing extreme technological risk* (2017). To watch the video, go to www.thinkunthink.org/digital-footnotes.

[391] 'Growing the artificial intelligence industry in the UK', report by Professor Dame Wendy Hall, Southampton University, and Jerome Pesenti, CEO Benevolent Tech, speaking on *Today*, BBC Radio 4, 30 December 2017.

[392] Remarks by Dr Stephen Cave, Executive Director of the Leverhulme Centre for the Future of Intelligence, *Today*, BBC Radio 4, 30 December 2017.

[393] 'Why machines do not have to be the enemy' by Sarah O'Connor, *Financial Times*, 1 November 2017. It quotes new research from the Organisation for Economic Cooperation and Development. 216,000 adults in 40 countries were put through a 50-minute assessment in a Survey of Adult Skills. One-third of workers use cognitive skills daily in their jobs, yet competency levels have already been matched by computers. 44% are still better than machines. 25% have jobs that do not use their skills every day. See also House of Lords Artificial Intelligence Committee, *AI in the UK: ready, willing and able?* Report of Session 2017–19 – published 16 April 2018 – HL Paper 100.

[394] 'Rise of the robots: are you ready?' by MIT roboticist Daniela Rus who explains 'why we need to collaborate rather than compete with artificial intelligence', *Financial Times*, 7 March 2018.

[395] 'Robot behaviour demands AI transparency' by Anjana Ahuja, *Financial Times*, 3 August 2017. Research quoted from Bath University presented at a conference at Sussex University.

[396] *The malicious use of artificial intelligence: forecasting, prevention and mitigation*, report by 26 authors from 14 institutions, spanning academia, civil society and industry, 20 February 2018. Also see: 'AI ripe for exploitation, experts warn', *BBC News* website, 21 February 2018.

[397] Jack Clark, head of policy at Open AI in San Francisco, quoted in 'AI progress sparks fears over cyber weapons' by Richard Waters, *Financial Times*, 21 February 2018.

[398] Interview with Seán Ó hÉigeartaigh, Executive Director at Centre for the Study of Existential Risk, *Today*, BBC Radio 4, 21 February 2018.

[399] Keynote address to the Hay Festival, 27 May 2017.

[400] Remarks to the Hay Festival, 29 May 2017.

[401] Lord Martin Rees in op cit. *Managing extreme technological risk* (2017).

[402] Summary of his book *What I learnt: what my listeners say – and why we should take notice* to the Hay Winter Weekend, 25 November 2017.

[403] 'Special report: AI in business', *The Economist*, March 31st–April 6th 2018.

[404] 'Emmanuel Macron talks to Wired about France's AI strategy', *Wired*, 31 March 2018.

[405] 'The technologist's dilemma' by Mustafa Suleyman, RSA President's Lecture, 14 November 2017.

[406] *Asilomar AI Principles*, Future of Life Institute, January 2017.

[407] Max Tegmark talk at Second Home, Spitalfields, London, 31 October 2017.

[408] Professor Huw Price, 13 July 2017.

[409] Chaired by Stephen Metcalfe MP and Lord Tim Clement-Jones, and with support on content from the Big Innovation Centre.

[410] The RSA, formally the Royal Society for the encouragement of Arts, Manufactures and Commerce (a title dating from the 18th century) advocates social and political change. The mantra of its CEO, Matthew Taylor, is 'Think like a system, act like an entrepreneur.'

[411] *The age of automation: artificial intelligence, robotics and the future of low-skilled work* (2017) report by Benedict Dellot and Fabian Wallace Stephens. London: RSA.

28

'YOU GUYS ARE IN THE STONE AGE'

Companies in the huge global insurance business face a massive pressure to reinvent themselves. They must ensure their relevance and a new level of digital efficiency. Their priority is to think both unthinkables and unpalatables for their business to thrive and survive. 'We are one of the last industries to be truly disrupted,' says Mark Wilson, CEO of Aviva.[412] So there has to be fundamental change.

In 2013 he set out to disrupt Aviva from within. The message was: 'If we don't change, we are going to die.' He was echoing the warnings in 2012 from the then Chairman John McFarlane.

The insurance market is smart and evolving rapidly. A fast-growing number of customers are impatient. They want risk cover. They want it almost instantly. They want the process to be super efficient. And they want to buy it online without fuss. But how would insurance providers – many of them global giants – be able to respond? They face unthinkables and unpalatables from new rival businesses, plus disruption from new efficiencies created by AI, machine learning, systems thinking and quantum computing.

British-based Aviva has a market cap of £21 billion. It has 33 million customers across 16 countries and employs almost 30,000 people. It has invested in new partnerships and acquisitions, and has more plans. So it is doing well. But since taking charge in January 2013, Wilson – a New Zealander who often wears jeans to the office – made clear to his staff that market success can never be assumed. They had to evolve into a different business. Fast.

From the moment he took over after his predecessor's 'unpopular tenure', Mark Wilson made clear that complacency had no place. 'I do turnarounds' was his mantra. Capital had to be boosted, costs had to be cut, and share price falls had to be reversed. In five years he achieved them all.[413] Processes like Systems Thinking meant many insurance payouts which used to take six weeks were being made in six hours. Where systems thinking was applied, customer satisfaction tended to increase measurably.

Attempts at dramatic digital innovation within Aviva had made little headway at first. Many ideas had been 'torn up'. Processes remained stuck in the legacy past, with a focus on failure-management. For example, staff efficiency in call centres used to be measured by how many calls were answered, not how many customer issues were resolved correctly. Call volumes were far higher than necessary because dissatisfied customers kept calling back! These call targets are gone now and people focus on how effectively they can resolve the customer's issue.

Dramatic innovation would be vital. So would diversification into fintech using inspiration from its newly created Digital Garage. This is a standalone startup staffed by newly recruited data engineers at a new off-site location in East London.

Digital Garage was the next and more radical shot. It was not a subculture. It was a standalone with a 'very different vibe'. Aviva had been struggling to hire digital innovators. (After all, what kind of data geek would want to join a 'boring' insurance company?) Not at Digital Garage. They convinced people with very different experiences in the gaming world to join them from the likes of Call of Duty on PlayStation 4 and Xbox.

Aviva's aim was to get into breaking up established business models. How could a big old corporate beast acquire a new startup mindset? 'It's not a lab. It's a business. Its objective is to make money,' Mark Wilson explained.

The Wilson principles were clear. Every possible new frontier was in Aviva's sights for consideration. Up to £100 million a year was budgeted to be spent on digital transformation internally. A venture capital fund had another £100 million to invest by 2020.

Wilson wanted new ideas from everyone inside Aviva. Many would be tried out and implemented. If they did not work, then the risk would have been worth it. No one would pay a price for proposing ideas that failed. Quite the opposite. A sense of premium was placed on innovation and the view that a good idea can come from anywhere.

Insiders point to the language of disruption which started in 2013. The message was to cannibalise your own business: 'If you are not disruptive yourselves, then someone else will be.'

'I remember us all being struck first by disruption being used as a sort of very positive attribute internally. It wasn't just a passing fad. It became very entrenched, a very sort of dominant part of the culture,' Sam White, Group Sustainability and Public Policy Director told us. 'There was that sort of willingness to try something for a year, and it didn't work. ... Rip it up and try something equally large or more ambitious, but different.'[414]

'Obviously some people react better to disruption than others. I think we've seen quite a lot of turnover at senior levels of people sometimes because they weren't willing to embrace it or deliver. I think the organisation has faced an awful lot of change. But Mark tends not to be ... saying, "We'll back off now." He tends to say: "Look, you're seeing a lot of change. You need to be ready for more, because this is now the culture we are. If you don't feel you want to work for an organisation that is going to be in perpetual change, then it's not going to be the one for you."'

Aviva has pushed ahead with new and aggressive determination on multiple tracks.

To save costs it withdrew from some foreign markets. It rationalised more costs and doubled down on its liabilities by mergers with Friends Life in the UK, plus deals in Ireland and Canada. Then to capture more market and impress customers it invested very heavily in what Wilson calls 'game-changing' new devices designed eventually to end most of the human contacts with Aviva for customers. 'No one has ever done this before.'[415]

'Ask It Never' removes a lot of human contact. It short-circuits all the time-consuming hassle of filling in forms – and probably talking to an agent by phone, who then asks questions you don't know the answer to! The catchline is 'Get a quote, not a quiz.'[416] By using the vast amount of data out there more intelligently, Aviva wanted to offer a pre-underwritten and pre-approved quote. 'Our customers want us to save them time as well as money. So our plan is to ask customers questions – once,' said Wilson.[417] The firm intent is to go from asking hundreds of questions 'to asking none – zero!' This is because of extraordinary leaps in the digital ability to read basic facts off public databases like house details and the risks for flooding. 'There is an awful lot of data you don't need to send us anymore.' As a result, 'we will pre-underwrite, pre-approve and give you a massive discount on what you are paying, probably 20% cheaper.' 'Ask It Never' does not end human intervention with customers. But it brings that reality much closer. And much quicker.

Then comes 'MyAviva'. It is a new digital dashboard which means customers can see all their policies in one online e-hub. There is no longer the need to check out five personal policy folders from one company or five different companies.

Another first for the company was experimenting with Amazon's voice-activated Echo. Aviva was the first UK insurer to launch an Alexa 'skill'. It lets people ask questions to demystify insurance jargon. So, for example, you could say, 'Alexa, what's an annuity?' and she'd give you an explanation. What stands out is that it was an example of the cultural change, trying to innovate at pace. From the Echo device coming out in the UK to getting something to market was less than 12 weeks. It wasn't about getting it perfect first; it was about moving fast to dip a toe in the water. The new culture was 'test and learn'.

The spirit and principles are all brought together in Aviva Quantum. This is a new global data science practice. It is conceived as an exchange of ideas and data sets to create a 'rich understanding' of new correlations of risks. The result will be new pricing structures and new identification of fraud, for example.

What has been the internal impact of this new solutions-based approach?

'No one bounces through a huge transformation process where your roles are at risk, and your colleagues' roles are at risk. With the best will in the world, it takes a while to get through every part of the business, every level of the business. So there's a period which is difficult. If it's not difficult for you, it's difficult for someone sitting within earshot of you. Humans are going to respond emotionally to that. I know I do,' Sam White told us.

What about the attraction for the NextGen of working at Aviva? Recruitment remains healthy. It is strengthened by a clear message from the C-suite that new arrivals can have an equal and vital voice in innovation. The feedback loop is vibrant and healthy by way of 'unblocking sessions' and 'culture action teams'. The internal GROW scheme is a digital learning platform to make sure staff shed conformity and understand the imperative for change and innovation.

'I've had a few of the graduates on my team in the last years,' said Sam White. 'It's brilliant; it's a really great opportunity. The graduate I had last: she was of the millennial generation, early twenties, and very confident. She was very competently able to articulate what we were doing wrong, and what we could be doing better in my team. [This] was actually incredibly welcome, very useful. I ended up having her reverse mentor me.

What was the impact of reverse mentoring? 'Great! Really refreshing and really interesting to understand how she saw some of the digital tools we used and thought about them differently.'

Why was her innovative engagement so important? '[She said:] "You guys are in the Stone Age in terms of your digital management." I really respected that. There's a vast stream of more intel and data and understanding of what's working and what's not working. But we were just not tapping into this a few years ago. She had the guts to publicly in the room challenge us on it; [she] was absolutely right.'

More than any business, insurance companies like Aviva must calibrate risks from unthinkables. In the extreme, failure could threaten its survival, a reality CEO Mark Wilson both thrives on and has to live with. But since 2013 a new aggressive enlightenment on innovation has strengthened its market position.

The £21 billion market cap confirms that. But one or two major unthinkables in future could soon deplete this impressive, enhanced value if Aviva and its CEO make the wrong risk calculations.

End notes

[412] 'Aviva on the hunt for acquisitions as CEO says: "We want to turn Aviva into a fintech"' by Oscar Williams-Grut, *Business Insider UK*, 25 May 2017.

[413] 'Aviva Chief Mark Wilson spins off in unexpected directions' by Patrick Jenkins, *Financial Times*, 22 March 2018.

[414] Interview, 19 March 2018.

[415] 'Aviva boss promises to slash prices AND let customers buy policies without filling out endless forms' by Mark Wilson, *The Sun*, 19 April 2017.

[416] To see the video promotion, 'Get a Quote not a Quiz' go to www.thinkunthink.org/digital-footnotes.

[417] 'Aviva to debut "game-changing" idea that will cut prices', *Insurance Business*, 19 April 2017.

29

'YES, THE STAKES ARE HIGH'

In sum, the nervous system of the world has become deeply fragile.[418] The international order of the past 70 years is fraying, maybe even breaking down.[419] Assuming that this is just a passing, inconvenient phase is not just flawed. It is irresponsible. For a multitude of reasons we are only in the foot hills of what threatens to become a rugged mountain of disruption. There are constant and compelling arguments to echo Al Jolson in saying that you ain't heard nothing yet. The very foundations of all we assume to be robust are being shaken – even the basic principles on which corporate wealth is built. Voices of anxiety are starting to break cover.

'Societal attitudes are changing in a way it is hard to tap into,' conceded one CEO of a major global corporate.[420] 'We need open leadership. There is a need for leaders to open up to public debate,' said another.[421]

Some at the very top now go even further. 'The capitalistic model no longer works,' was the remarkable alert from Mark Bertolini, CEO of the health insurance giant Aetna, to one hundred top fellow CEOs gathered in New York City.[422] As we have reported, Bertolini added that if corporates further alienate the public, 'we are in danger of losing our operating licence'. The FT City Network of 50 top C-suiters produced the same alert from different evidence. Capitalism has 'lost its way' and taken a number of 'wrong turnings'.[423] Then came New Zealand's Prime Minister Jacinda Ardern. She took office while labelling capitalism a 'blatant failure'.[424] While confirming growing good reasons to define the global predicament as the 'edge of chaos', there are voices that venture optimism. There is the controversial idea for a Blueprint for a New Democracy from the celebrated Zambian-born economist and 'democratic capitalist' Dambisa Moyo.[425]

The system's moral compass has begun to swing, catalysed in part by those who have done so well from it. Profit and loss is no longer the way that compass is necessarily calibrated. The Milton Friedman principle that 'there is only one social responsibility of business – to … increase its profits' is increasingly considered to be not just well past its sell-by date but now down right counter-productive. There is too much push back these days, especially from millennials and NextGens. 'If people want to do things in their private lives with social factors, why would they not want the companies they invest in to do the same?' asked the Nobel economics laureate Oliver Hart.[426] Some former business leaders are forcefully raising similar searching questions. 'The way companies are being run today morally offends me. A lot of people losing a lot of money because of the mediocrity that's going on. … That is wrong. I am an optimist,' came from Mike Rees. Until 2016 he was the deputy managing director of Standard Chartered Bank.[427]

There are CEOs who now say that their companies no longer want to attract investors like hedge funds who only want the biggest possible short-term returns.[428] In a time of structural disruption they create unnecessary existential threats to corporates who have increasingly become hostages to short-termism.

That is why Larry Fink's warning to CEOs in his annual 'letter' deserves to command great attention and defy the voices of inevitable sceptics, whose disparaging irritation we have heard in private. Fink wrote: 'The public expectations of your company have never been greater. Society is demanding that companies, both public and private, have a social purpose.'[429] Otherwise 'it will lose its licence to operate from key stakeholders'. Others are catching on too. One of Fink's arch-rivals is Bill McNabb, Chair of the Vanguard Group. He convenes the grandly named CEO Force for Good. He wrote in a critical tone to fellow CEOs a few weeks later: 'For too long, companies have sacrificed long-term value creation to generate short-term results.' Gillian Tett of the Financial Times added her comment. 'Mr McNabb's letter shows is that (Milton) Friedman's vision of capitalism is starting to look almost as passé as big shoulder pads.'[430] There are other trendsetters on the push away from the obsession with returns and the short term.

Joe Kaeser, president and CEO of the global engineering giant Siemens, has gone public with a matching scale of alarm. He has broken cover to write what many leaders increasingly fear but few want to talk about in public. He spoke out to broaden and build on what for a long time have been the pioneering footsteps of Paul Polman, CEO of Unilever, who had mounted almost a one-man global campaign to highlight the failings of leaderships and what they could do better.

Unlike its arch competitor GE, Siemens is a smart winner so far in the struggle to restructure and embrace the new renewable energy opportunities.[431; 432] Dr Kaeser labels disruption as a revolution. His warnings are remarkable. Close attention needs to be paid to them. 'Yes, the stakes are high,' wrote Kaeser. 'If we get the revolution right, digitalisation will benefit the nearly 10 billion humans inhabiting our planet in the year 2050. If we get it wrong, societies will be divided into winners and losers; social unrest and anarchy will arise; the glue that holds societies and communities together will disintegrate; and citizens will no longer believe that governments are able to fulfil their purpose of enforcing the rule of law and providing security.'[433]

Iain Conn, Group CEO of Centrica, the UK gas provider, has also made it a public issue. 'Business has to form a different relationship with society and government. And right now it is at a low point in my view. ... We're going to have to find a way to be trusted. Power is shifting to the customer because they have more choice, and digitisation is accelerating the whole thing.'[434]

And increasingly anxious stakeholders from every generation are boldly raising their voices. We heard one top CEO confide how the disquiet of his nine-year-old daughter had made an impact on his thinking about renewables and what the next generation expect. One evening she had wondered out loud to him. How could she be the daughter of a father who heads up a huge, oil-producing energy company which Greenpeace thought was a bad organisation? The thoughtful way in which this CEO told the story made clear the effect of her words on the direction he realised he must take the company.

This growing cohort of top-level alerts illustrates a core finding of our **Thinking the Unthinkable** work. Social unrest and anarchy?

Governments losing authority and credibility? To a vast majority, the warnings from Bertolini, Fink and Kaeser are off the wall and unthinkable. The sceptical minds of conformists might ask something like: 'Jeez, what are these guys smoking?' Yet the evidence on which they base their warnings is stark and potentially bone-shaking. It should not be questioned. A serving government minister told us that in his view 'there is already a degree of anarchy, and the anarchy will get worse if you don't involve people.'[435] Such analysis must not be dismissed as delusional or unthinkable. In reality such scenarios must be viewed as plausible, even if they are also unpalatable. In line with Lord Macpherson's frank admissions of a 'monumental, collective, intellectual error', too often since 2014 there have been clear trends with evidence which should have been identified and highlighted, not written off as unthinkable.

End notes

[418] Ian Goldin in a presentation on 19 May 2017 about his books, *The age of discovery: navigating the risks and rewards of our new renaissance* (2016; London: Bloomsbury) and *The butterfly defect: how globalisation creates systemic risks and what to do about it* (2014; Princeton: Princeton University Press).

[419] *Financial Times*, 31 October 2016.

[420] Private remarks, 15 February 2018.

[421] Private remarks, 15 February 2018.

[422] Fortune CEO Initiative, Ritz Carlton Hotel, New York, 25 September 2017.

[423] 'Greed and tax dodges leave capitalism ripe for reform, say business leaders' by Patrick Jenkins. *Financial Times*, 23 October 2017.

[424] 21 October 2017.

[425] *Edge of chaos* (2018) by Dambisa Moyo. New York: Little Brown.

[426] Presentation to the World Knowledge Forum, Seoul, 17 October 2017.

[427] 'Standard Chartered veteran Mike Rees set for £500k a year pension' by Jill Treanor, *The Guardian*, 10 January 2016.

[428] Voices heard during an on the record debate among one hundred CEOs at the op cit. Fortune 'CEO Initiative', 25 September 2017.

[429] op cit. Larry Fink, 16 January 2018.

[430] 'In the vanguard: fund giants urge CEOs to be "force for good"' by Gillian Tett, *Financial Times*, 1 February 2018.

[431] 'GE to slash dividend and sell off oldest divisions in revival push' by Ed Crooks, *Financial Times*, 14 November 2017.

[432] 'Flying too far from the sun' by Ed Crooks and Patrick McGee, *Financial Times*, 13 November 2017.

[433] *The world is changing. Here's how companies must adapt*, World Economic Forum, 25 January 2018.

[434] op cit. Iain Conn, 9 March 2018.

[435] op cit. Interview with Lord Mark Price, 25 July 2017.

30
POLITICAL INSURGENTS 'SHATTER THE MOULD'

Europe's migration crisis in 2015 is a classic example of the stability of the system being rocked by apparent unthinkables. But it is too easy for those at the top of governments across Europe – especially in Germany – to say they were caught out by unthinkables. There was plenty of evidence with many warnings. But governments viewed them as unpalatable.

For two years the UN High Commissioner for Refugees (UNHCR) and the International Organisation for Migration (IOM) had issued increasingly blunt warnings to European nations. They were threatened by an impending build-up of hundreds of thousands of desperate displaced people and economic migrants from Syria, Turkey, North Africa and further afield. Instead EU governments viewed the numbers as unthinkable and the warnings as scaremongering. 'It was a big shock. 1.5 million people. We should have seen that,' the then EU Humanitarian Affairs commissioner Kristalina Georgieva confirmed to us.[436] 'As Europeans found out, the refugee crisis was like a slow-moving tsunami. It did come, and it did hit us.'

The mass tide of humanity was desperate enough to take enormous risks to find somewhere better to live. What literally no one in power had foreseen was the incredible ability and ingenuity of the huge numbers on the move to organise themselves and share with each other logistics advice via mobile phone. They did it cost-free via SMS, WhatsApp, Instagram and other pop-up digital platforms that facilitated instant communications. The advice to each other flowed freely and unencumbered across borders, sharing information on best routes and where governments were trying to obstruct and reverse migrant flows.

National security agencies found themselves blindsided and wrong-footed. Police and security forces could only act belatedly, rushing to erect razor wire and enforce usually control-free EU borders. They were behind the curve, while the migrants and refugees had the initiative. They commanded both the digital and humanitarian high ground. It meant they could circumvent many of the heavy-handed, official efforts to block and control the waves of people on the move right across south-eastern Europe.

Remarkably, through spring and summer of 2015, European leaders had failed even to conceive of these unthinkables. They had not believed the forecasts. The evidence and warnings were there. But they were unpalatable. One top interior ministry official confided that his department had predicted to ministers the likelihood of the mass migrant wave. But the forecasts had significantly underestimated the scale. As several have confided, they viewed the likelihood of huge numbers as unrealistic, and the implications as simply too unpalatable to contemplate. 'We were too busy trying to save the Euro, under instructions from Chancellor Merkel,' was how one very senior German official described the government position in Germany during July and early August that year.[437]

So governments largely sidelined the evidence and ignored the threat. As a result they were unprepared when the waves of human desperation risked crossing the Mediterranean or Aegean in massive numbers. 'We failed to see it because we were too politically correct,' one European president confessed belatedly to our project.[438] The humanitarian and political cost was enormous. Governments resorted to draconian emergency measures to tighten border controls and internal security – partly to convince domestic populations that there was a tough policy. But toughness and images of riot police with razor wire were as much to cover the political failures of not listening to the warnings from the UNHCR and IOM.

For multiple reasons, the decisions of many EU nations to dismiss those warnings as unpalatable has had a profound and probably irreversible impact on European politics and societal cohesion for at least a generation. They help to justify the nature of the warning from

Joe Kaeser, CEO of Siemens. As they struggled to catch up, many leaders were viewed as having failed in their duties.

This swiftly stunned political establishments by awakening the long-slumbering resentments of populists and nationalists in many countries. Instead of projecting bold IMAX-scale ideas and images for noticeable improvement, politicians engaged in what could be called political pixilation:[439] the self-serving recycling of often-stale thinking. Only after they leave power do leaders realise how out of touch they were. The former UK prime minister Gordon Brown conceded he had been the wrong prime minister for the social media age.[440] Suddenly, new leaders with alternative thinking found new ways to riff. Even age did not matter. In the US Bernie Sanders and in the UK Jeremy Corbyn attracted huge numbers of the young who feel politicians are out of touch.[441] They used social media more effectively.[442] They generated unexpected popularity and support, like the surprise impact when Labour's Corbyn did the unthinkable of appearing on stage at the 2017 Glastonbury Festival.[443]

The mishandling of the migration wave sparked an earthquake of discontent. It cracked and fractured the usually robust walls of traditional politics, most notably for Chancellor Merkel in Germany, who barely survived an election rout in September 2017. It vaporised many traditional political parties. Merkel's routine restating of a mantra that Germans 'have never had it so good' failed to convince many voters who were disillusioned.[444] In France, Emmanuel Macron's new En Marche movement blew most of the old, well-established parties out of the water, apart from the National Front with its core anti-immigrant policy. 'He went into battle with a fan club instead of a party, armed with themes rather than policies. Initially he seemed a mere will-o'-the-wisp of the social media age.'[445] It had been unthinkable. 'We never saw it coming,' conceded one Paris-based ambassador.[446] The dramatic change in public mood secured Macron the presidency, a huge majority in parliament and unprecedented public expectations. 'I am profoundly optimistic about our country,' said the distinguished political scientist Dominique Moïsi.[447] He had an upbeat assessment for France which is not heard for many other nations. Macron is 'the right man at the right time in the right place. ... A majority [in France] believe in revolution and change.'

Elsewhere there was a similar public push back against anything establishment. Warnings from the more enlightened like Mark Rutte, the Dutch Prime Minister, in late 2016 did not create fundamental political awakenings by traditional parties. 'The voters are not wrong. When voters move in another direction, it means the mainstream parties have to be more successful in showing we can solve these problems.'[448] They could not. Instead those 'wrong' voters fuelled a new conservative and nationalist radicalism, first in Hungary and Poland, then Austria, the Czech Republic and Sweden, followed by Italy. Across all those countries and more, political insurgents had found the key to 'shatter the mould'.[449] This is even though before elections, the traditional parties would not admit to the scale of the threat to them and their way of doing politics. Many seemed to assume the invincibility of the political framework they served. How wrong they were. They did not understand the overwhelming public mood that 'mainstream leaders have conspicuously failed.'[450]

'We have stuck to old patterns,' admitted Norbert Röttgen, one of the highest-level centre-right figures after Chancellor Merkel's vastly diminished election victory in Germany in September 2017. Usually the formation of coalition governments in Germany can be agreed in days. This time the new political realities meant the process took an astonishing six months.[451] In the March elections in Italy, the Five Star anti-establishment movement confirmed the scale and nature of political upheaval. It was picking up greater momentum and having profound impact. The EU's High Representative Federica Mogherini, herself Italian, identified a 'major shift to anti-system messages'.[452] She confirmed what many viewed as an ominous trend. Once again the traditional leadership class was being humiliated. 'It is a big shift [and] … went beyond our worst expectations,' was how one Italian official summarised the political bombshell. 'There is a feeling of loss of direction, and it is so deep. It proves that we are facing a very big failure of the ruling class.'[453]

And this 'major shift to anti-system messages' after 2015 has had further sinister implications. It rammed open a door that allowed an 'increasingly aggressive' Russia to exploit outdated election laws and old fashioned voting systems in order to meddle in elections worldwide.[454]

Moscow found ways to interfere digitally in order to destabilise countries to its own pro-Putin agenda and strategic advantage.[455] The implications of this are far greater than most are prepared to even listen to, let alone accept.[456]

A few years ago, such a scenario and chain of events relating to Russia would have been considered unthinkable. After all, since 2009 a spirit of 'reset' had been agreed to improve Russia-US relations. Now sombre, uncomfortable new realities are removing bite-sized chunks from the once-strong foundations of all that has long been assumed.[457]

There had been evidence to signal what loomed and threatened with Russia. But it was largely viewed by political leaders as 'off the wall' and unpalatable – until far too late. This goes a long way to confirming the anxiety that leaderships remain irresponsibly out of sync with the reasons for the nature and scale of disruption that now both weakens and undermines them. Treaties, agreements and contracts designed progressively over many years to create and embed stability have been dramatically shredded by opportunism and bloody-minded rejections of so much that had been achieved. There is now a 'game with no rules. Rules do not apply. There is nothing to replace those rules,' said one very high-ranking UN official.[458] The blame for this can be laid squarely at the feet of both Trump in Washington and Putin in Moscow.

So what is the takeaway for leaders facing similar unthinkables and unpalatables that are approaching unnoticed like a slow-moving tsunami? Hillary Clinton summarised the reason why those of her leadership generation have become so disconnected from the new truths. 'Our immune system has been slowly eroded over years,'[459] she wrote. The former US Secretary of State Madeleine Albright told this project: 'There is not enough leadership. It is a blindness to what is inevitable. It is a matter of planning. Difficult! Planning for the worst. [But] that is never a great encouragement for leaders.'[460]

Importantly there must be that planning even if leaders and their staff cannot believe in the possibility of the unthinkable happening. These days, there is an inevitable chance that it will.

End notes

[436] op cit. Kristalina Georgieva, 9 March 2018.

[437] Senior German official speaking off the record, October 2016.

[438] President Kolinda Grabar-Kitarović of Croatia, GLOBSEC conference, Bratislava forum, 15 April 2016.

[439] Adapted from a phrase used in 'Tory conference was a chance for renewal – and they blew it' by Matthew d'Ancona, *Evening Standard*, 4 October 2017.

[440] *My life, our times* (2017) by Gordon Brown. London: Bodley Head.

[441] 'Politicians out of touch with issues that matter most to us, say young people' by Barney Davis, *Evening Standard*, 13 June 2017.

[442] 'Tories trounced by Labour in social media election battle' by Nicholas Cecil, *Evening Standard*, 14 June 2017.

[443] 'Jeremy rocks Glastonbury Festival as politics once more feels the power of pop' by Anne McElvoy, *Evening Standard*, 26 June 2017. Also: 'The Corbyn surge is real and Labour is transformed' by Simon Fletcher, a chief of staff and campaign director for Corbyn, *Evening Standard*, 26 June 2017.

[444] 'Germans "have never had it so good" says Merkel' by Stefan Wagstyl, *Financial Times*, 24 November 2016.

[445] 'To heal his nation, Macron will have to make France less French' by Patrick Bishop, *Evening Standard*, 8 May 2017.

[446] Lord Peter Ricketts, UK ambassador at the time, conversation on 7 December 2017.

[447] op cit. Dominique Moïsi, 14 February 2018.

[448] 'Europe risks falling "over the edge" – mainstream parties must learn from populist surge, warns Dutch Prime Minister', interview with the *Financial Times*, 12 December 2016.

[449] 'Insurgents shatter the mould in Italian politics' by James Politi, *Financial Times*, 5 March 2018.

[450] Sir Nigel Sheinwald, former senior UK diplomat and Visiting Professor at King's College London, closed remarks to the Oslo Energy Forum 2018, 14 February 2018. Released by agreement.

[451] Norbert Röttgen, remarks to Brussels Forum, 5 March 2018.

[452] Federica Mogherini, remarks to Brussels Forum, 8 March 2018.

[453] op cit. James Politi, 5 March 2018.

[454] Speech by UK Prime Minister Theresa May at the Guildhall, City of London, 13 November 2017. 'We know what you are doing. And you will not succeed,' she warned President Putin directly.

[455] Interview with MI5 Director Andrew Parker, 31 October 2016. Russia 'is using its whole range of state organs and powers to push its foreign policy abroad in increasingly aggressive ways – involving propaganda, espionage, subversion and cyber-attacks. Russia is at work across Europe and in the UK today. It is MI5's job to get in the way of that.'

[456] op cit. Larisa Brown and Chris Greenwood, 8 March 2018.

[457] *Modern political warfare: current practices and possible responses* (2018) by Linda Robinson et al. Santa Monica: RAND Corporation.

[458] Private remarks, 20 January 2018.

[459] op cit. *What happened?* by Hillary Clinton, p. 326.

[460] Remarks at the German Marshall Fund's Brussels Forum, 9 March 2018.

31

'TOTTERING TOWARDS AN OUTSIZED, WORLD-SHAPED EARTH WRECK'?

Will leaders accept this kind of challenge to their complacency? Will they learn from the shock?

Populism is not vanquished. Quite the opposite. The reasons for it and the disillusionment with politics to represent the anxieties it represents are becoming ever sharper, and will get worse.[461] Populists are becoming mainstream.[462] 'They want to do politics in another way. They are looking for protection in a world that is more uncertain and dangerous.'[463] As a result, their head-on challenge to established attitudes and systems has great momentum and attraction. They are asserting themselves and undermining governance in ways that were unthinkable until very recently.[464] The implications are profound for leaders. But how many will be open-eyed and radical enough to first identify then embrace the challenge? How many will accept alerts they don't want to hear? 'You really need someone giving awkward and unvarnished truth, saying actually it is not going very well.'[465] But for most, these are not the politics they know or feel comfortable with.

Hillary Clinton knows the political cost of not knowing or realising. 'I had been unable to connect with the deep anger so many Americans felt, or shake the perception that I was the candidate of the status quo.'[466] She added: 'When people are angry and looking for someone to blame, they don't want to hear your ten-point plan to create jobs and raise wages. They want you to be angry too.'[467] Clinton did not get that. Trump did. That is the price for sticking to those 'old patterns' in a new world of 'anti-system messages'.

Should there be shock or surprise? Why is greater resilience and adaptability not a part of executive DNA? Centuries of history will always remind us how 'shit happens', including for the most eminent and distinguished of leaders. The unexpected has to be expected. Indeed, in the financial world, crises 'follow a nature-like rhythm: they peak and purge, swell and storm'.[468] In many ways, that is both the attraction and hazard of being a leader. 'You never expect it to be easy. But that has been the "come-on" to being a leader. Now it is more difficult than ever. If you get things wrong, you can end up in jail,' confided one CEO.

Is this predicament for leadership worse than ever, especially the need for change both in leaders themselves and those they lead? Can leaderships today overcome the 'distress' of being 'scared' and 'overwhelmed'? If so, how?

There is some reassurance at least. Decades of monitoring leaders has confirmed the scale of what all of them have to confront in order to embrace 'adaptive challenges'. Here, for example, are two critical observations from one important analysis in 1997.[469] They confirm the current scale of the problem and the behavioural challenge. 'First … executives have to break a long-standing behaviour pattern of their own: providing leadership in the form of solutions. … Second, adaptive change is distressing for the people going through it. They need to take on new roles, new relationships, new values, new behaviours, and new approaches to work.' Overall, it 'generates distress'.

The veteran politician and diplomat Lord Chris Patten repeatedly emphasised the scale of that leadership deficit in his magisterial effort to ask What Next? Surviving the Twenty-first Century.[470] In his book he even asked presciently, 'Does economic globalisation – and the social and environmental changes that accompany it – run too far ahead of the ability of politics to cope?' That was 2008, and he was right. He also feared that 'we are tottering towards the precipice of an outsized, world-shaped earth wreck'. Again he was right. But it did not stop the march to what now, ten years later, seems to be a cliff of despair – that abyss – which leaders somehow have to face up to and cope with.

Yet few, if any, appear to have taken any notice of – or at least factored into their attitude to their responsibilities – this reality of unthinkables.

By now it should surely have been embedded in every leader's DNA. We have seen the eminent historian Margaret MacMillan point her finger at audiences of senior executives and warn them that disasters like World War One happened in large part because leaders were 'smug' or 'complacent'. Yet such realities of history do not mean that those at the top today are more aware or better prepared for the scale of unthinkables. Quite the opposite. Being hyper-connected and instantly informed in our new digital space does not seem to guarantee the rounded wisdom and insight needed to lead in the new turbulent times of 2017. Instead it seems to reinforce prejudices that become baked into leadership psyches. It can be regarded as a comfort blanket created by self-deception.

Hence once again the red alert, and a warning that we are only in the foothills of new unthinkables. History has many lessons, but few leaders seem to know or remember what they are in ways that will inform them for the challenges they face today or tomorrow.

The long shadow of Al Jolson lives on. You ain't seen nothing yet.

End notes

[461] See for example *Us vs them: the failure of globalism* (2018) by Ian Bremmer. New York: Penguin.

[462] See 'A dangerous waltz – Europe's populists are becoming more intertwined with the mainstream', *The Economist*, 3–9 February 2018, pp. 18–20. Also 'Threat and opportunity: how to learn from the populists' pp. 13–14.

[463] Private remarks by a leading adviser to President Macron of France, 1 December 2017.

[464] See *Global trends 2017–22: the centrality of governance*, AT Kearney Global Business Policy Council, 6 October 2017.

[465] op cit. Sir Lawrence Freedman, 9 October 2017.

[466] op cit. *What happened?* by Hillary Clinton, p. 386.

[467] ibid. p. 398.

[468] From a summary of *Manias, panics and crashes: a history of financial crises* (2015) by Charles P Kindleberger. New York: Palgrave Macmillan. First published 1978, multiple editions updated by Robert Z Aliber and Robert M Solow.

[469] op cit. Ronald A Heifetz and Donald L Laurie.

[470] *What next? Surviving the twenty-first century* (2008) by Chris Patten. London: Allen Lane.

32
'GOVERNING (AND SACKING) BY TWEET'

So a new disruptive reality has taken our planet by storm. The impact goes well beyond geopolitics.

Suddenly it is fashionable to be nasty. There are 'free speech wars' where 'everyone's shouting, nobody's listening'.[471] Increasingly 'there are a lot of people who just do not believe in compromise'. [472]'Our politics have become almost exclusively accusatory and bombastic. We leap to a conclusion – I'm right and you're wrong – without any intervening exchange.'[473] In the US, women built a huge new movement pressing for equality and an end to sexual abuse. In the UK, rectifying the usually dramatic gender pay gap took off belatedly as a major public issue. In the US, racial divisions were inflamed once again via police killings of non-white people which catalysed the Black Lives Matter movement. The US Department of Justice had excoriated the Chicago Police department for violating citizen rights without accountability, especially African Americans and Latinos.[474] In the UK the ugly spectre of antisemitism suddenly emerged like a dark cloud over public life.[475] The Archbishop of Canterbury published a new book warning that in Britain such new emotions are leading to 'cracks in our society ... the growth of intolerance and above all an inward turning' in a 'self-protective society without generosity, arising from a lack of confidence'.[476] Traditional loyalties have largely gone. 'Everything is more difficult and fluid. ... [It is a] period of considerable political difficulty across the western world.'[477] Overall in the UK (at least) 'there is an awful kind of quarrelsome, bitter, sometimes savage debate going on. ... We must recognise that this is a very, very nasty place to be.'[478]

It has also become politically fashionable to label inconvenient facts as 'fake'. If the US President can get away with claiming the truth to be fake, then why can't you and others? To try to get his way, Trump and his acolytes loudly blame the media for being 'dishonest people' who publish 'fake news' based on lies which they concoct maliciously. The President starts governing by tweet at 6 in the morning to seize the agenda with often stark, contrarian thoughts that grab the high ground.[479] Policy is generated spontaneously via his touchscreen as he watches Fox News. The presidency was no longer configured for sound bites. Trump was the 'tweet bite' president![480]

'I am not involved in how the president constructs his tweets, when he tweets, why he tweets, what he tweets,' said the then Secretary of State Rex Tillerson.[481] Trump creates 'alternative facts' and makes false claims in order to show he is right, and the sceptics or political adversaries are wrong. He even sacked his Secretary of State by tweet without even the courtesy of a phone call.[482] He then announced the departure of his National Security Adviser H R McMaster by tweet.[483] He belittles in equal measure the adversaries he dislikes (like 'Little Rocket Man',[484] the leader of North Korea) and those who have failed him (like 'sloppy Steve' Bannon[485] after the publication of Michael Wolff's explosive revelations about Trump's White House in Fire and Fury, or former FBI Director James Comey who he labelled a 'slime ball', leaker and liar).[486]

We are in a place where the US President does not care about being disparaged for his 'childish Twitter rampage', or the accuracy of what he says, or the fact that he 'has tweeted himself into a corner' on unsubstantiated allegations.[487] Even the White House Communications Director believes she can somehow get away with telling 'white lies' to protect the president in a nine-hour congressional hearing. (She resigned the next day)[488] As Hillary Clinton concluded after a year of campaigning and trying to knock out Trump politically: 'It almost felt like there was no such thing as truth anymore.'[489] But it did not matter to voters. He became US president.

But then comes the thunderstorm of doubts. After almost a year in office, Trump responded to all the bitter criticism about what he had done over 12 months and scepticism about his mental health with the blithe tweet assessment that he is a 'very stable genius'.[490] This further exacerbated the turmoil of judgements about his mode of leadership. Does the President mean what he writes? Does he write what he means? Does he really understand the facts and arguments behind his own policies? And the President himself seems unapologetic if he makes a mistake or what he called a 'clinker'.[491] His spokesperson tries to push back on the impact, saying allegations that his predecessor ordered unnamed people to 'tapp' (sic) his phone should not be taken literally![492]

So if the US President's tweets might be wrong (or not as right as they should be), who do we believe? In this context, his tweet announcing his agreement to a hyper-risky meeting with North Korea's 'little rocket man' was even more stunning.[493] He had not even consulted his Secretary of State Rex Tillerson, who was abroad. Nor did he consult US 'experts' who have spent their careers mastering the minutiae of North Korea's deceptions, programmes and intentions for years.

This goes a long way to confirming what has been labelled the US President's 'doctrine of obliteration' which so many others increasingly seem to want to mirror. It appears to be based on the principle 'rip things apart and make someone else fix them'.[494] Russia under Putin also prides itself in being just as destructive, again on the president's own unchallenged terms. The intentions of China and others seem ominously similar.

Unthinkable? Yes! But that judgement is framed by the well-established norms of conformity.

How relevant are those norms these days? Leaders now face a whole new disrupted world. And it is nothing like they think they are prepared for because of the way they qualified to get to the top.

End notes

[471] 'Free speech wars: everyone's shouting, nobody's listening', *Prospect*, March 2018. There is a big selection of articles on this at prospectmagazine.co.uk.

[472] op cit. Hillary Clinton, 18 October 2017.

[473] op cit. John Kerry, Ditchley Lecture, 8 July 2017.

[474] 'Chicago police violated citizens' rights, DOJ reports' by Lindsay Whipp, *Financial Times*, 14/15 January 2017.

[475] In the days leading up to a tense rally outside parliament in London, 26 March 2018.

[476] *Reimagining Britain: foundations for hope* (2018) by Justin Welby. London: Bloomsbury.

[477] Professor Robert Tombs, speaking on *The World at One*, BBC Radio 4, 24 December 2017.

[478] Professor David Marquand, speaking on *The World at One*, BBC Radio 4, 24 December 2017.

[479] 'Trump on vacation: work, play, tweet' by Peter Baker, *The New York Times*, 9 August 2017.

[480] Richard Levick, chair of the Levick communications consultancy in Washington DC, quoted in 'Tweet bite Trump keeps old media at a distance' by Barney Jopson and Anna Nicolaou, *Financial Times*, 3 December 2016.

[481] Quoted in 'US global leadership is missing in action', editorial, *Financial Times*, 12 July 2017.

[482] 13 March 2018. Secretary Tillerson was in Africa. Unlike the President, he did not use Twitter.

[483] 22 March 2018.

[484] 22 September 2017.

[485] 4 January 2018.

[486] 'Trump calls Comey "untruthful slime ball" as book details released' by Michael D.Shear and Alexander Burns, *The New York Times*, 13 April 2018.

[487] Editorial by *The New York Times* editorial board, 6 March 2017.

[488] Hope Hicks speaking after the hearing on 27 February 2018. She was also a 'person of interest' for the Special Counsel's investigation into alleged Russian meddling in the 2016 US election campaign.

[489] op cit. *What happened?* by Hillary Clinton, p. 8.

[490] 6 January 2018.

[491] *Financial Times*, 3 April 2017.

[492] 'Using air quotes, White House walks back "wiretap" talk' by Julie Hirschfeld Davis, *The New York Times*, 14 March 2017.

[493] 8 March 2018.

[494] 'Trump's way: a doctrine of obliteration' by Thomas L Friedman, *The New York Times*, 19 October 2017.

33

'RIPPING APART OUR SOCIAL FABRIC'

The trend is clear but unpalatable.[495] The unthinkable is about a whole new way of governing through active distraction or diversion, or greater autocracy and authoritarianism, even if those in power were technically elected democratically. There are implications for all of us.

Digital subversion and the destabilising of nations viewed as adversaries via the weaponising of information is considered a valid strategy. Equally sinister is the fact that many leaders less respectful of accountability are watching as Trump actively weakens the cause of liberal democracy.[496] He runs what one leading US lawmaker described as 'an adult day care centre',[497] and he unmakes the world the US made in his 'permanent war with reality'.[498] There is a democratic recession where Trump is viewed by many 'as a clown – but he is the most powerful one in the world'.[499] So they are rubbing their hands at the prospect of new opportunities to oppress and suppress to their advantage.[500] Emboldened by others peddling 'malign influence' and a 'disdain for democracy', they are actively working on how they too could roll back good governance like Trump in order to remain unchallenged at the top.

Like Trump or Putin, what could they get away with too? Respect has been devalued. After all, Trump made a career in business through being just transactional on deals then dishonouring the contracts he signed.[501] 'His reputation was for being a litigious client, slippery, untruthful, loud, wily and knavish. He was prepared to use vexatious and underhand tactics that toppled into absurdity.'[502] In the White House he continued the same vindictive tactic of denigrating and diminishing those he fired. They had once been 'distinguished leaders' who he praised lavishly when he appointed them. In the same exploitative vein, Putin does not respect hard-won international treaties that took years for his predecessors to negotiate.

But there are contradictions. While 'media has become the least-trusted global institution for the first time',[503] circulation of the satirical British magazine Private Eye has had an 'extraordinary boost' – to its highest level ever.[504] It's the same for the New York Times, with subscriptions up 600,000 despite being in the Trump crosshairs for its daily revelations of failings in what the President boasted was his 'well-oiled' White House administration.[505] It is boom time for traditional TV. Channel bosses gleefully report that viewers are surging back in a search for a mix of comfort, reassurance and consolation so they can be sure they are not alone in their astonishment.[506]

Some of the top leaders renowned as the smartest, wealthiest and most farsighted have been forced to admit that new unthinkables have caught them out. The super-rich, super-big tech companies led by Google and Facebook together command 60% of all digital advertising revenues. Suddenly they started feeling the intense heat of public disgust. They were accused of the unthinkable of antisocial behaviour and creating 'anti-social media'.[507]

Before Facebook was hit in mid-March 2018 by evidence that the data of up to 87 million users had been compromised to help Donald Trump get elected, at least one former senior Facebook executive had said the accusation was justified.[508] Remarkably, neither digital giant had appeared to want to scope unthinkables which could conceivably destroy their reputation in minutes. They had not defined or brainstormed extreme risks, nor crisis-managed what might happen on their platforms, or (if it did) how to control it. 'In the deep, deep recesses of our minds we kind of knew something bad could happen,' Facebook's former Vice President of User Growth Chamath Palihapitiya revealed.[509] Overall 'we have created tools that are ripping apart the social fabric of how society works'. After his eight years in office, President Obama warned that continuing current trends of harnessing the new technology threatens a new 'Balkanisation of society' among the next generation.[510] He urged 'we must make sure that they don't think that just sending out a hashtag, of itself is bringing about social change'.

The Cambridge Analytica revelations forced Facebook's Mark Zuckerberg to concede how narrow was his mega company's view of responsibility. Vast wealth and commercial success had not generated the worldly capacity for wisdom that many expected. 'Today, given what we know . . .I think we understand that we need to take a broader view of our responsibility . . .That we are not just building tools, but that we need to take full responsibility for the outcomes of how people use those tools as well.' This was clearly a revelation.[511] After being grilled by two US Congressional committees Zuckerberg said it would take three years to fix the nature and scale of the problems revealed by others about Facebook's failings.[512] Another FB executive conceded 'there is an awakening that is taking place inside the company where the mentality is very much all hands on deck. People have to see how we perform on our promise.'[513] Despite those 'deep, deep' private anxieties revealed by Chamath Palihapitiya, the leaders of the tech giants had failed to collectively think through the likely 'negatives' of extreme risks which might hit them one day. What about the damaging perceptions created when their algorithms position revenue-generating ads next to vile videos?

Insiders from one major tech company told **Thinking the Unthinkable** that top executives had discussed this possibility in the past, but not with any great enthusiasm or realisation of the possible implications. They had decided it would require an enormous scale of human intervention to screen and filter material. 'It could not be done reliably with software' and 'it was not considered threatening enough. ... There was not a big realisation of the damage it could do.'[514] The cost escalation would be enormous. The threat was viewed as so small that it did not justify spending on the level of resources which would be needed.

So they would wing it. But when crisis hit, winging did not work. This was in line with an overarching Silicon Valley principle. Ethics should not get in the ways of compelling new tech developments. Unthinkables were rarely on radar screens. 'The attitude is move fast and break things,' confirmed Greg Sherwin, a 25-year veteran of the Valley.[515] Until 2018 he was Vice President for Engineering and Information Technology at Singularity University. 'Companies must be more than just out for profit ... They want to be light footed ... They don't want to spend until they need to.' But he said that the culture of big tech will now have no option but to change. This is because new engineers and graduates emerging from college are 'more holistically aware'. This means that on the ethical implications, tech corporations will to be 'more receptive to that message'.

But for the moment, in the first months of 2018, the strength of the public outrage, corporate backlash and political anger forced the hands of the monster tech corporates who had believed they could do no wrong. YouTube revealed it had to pull 8.3 million videos from its site between October and December 2017. More than 80% were identified by software and machine learning, not humans.[516]

In March 2018, following the Facebook catastrophe of unauthorised data harvesting and its apparent impact on voter decisions in the US election, that had to change at super-high speed. Mozilla, a major advertiser on FB, 'paused' its spend. The reason was dynamite. 'We feel that the social structure is being hacked, and also that individual consumers and citizens are being hacked.'[517] Even more significantly, with that data 'it turns out you can understand a human being in some ways better than that human being understands themselves'.

A core principle among most tech giants was being exposed. Techies and data engineers were employed to develop great new digital ideas, not to concern themselves with the eventual social implications or possible downsides. 'I do not want engineers to develop self-awareness. Their job is [just] to be engineers,' we were told by the President of Baidu, China's leading search engine.[518] And the implications of AI? That is 'sent off site to other companies to think about'. But swiftly, and in many ways unexpectedly, such complacency has ended up leaving them open to the pillorying of their brands. They are even accused of turning blind corporate eyes to the way their algorithms facilitate a host of antisocial phenomena, like the creation of pop-up brothels which exploit and violate migrant women.[519]

But public anger suddenly pressed hard against a corporate complacency which 'refused to accept responsibility or take action that would entail any significant change to their business model'.[520] Big spenders for online advertising went for the jugular. Major brands like Coca-Cola, Johnson & Johnson and Volkswagen withdrew advertising from YouTube because their ads were positioned around extremist or derogatory videos.

Facebook introduced new rules.[521] They were not enough. 'Unilever will not invest in platforms or environments that do not protect our children, or which create division in society, and promote anger and hate,' warned Keith Weed, Unilever's chief marketing officer.[522] 'We cannot continue to prop up a digital supply chain ... which at times is little better than a swamp in terms of transparency.'

There was a new imperative for a new social responsibility. But was there really a seismic change in attitudes? 'People are realising you have to think ahead of time about problems that may [emerge],' according to Demis Hassabis, co-founder of DeepMind, which was bought by Google in 2014.[523] 'Collateral problems you did not necessarily realise when starting to make the technology. But you need to think harder about that at the beginning, not wait till the problems appear and then try to catch up.' Certainly governments are struggling to even get close to catching up with new digital realities. 'The way we work is changing rapidly, but our institutions – such as the tax system or rules governing the labour market – simply haven't kept pace,' said Rohan Silva, the former Downing Street adviser turned digital startup entrepreneur.[524]

There had already been noticeable signs of a new awareness and 'massive change in the Valley [Silicon Valley]' since mid-2017.[525] Stanford University had started a new programme to initiate a change of attitudes in the Valley.[526] In his 2018 New Year message, Mark Zuckerberg, the founder and boss of Facebook, had already conceded that even his vast wealth failed to provide him with the leadership skills needed to imagine the ways that disruption would impact a world where Facebook is one of the top five wealthiest companies. He wrote: 'We currently make too many errors enforcing our policies and preventing misuse of our tools.'[527] He added that 2018 must be a 'serious year of self-improvement'. Self-improvement? 'How many leaders are prepared to even concede their vulnerabilities in this way, let alone accept that they have to improve themselves? Zuckerberg had no other option.

But ten weeks later he and Facebook found 'self improvement' being forced on them by the data harvesting outcry. Zuckerberg and FB took a huge hit on their joint credibility. They were floored by their own failure to control outside developers, to do more than just take them at their word, and above all ensure that only FB controlled the data of its customers. Zuckerberg did rare TV interviews expressing 'regret' and that they 'got that wrong.'[528] Unthinkable? No – unpalatable. By confirming FB would now spend enormous amounts of money by 'massively ramping hiring' of personnel to retro-address issues, the company admitted it should have identified and nailed down the vulnerability much sooner.[529] It would now cost tens of billions of dollars in revenue, profits and value. And therefore their global reputation.

This coincided with a devastating assessment of Facebook in Wired magazine. It was marked by a cover image of Zuckerberg's face with bruises photo-shopped on to it. The piece reported interviews describing 'the same basic tale' of 'a CEO, whose techno-optimism has been crushed as they've learned the myriad ways their platform can be used for ill. Of an election [US] that shocked Facebook, even as its fallout put the company under siege. Of a series of external threats, defensive internal calculations, and false starts that delayed Facebook's reckoning with its impact on global affairs and its users' minds. And – in the tale's final chapters – of the company's earnest attempt to redeem itself.'[530]

The 2018 Facebook crisis has been an object lesson for all leaders. So take note: it is not just a Facebook problem.

These are weird times by the standards that have framed the majority of our lives in the most recent couple of decades. Suddenly unthinkables have upended many norms, traditions and accepted ways of doing things. The disruptors are emboldened and exhilarated by the fast-growing public resentments they have mobilised, plus the accompanying skyrocketing revenues. They rub their hands in delight at the hurricane of discomfort they have created, and the fact that the 'swamp' of out-of-touch elites is being drained, just as President Trump promised during his 2016 election campaign. Those the disruptors label as conformists find themselves like a losing boxer who is on the ropes being pummelled physically and mentally.

End notes

[495] op cit. Michael J Abramowitz, pp. 2–3.

[496] 'Global disorder and the fate of the West' by Martin Wolf, *Financial Times*, 3 January 2018.

[497] Remarks by chair of the Senate Foreign Relations Committee Bob Corker (described by President Trump in his tweets as 'Liddle Bob Corker'), 8 October 2017.

[498] 'The rise and fall of American leadership' by Martin Wolf, *Financial Times*, 31 May 2017.

[499] 'Trump is a clown – but he is the most powerful one in the world' by Matthew d'Ancona, *Evening Standard*, 8 November 2017.

[500] op cit. Michael J Abramowitz.

[501] 'Trump is poisoning global trade' by Edward Luce, *Financial Times*, 19 October 2017.

[502] *Collusion: how Russia helped Trump win the White House* (2017) by Luc Harding. London: Guardian Books, p. 303.

[503] op cit. 2018 Edelman Trust Barometer.

[504] *Private Eye* Editor Ian Hislop on *Broadcasting House*, BBC Radio 4, 19 February 2017.

[505] White House press conference, 16 February 2017.

[506] 'For solace and solidarity in the Trump Age, liberals turn the TV back on' by Michael M Grynbaum and John Koblin, *The New York Times*, 12 March 2017.

[507] 'Have we reached peak Facebook?', *The World at One*, BBC Radio 4, 16 February 2018.

[508] 'Ex-Facebook President Sean Parker: site made to exploit human "vulnerability"' by Olivia Solon, *The Guardian*, 9 November 2017.

[509] 'Former Facebook executive: social media is ripping society apart' by Julia Carrie Wong, *The Guardian*, 12 December 2017.

[510] op cit. President Obama, 27 December 2017.

[511] Press conference, 4 April 2018.

[512] 'Mark Zuckerberg says it will take 3 years to fix Facebook' by Steven Levy, *Wired*, 1 May 2018.

[513] op cit. Campbell Brown, 22 March 2018.

[514] Private remarks from a former senior Google executive, 19 March 2018.

[515] Interview at the Horasis Global Meeting in Estoril, Portugal, 6 May 2018.

[516] 'YouTube announces it has removed 8.3m videos from website' by Aliya Rem, *Financial Times*, 24 April 2018.

[517] Interview with Mitchell Baker, Executive Chair of Mozilla, *Channel 4 News*, 23 March 2018.

[518] Conversation with the President of Baidu and former Vice President of Microsoft, Ya-Qin Zhang, at the World Knowledge Forum in Seoul, 17 October 2017.

[519] 'Google and Facebook among giants "making profits" from pop-up brothels' by Tom Harper, Tim Shipman, Mary O'Connor and Danny Fortson, *The Sunday Times*, 4 March 2018.

[520] 'Advertisers' challenge to Facebook and Google', editorial in the *Financial Times*, 13 February 2018.

[520] 'Facebook changes ad rules to protect brands' by Hannah Kuchler, *Financial Times*, 14 September 2017.

[522] 'Unilever warns Big Tech to drain online ads "swamp"' by Shannon Bond, *Financial Times*, 12 February 2018. Advance reporting of Unilever Chief Marketing Officer Keith Weed's planned remarks to the Interactive Advertising Bureau conference the same day.

[523] Interview on *Today*, BBC Radio 4, 27 December 2017.

[524] 'The self-employed will benefit when we catch up with the digital revolution' by Rohan Silva, *Evening Standard*, 12 July 2017.

[525] op cit. Francis Fukuyama, Stanford University, closed remarks to the Oslo Energy Forum 2018, 14 February 2018. Released by agreement.

[526] The Global Digital Policy Incubator. The Executive Director is Eileen Donahoe.

[527] 4 January 2018.

[528] op cit. CNN interview re-run on *Channel 4 News*, 22 March 2018.

[529] op cit. Sheryl Sandberg interview re-run on *Channel 4 News*, 22 March 2018.

[530] 'Inside the two years that shook Facebook – and the world' by Nicholas Thompson and Fred Vogelstein, *Wired*, 12 February 2018.

34

'GET OUT OF YOUR COMFORT ZONE'

To repeat the Al Jolson principle: 'you ain't heard anything yet'. As we analyse in detail, coming down the track of disruption are the digital brilliance but sinister implications of the three As: Artificial Intelligence (AI), Algorithms and Automation.

There will be new efficiencies that rival and overtake the capacities of humans. But they also have the capacity to decimate all modern-day assumptions of the nature of work and wealth. How much further will leaders be left flailing and outside of what was once their comfort zone? Even criminals have adjusted. Digitisation means they can do their thing differently. 'You can now rob a bank from your lounge [on a laptop, tablet or mobile phone] without a gun and mask.'[531]

The unthinkable in the world of work is the question: will most humans soon be marginalised – whether cab drivers or warehouse workers at the lower end of the spectrum, or back room functionaries and lower level managers, plus professionals like lawyers, accountants and bankers at the higher end? If so, the working assumption must be that the middle class will be hollowed out as jobs for humans disappear. Attitudes to work and jobs will have to change radically. There must be a mass drive for constant re-skilling.[532] The trouble is that minds are stuck in the industrial era, when they should already be in the new era of algorithms, digital and artificial intelligence. 'People need to work differently for a longer period. Now we must learn to work continuously.'[533]

If AI and algorithms can draft contracts and check spreadsheets in a nanosecond, why are even highly qualified people needed to do the same, charging anything from $100 to $10,000 an hour? 'Get out of your own lane and comfort zone. Technology will push you out,' was a blunt warning we heard given to lawyers.[534] 'Will society value your skills as they have done?' Your jobs and roles 'will not necessarily be done by humans any more. ... Technology will replace process-oriented work.' Overall, lawyers 'have absolutely no idea what to do about this'. Estimates travel in one direction. But there are big differences on the scale of what is coming down the track, and where will be most affected. 'The proportion of jobs at high risk of automation by the early 2030s varies from 22% to 39% for different UK constituencies,' according to analysis by Future Advocacy.[535] [536] In one forecast, the Bank of England warned that 15 million jobs in the UK alone are at risk.[537] Another more radical forecast suggested that barely 5% of current jobs in many sectors will survive beyond 2030. The future of companies is also at risk. 'The structure of the firm will have to change. It will be driven by clients.'[538]

Yet to a vast majority these remain unthinkables. What is critical here is the following.

Ahead lies the probability of an 'even greater disjointed world ... [where] the majority of society will be left behind'.[539] As a result, those who are fortunate enough to have adequate or generous earning power and cash availability now must assume they are likely to have much less of it in future. How will communities adjust as they too are hollowed out by this vaporisation of wealth among highly skilled people who believed they had it made for life and could spend without too much concern? The trickle-down implications from the slowing down of human economic activity are potentially life-changing in ways that most people cannot even bring themselves to think about.

Are these unthinkables? Political and corporate leaders might hope so. But in reality the imperative is to view them as unpalatables which such leaders – especially those at the top of government – must first appreciate then concede are likely to happen. They must plan for them in order to merely preserve stability in society. This is even if it has to be with a new equilibrium between all the new, unthinkable variables that are emerging.

After his extraordinary trouncing of traditional politics in 2017, President Macron of France has already found himself on borrowed time with an ever-shorter timeline. Enormous populist hope is invested in him and his politically brave vision. But 'you are right to say there will a be a test on delivery and expectation. The real test will be the unemployment rate and creating growth.'[540] Despite reactions of horror and accusations of scaremongering in our early stages, **Thinking the Unthinkable** has already warned long ago of this unthinkable of a shredding of the unwritten contract between leaders and the led. The CEOs Paul Polman from Unilever, Joe Kaeser from Siemens, Larry Fink from BlackRock and Indra Nooyi from PepsiCo are the vanguard of corporate voices now echoing the same warning.

Which is why you must recall again the warning right at the start of this book. All these new unthinkable challenges are akin to learning how to cope and reconfigure everything in wartime. These new unthinkables are 'overcoming the capacity of national and international institutions'.

End notes

[531] Remarks by Craig Hancock, Global Chief Information Security Officer for Telstra, at the Procurious summit of procurement executives in Melbourne, 30 October 2017.

[532] op cit. Director's report on the conference 'Machine learning and artificial intelligence', 8–10 December 2017.

[533] 'Workplace learning starts here', presentation by Heather McGowan, Co-Founder, Author and Advisor for Work to Learn, to OEB17 in Berlin, 8 December 2017.

[534] Azeem Ibrahim, entrepreneur, investor and philanthropist speaking at the Legal Week Connect conference, London, 29 November 2017.

[535] *Where will automation hit hardest?* (2017). Future Advocacy.

[536] An OECD paper suggested there would be significant international variations: *The risk of automation for jobs in OECD countries: a comparative analysis* (2018) Paris: OECD.

[537] See an extensive list of probabilities of jobs disappearing in 'These are the jobs most at risk of automation according to Oxford University: is yours one of them?' by Patrick Scott, *Daily Telegraph*, 27 September 2017.

[538] Ahmed Shaaban, Managing Director of Fulcrum GT, to the Legal Week Connect conference, London, 29 November 2017.

[539] Remarks by Larry Fink, Chairman and CEO of BlackRock to Future Investment Initiative, Riyadh, 25 October 2017.

[540] Private remarks by a leading adviser to President Macron of France, 1 December 2017.

35

'WAITING FOR MIRACLES DOES NOT CONSTITUTE POLICY'

In the weeks before publication of this book, an equivalent of 'wartime' gripped the city of Cape Town in South Africa. It is one of the country's two joint capital cities. The conurbation's leaders and institutions confronted what national and regional leaders viewed for years as the unthinkable: that the reservoirs and taps would run out of water. **Thinking the Unthinkable** was there to report the scary predicament. For weeks the online app and its countdown clock[541] forecast that in April 2018 the taps would have to be turned off. Catastrophe was averted. But it was close run.

Cape Town, a city of four million with probably two million more unregistered people, had been forecast to be the first city in the world to run out of water. In early 2018 the growing fear was of disease and a violent citizen backlash. How could society prepare and cope? How could leaders have failed to provide one of life's basic needs to their city? Unthinkable! Yes. But by their own admission, over 13 years, few leaders in power ever took seriously the unpalatable warnings of climatologists and hydrologists about the inevitability that Cape Town would be a waterless city. The same fate could face 11 other major world cities.

Severe measures from January to March managed to conserve the little water that was available. It meant a postponement for Day Zero. This was 'largely down to one of the most drastic civic water conservation campaigns ever conceived'.[542] But every leader can learn the message. Cape Town's unthinkable crisis should never have become one. And there are sombre lessons for at least another ten cities around the world which face severe water stress.

Lord Nicholas Stern, author of the Stern Review on climate change,[543] told us that Cape Town's narrow escape is a metaphor for what top climate change experts see as a major challenge for global leaders over the next two to three decades. It is the questionable viability of their country's fast growing urban sprawls. 'The Cape Town example is embedded in all of this. We've got to manage the growth of cities.'

This is why we analyse what happened in Cape Town. Was it unthinkable? Or was it just indifference to the unpalatable evidence that made very clear what the city faced? If so, why did leaderships marginalise the scale of what threatened? What are the lessons for leaders?

For a year there had barely been measurable rainfall. For three years there had been drought in the Western Cape. In January 2018, the Mayor, Patricia de Lille set a date for the day which would be the 'point of no return'.[544] The city's predicament had gone from 'the realm of possibility to probability'. The alarm was dramatically reinforced by the live app. Around the clock, Capetonians could watch a live countdown of the crisis 24/7 on their mobile phones, with immediate access to the alarming data about the steadily reducing water and reservoir levels. It counted down to the date when the 'taps will be turned off'.

The warnings in the first weeks of 2018 were that dams would be below the critical level of 13% capacity on the 12th of April. That date advanced suddenly by ten days at one point. From February, the daily water allowance was just 60 litres, down from 87 litres in the previous month. The city prepared for Day Zero by setting up 200 water-collection points. Residents would have to endure queues alongside armed guards for a daily water allowance of just 25 litres.

There was an increasingly urgent and desperate struggle to work out how Cape Town would be kept functioning, with its citizens adequately hydrated. Water could not just be created. It has physical mass and presence. Shipping in even the minimum amount of water needed would require superhuman logistics capacities and be hugely expensive. Emergency funding of R3 billion ($252 million) could not suddenly provide new infrastructure. It was impossible for the proposed emergency supply developments – groundwater extraction, four desalination plants, and water reuse— to be online before Day Zero.

The challenges to communicate and reassure an increasingly anxious and frightened public were immense as Day Zero approached. The shock tactics worked. The public discipline in slashing water use pushed the date back to August, even though the water in the dams was down to 10% in early April. This delayed the crisis. It did not end it.

How did Cape Town and South Africa's government allow a largely modern conurbation to get to this point of crisis which threatened human survival along with public health and public security? Had it really been unthinkable?

'A well-run city does not run out of water,' Mayor de Lille told a briefing on the city's water resilience plan on 17 August 2017.[545] But was Cape Town well run? 'No,' said water experts and urban planners. They blame the city's unwillingness over many years to even consider the dramatic scenario of extended drought caused by a lack of rainfall. The prospect was unpalatable. But the evidence was there, even if it was unthinkable.

'It's increasingly unpredictable as to when that rain will fall,' Kevin Winter, an environmental scientist at the University of Cape Town warned in March 2017. 'That's in line with some of the climate predictions that go back to at least ten years ago: very uncertain weather variabilities, warmer and drier periods, followed by short periods of rainfall.'[546]

As the scale of the crisis became clearer, Helen Zille, the Premier of the Western Cape, claimed: 'This drought could never have been foreseen'. This was because even climate and meteorological models had not predicted the drama of a lack rainfall on this scale. 'The South African weather services have said to me that their models don't work anymore, in an era of climate change ... when the experts can't predict anything anymore. We have to make sure that we control what we can control, which is our own behaviour.'[547]

But surely this uncertainty should have been factored into the planning? Michael Muller, former Director-General of Department of Water Affairs, says 'Yes.' In 2007, his department published a study for the Western Cape Supply System.[548] It recommended that water sources must be augmented between 2012 and 2015. This was due to the increasing unpredictability of rainfall patterns, the greater likelihood of drought, and Cape Town's growing population, which is believed to be as high as six million compared to the four million currently registered. Muller said the study came 'with the warning ... that by 2015 you are going to have to do some of these things. And they weren't done. ... Cape Town, in particular, thought they would be able to get away with doing nothing until 2022.'[549]

Good rainfall in 2013-14, plus more disciplined use of water in cities and on farms, generated complacency. Muller labelled this a 'very serious mistake'.[550] It appeared that more water was available than was the case. The authorities congratulated themselves. Water saving measures showed they had responded appropriately to the Water Affairs Department's report. These included 'water demand management strategies' like replacement of water meters, free plumbing repairs and leak detections.[551]

'They were warned,' Muller concludes. But 'they chose to ignore the warning on a number of occasions; they even boasted about how effective their water-saving campaigns had been and that it would only be in 2022 [that they'd] need more water. ... Overconfidence led to bad management decisions and it meant that interventions that could have been started haven't yet been actually initiated.'[552] There were also the inevitable concerns about overspending on big water projects which did not seem needed at the time. Despite escalating warnings from scientists, this produced 'a degree of optimism and a degree of belief in the effectiveness of these local measures that perhaps misled people,' said Kevin Winter, from University of Cape Town (UCT)'s department of Environmental and Geographical Science, and Future Water Institute.[553]

David W Olivier, of the University of Witwatersrand's Global Change Institute, has a more positive view. The 'first official warnings of potential water scarcity, and of the need to diversify the city's water supply using ground water and other sources', came from Cape Town's consultants as early as 2002.[554] He says that Cape Town took the 2007 warning seriously 'and acted quickly'. However the problem with leadership in water policy is systemic. Scientists' research is always hampered by governmental red tape between the various governments. He said that research on groundwater projects was at an advanced stage by 2006. 'Why [the city didn't move into the next phase], I don't know,' said one unnamed researcher. 'Probably because it rained a lot.'[555]

Water-saving policies 'were so effective that the city met its 2015-2016 water-saving target three years early'. Based on the data and projections they had at the time, the augmentation projects described by Muller's 2007 report were appropriate for what Cape Town needed. But then came the unthinkable: the most severe drought in the Cape's modern history.[556] When it comes to unthinkables and unpalatables, there are certainly signs of denial. Olivier acknowledges that the panic in Cape Town's political offices 'came 15 years too late'.

'Crisis' is a word which is too freely used sometimes. But by early 2018 that is what had engulfed Cape Town. Other major cities which faced similar likely water stress and major shortages watched with increasing anxiety. How would Cape Town cope, not just with the absence of water, but also the consequences for governance, health and social stability?

Cape Town's predicament was exacerbated significantly by the political tensions between the national government of the African National Congress (ANC) and the regional government of the Western Cape run by the Democratic Alliance (DA). The Mayor of Cape town won a vote of no confidence brought by her own DA party who accused her of maladministration. Her Deputy was put in charge of the water crisis.

'The attitude within and across political parties is that there's political capital to be gained at the expense of this crisis, rather than communicate with each other. The way one deals with crises shouldn't be a crisis in itself,' said Erwin Schwella, Professor of Public Leadership at Stellenbosch University in the Western Cape.[557]

David W Olivier says the ANC national government carries heavy responsibility. It has the responsibility of making water allocations to agriculture. In 2015, despite a major drought, it allocated 60% of the Western Cape's water to Cape Town and almost all of the rest to agriculture. Fruit farms and vineyards on the Cape have political and commercial clout. They consume vast amounts of water. As a result, the drought soon took a toll on dam levels. But the national government took no action. The agricultural water allowance in 2015/16 stayed at the same level. Olivier says that this 'pushed demand for water beyond the capacity of the supply system and consumed Cape Town's safety buffer of 28 thousand megalitres.'[558]

The low winter rainfalls of 2015 signalled alarms locally. The government of Western Cape applied to the national government for R35 million ($2.9 million) to increase water supply by way of boreholes and recycling. But the response from Pretoria was the political equivalent of a deaf ear. Because the dams were 75% full, the national government rejected the request.

In 2016, the national government agreed to recognise only 5 of the 30 Western Cape municipalities as drought disaster areas. Significantly, this did not include Cape Town. Despite having promised financial aid, the government did not release the agreed funds until October 2017.

Inaction by the national government is regarded as the main source of blame for the acute water crisis. It has been exacerbated by mutual partisan blame-hurling between the ANC and the DA. Additional factors are spiralling mismanagement, debt and corruption scandals at the national Department of Water and Sanitation. 'Had systems in national government been running smoothly, Cape Town's water crisis could have been mitigated. … With timely responses to disaster declarations, water augmentation infrastructure could have been up and running already,' said David Olivier.[559]

But the Western Cape and Cape Town governments must shoulder some blame. Benoit Le Roy, CEO of the NGO, Water Shortage South Africa, said: 'They are indirectly responsible through inaction, because they are not responsible for the provision of bulk water. … Hoping for rain and relying on national government to make provision was a big mistake.'[560] As the local newspaper the Daily Maverick put it, 'Waiting for miracles does not constitute policy.'[561]

No matter where they place the most blame, the scientists agree on one thing: The Cape Town water crisis is not so much a 'once-in-a-thousand-year' drought. It is a crisis of leadership and foresight, and failure to think the unthinkable. The signs were stark but unpalatable. They should have been taken seriously and acted upon when the prospect of severe drought was merely a warning.

It is not just Cape Town; 11 other global cities also face severe water stress. These dozen cities are only the most extreme examples. Resources for cities is fast becoming a major global issue as the population of cities expand massively in the coming decades. 'They're going to double in 40 years and the decisions we take in the next 10 or 15 are going to shape what that doubling looks like,' Lord Stern told us. 'It's the whole shooting match. It's energy, it's water, it's the ability to move around, you know, it's sewage and pollution, it's the whole lot. In many ways, I think it is the biggest [issue of our time]. It's one of those predictions that's about as solid as you can get. We're 50% or so urbanised now. It's a pretty fair bet that by mid-century, or 40 years from now, we'll be 70% or so. And the population is now seven-and a half billion and it will be nine and a half.'[562]

So water stress is not unthinkable. The growing scale and threat are unpalatable. Therefore they have to be taken seriously in order to satisfy citizens who expect a supply of clean water as their human right.

Cape Town's bleak experience highlights all too graphically the importance of that new, brave language and alert from Joe Kaeser, President and CEO of Siemens. To repeat him: if leaders get things wrong he warns of 'social unrest and anarchy', that 'the glue that holds societies and communities together will disintegrate', and that 'citizens will no longer believe that governments are able to fulfil their purpose of enforcing the rule of law and providing security'.

End notes

[541] Day Zero is postponed to 2019. Visit www.thinkunthink.org/digital-footnotes for a link to the Day Zero dashboard.

[542] 'How Cape Town beat the drought' by Joseph Cotterill, *Financial Times*, 2 May 2018.

[543] Interviews with Lord Nicholas Stern, 5 February 2015, 13 November 2016 and 7 February 2018. The Stern Review: *The economics of climate change*, HM Treasury 2006.

[544] 'Cape of storms to come' by Diana Neille, Marelise van der Merwe and Leila Dougan, *Daily Maverick*, 27 October 2017.

[545] 'Cape Town will not run out of water' by Monique Natlock, *Eyewitnessnews*, 17 August 2017.

[546] 'Waiting for the rain in parched Cape Town', *Deutsche Welle*, 31 March 2017.

[547] Helen Zille interview, *BBC Newsnight*, 24 January 2018.

[548] op cit. 'Cape of storms to come'.

[549] ibid.

[550] ibid.

[551] ibid.

[552] ibid.

[553] ibid.

[554] ibid.

[555] ibid.

[556] 'Cape Town's water crisis: driven by politics more than drought' by David W Oliver, *News24*, 14 December 2017.

[557] '"Day zero": how drought, water mismanagement, politics led to crisis' by Morgan Winsor, *ABC News* website.

[558] ibid.

[559] ibid.

[560] op cit. 'Cape of storms to come'.

[561] ibid.

[562] op cit. Interviews with Lord Stern, 5 February 2015, 13 November 2016 and 7 February 2018.

36

THE BLOCKERS STOP LEADERS KNOWING WHAT THEY NEED TO KNOW

Whatever your role or position, are you not just aware but ready for this? Are the implications close to the top of your mind?

The signs do not generate hope. How is it possible, for example, that on Brexit the UK government had to be warned by a parliamentary committee of a 'serious dereliction of duty' if it fails to prepare for the unthinkable that their negotiations could fail.[563] The committee concluded: 'The possibility of "no deal" is real enough to justify planning for it. The government has produced no evidence, either to this enquiry or in its White Paper, to indicate that it is giving the possibility of "no deal" the level of consideration that it deserves or is contemplating any serious contingency planning.' Could it be that the majority of Brits who voted for Brexit really wanted to back a possibility that 'Britain on its own will count for little on the world stage'?[564]

This confirms one core conclusion of this ongoing project. In interviews relating to an embarrassing succession of global events we have discovered how political correctness and career conformity have shamefully narrowed the options ministers and corporate leaders are given to consider. In too many cases, tabling a range of options, however extreme or surprising, has been viewed as a career killer. What mattered most has been conformity to a certain mindset on risk that is routinely dictated from the top.

In politics especially the acute expectation that any new minister must be across his brief within hours of being appointed is a severe impediment to detailed knowledge and making well-informed judgements. 'There's no training, no guidebook, no manual, no introduction. You leave the Cabinet Room with promotion ringing in your ears ... and walk straight into the department and start doing the job.'[565] So often the political imperative takes over. Expert advice is routinely relegated unless it fits the predetermined political line.

The scale and costs of this painful disconnect was highlighted by Thinking the Unthinkable in its first interim findings based on confidential conversations.[566] It was all confirmed very publicly during the dramatic resignation of Sir Ivan Rogers, UK Permanent Representative to the EU in January 2017. He summarily left his post because he said Downing Street routinely rejected his analysis and reporting, especially on issues relating to the UK's fractious relationship with Brussels following the vote to leave the EU.

On the day he resigned Sir Ivan send a blunt email of exasperation to his colleagues about negotiating with the EU, which the Prime Minister's office did not want to hear.[567] Inevitably it leaked, and what it contains needs to be read by every leader. It probably echoes the frustrations and obstructions in their (your?) organisations too.

Sir Ivan's 1350-word criticism of both the process and the deafness of those at the top to inconvenient facts was explicit. He urged them to 'challenge ill-founded arguments and muddled thinking ... and ... never be afraid to speak the truth to those in power'. He recognised what can be a lonely searching of conscience, especially over the imperative to work to the principles of the Civil Service Code. 'I hope you will support each other in those difficult moments where you will have to deliver messages that are disagreeable to those who need to hear them.'

This one public example revealed a pervasive mood of trauma, despair and heart-searching among many officials within the UK Civil Service. It mirrored so many examples we have seen or had shared with us. They highlight why unthinkables are routinely not thought about. In the UK's case, how could they put to their bosses the unthinkables or unpalatables that needed to be tabled without having their career 'legs chopped off', in the language used to us by one very senior government official?

Philip Stephens of the FT lifted the lid a little further. At the top of the UK government, 'Mrs May is roundly mistrustful of her senior civil servants. Officials are shut out of decision-making. Unvarnished advice invites histrionics from her political sidekicks.'[568] Environment Secretary Michael Gove reportedly embarked on a 'rant' against 'clock-watching civil servants' in a UK cabinet meeting.[569] He was said to have accused 'senior civil servants of blocking new policies'. He claimed 'No. 10 [Downing Street] has been captured by the civil service.'

But the Prime Minister's two closest 'sidekicks' paid the ultimate political price for what had become an embedded culture of control freakery after Mrs May's disastrous election gamble in June 2017. Nick Timothy and Fiona Hill were the Prime Minister's joint chiefs of staff. From their time with her as Home Secretary they were her eyes, ears and enforcers. They were also renowned for what was described widely as their bullying style in order to get what they expected. They were nicknamed the Gruesome Twosome.[570] It instilled fear in civil servants and denied the Prime Minister much information which might have been inconvenient but which she should have known by way of it being passed up the chain to her.

Instead this kind of briefing material was blocked routinely. It was a main reason why Mrs May lost her reckless election gamble in 2017. Timothy and Hill paid the price for this authoritarianism. They resigned immediately after the election debacle which had left Mrs May running a minority government instead of one with the enhanced Tory majority she believed would be delivered.

What if they – and therefore the Prime Minister – had allowed all voices on a possible election to be heard from her party leadership colleagues, including those with arguments against calling it?

As a remote, often self-contained leader who was full of self-confidence, the Prime Minister thought that she, and she alone, knew best. She did not. The unthinkables defeated and weakened her.

End notes

[563] *Article 50 negotiations: implications of 'no deal'*, UK House of Commons Foreign Affairs Committee, published 7 March 2017, para 60, p. 26.

[564] 'Britain will count for little on the world stage' by Sir John Sawers, former director of MI6, *Financial Times*, 21 June 2017.

[565] Quote from George Freeman, Parliamentary Under Secretary of State for Life Sciences 2014–2016, in *Professional development for ministers*, Institute for Government, 2018.

[566] op cit. *Thinking the unthinkable* (2016) by Nik Gowing and Chris Langdon.

[567] 3 January 2017.

[568] 'Brexit, Donald Trump and the threat to Europe' by Philip Stephens, *Financial Times*, 19 January 2017.

[569] 'Gove rants at clock-watching civil servants' by Tim Shipman, *The Sunday Times*, 21 January 2018.

[570] 'The Prime Minister ruined by her gruesome twosome' by Alasdair Palmer, *The Sunday Times*, 25 June 2017.

37
Angry consumers and angry citizens: who takes notice?

While the shock from unthinkables since 2014 has been seismic, it is nothing compared to those which imminently threaten the capacity of top leaders to handle them.

Despite the fears they harbour now, history is likely to record the unthinkables so far as relatively benign, modest and marginal compared to the disruptive threats that are now coming down the track at high speed. It has to be reckoned that they will swiftly compound the systemic shock that is already there – and not just from Brexit and Trump, or migration in Europe and the growing power challenges from Russia and China.

Together leaders must urgently dig much deeper to embrace the new nature of unthinkables and their likely impact. Not all will happen. But it needs to be assumed that many will. It is best to be prepared. But there is not the luxury of time that many might assume. The possible time frame is not the next 20 years, but 20 months, 20 weeks, 20 days – perhaps even 20 hours. Further disruption and destabilisation by unthinkables is that imminent.

The knock-ons from Artificial Intelligence (AI) and the digital power of algorithms threaten to convulse all assumptions about what makes a balanced, stable, contented society. This means that the pressures on corporate and political leaders will be even greater. This is especially if they are in some kind of state of denial about the scale of disruption unfolding.

It therefore must be asked: have we reached a point of 'peak everything'?[571] Peak democracy, peak western influence, peak progress and peak jobs, for example? In a way that is already well underway in critical ways that go far deeper than Brexit or Trump. A huge number of jobs will be made redundant by automation and robotics.[572] In the UK average earnings and disposable income for the next generation will fall.[573] A large majority will not have the good fortune of those born between the 1940s and 1960s.[574] Hence the major alert that eventually significant parts of the middle class will be hollowed out.[575]

The overall context for this is the new and likely stratospheric level of digital connectivity.[576] It will instantly promote public expectations because of the new possibilities. It will also foster even greater discontent. This will be because of mass disappointment at the failure of leaders who find themselves unable to shift from their conformist mindset in order to meet the new scale and speed of effectiveness that the public, customers and therefore voters or shareholders expect.

As we have chronicled here, this is already creating an existential threat to the viability and survival of both governments and corporates. These massive structural changes – unthinkables to most people – are in addition to the destabilising impact of the early stages of current unthinkables like Brexit, Trump, the Russian promotion of instability and the Chinese moves to dominate everything on their terms. How far have they (you?) even begun to recognise the scale and nature of these, let alone how they (you?) as leaders will handle them?

As we have reported, many leaders describe all-too-graphically how they are consumed by pressures from the immediate and short term, as our data confirms. 'I am overwhelmed. No time to think. Come back in six months,' confided one over a whisky. So how can they embrace the possible scale of unthinkables which they have no time to think about? Yes, the threat is extreme if those at the top don't embrace the scale of change instead of denying it, or at least trying to palm it away. Exaggeration? No! As we saw one top CEO in the global consumer market tell a closed-door gathering: corporates are in danger of 'creating angry consumers and angry citizens'. The reason? 'Society will not accept the speed of technological change' and its implications for them.

So if leaders and leaderships – by their own frank admissions – are already struggling to cope, how will they handle what else is now powering towards them in stark but immeasurable ways?

To repeat. This book is here to confirm unambiguously the state of unease about this new normal, even though it remains ill-defined for the time being. While raising the alarm bell loudly, that in itself should reassure all of you. So should the realisation that this is afflicting all their peers too.

In other words, the lily pads of executive concerns are starting to come together as they need to. But how will a sharing of fears and experiences (plus a speeding-up) be engineered and coordinated? Who will do it? Who has the resources to make it happen? And what options for solutions will there be?

Stay with us as we provide evidence of positives when CEOs open their minds to each other In order to share their experiences.

End notes

[571] op cit. Geoff Mulgan, 16 November 2016.

[572] For a detailed sample of the debate see: 'This is the future: the unstoppable march of machines' by Nick Clegg, *Evening Standard*, 23 January 2017.

[573] 'Now for the pain: the biggest squeeze on incomes for 60 years' by Nicholas Cecil and Joe Murphy, quoting the Resolution Foundation, *Evening Standard*, 23 November 2017.

[574] 'Predicted inheritance boom will arrive too late for many millennials' by Patrick Collinson, quoting findings of the Resolution Foundation, *The Guardian*, 30 December 2017.

[575] 'Robots march on "safe" jobs of middle class', by Nicholas Hellen, *The Sunday Times*, 5 February 2017.

[576] For a detailed taste of the scale of this challenge see: 'The robot economy' special issue of *Newsweek*, 9 December 2016.

38
OPENING MINDS TO BRAVE NEW IDEAS; LEARNING FROM EACH OTHER

One way for **Thinking the Unthinkable** to showcase potential solutions and new positives is to share core impressions left by conversations. Discretion is required to respect confidences and the frankness of what was said. But sampling the views from open exchanges between top executives can highlight a developing new willingness and value to think more radically about the challenge of unthinkables. Often open discussion and sharing of perspectives lubricates the path to solutions.

The energy business has been emerging from a hugely turbulent and disruptive period, with existential threats to operators. After the sudden Saudi decision in 2014 to slash crude oil prices by 60%, the economics of oil production were thrown into turmoil. For a long period after that dramatic Saudi move, crude prices bumped along at very low levels of $20 to $25 a barrel. For many, production became uneconomic. This is what the Saudis hoped would happen in order to force a thinning-out of production capacity. Many operators and service providers who got used to fat in the years of plenty had to slash costs just to stay in business. But these often-brutal new realities became an incentive to speed up the development of the technological attractions of shale oil. This unexpected success meant that for many reasons the Saudi gamble failed and lost them an estimated $100 billion of oil revenue each year.

By early 2018, remarkably there was a new equilibrium and profitability in the market, with oil prices back at $60 to $70 plus per barrel. Oil demand was rising and would keep rising, even with forecasts of the ever-greater importance of renewables in the energy mix by the years 2025 to 2030.[577] Indeed BP declared itself 'massively surprised by renewables', which it forecast would be not 4% but 14% of the energy mix by 2040. The sudden public concern about the devastating impact of plastic on the environment had also been a new unthinkable. But with costs down by up to 50%, a mix of the major operators and a new generation of upstream producers were seeing big new opportunities to buy into production capacity. Sellers like Maersk and Engie found buyers. This was despite the significant increases in energy production already being generated from renewables, especially wind and solar.

Until recently there has long been a strong sense that the oil and gas business reacted to crises like the unthinkable Saudi price cuts in 2014, as opposed to envisioning and preparing for them. The impression was often of wishful thinking and more than a whiff of complacency. Prices pre-2014 of up to $80-$100 a barrel had reinforced the sense that the good times would never end. That was even with the new production realities created by climate change and greater public demands for sustainable energy. Costs were not usually slashed in the expectation of a drop in prices. Instead it was only necessary after or when prices crashed which dictated that costs had to be slashed.

In 2018 the good times were back again, with prices, revenues and profits up significantly but different terms for trading. There were huge new investments, especially by oil companies buying the production assets of another. For example, the French giant Total bought Maersk's North West Europe production operations – mostly in the North Sea – for $7.45 billion. This purchase would be a generator of surplus cash to be shared with shareholders, with no risk of being a new cash drain.[578] Neptune Energy – an independent oil and gas exploration company backed by huge investment funds like Carlyle – bought Engie upstream, which produces 170,000 barrels a day in seven countries.

So how is a newly self-confident and profitable energy sector preparing itself for the inevitability of whatever new unthinkables might hit them? Judging by conversations among senior executives heard by TTU, there is a significantly different mood these days. It offers broader lessons to many others well beyond the energy business. Don't be complacent, and don't hang around. The new ways of working need to be embraced sooner rather than later. The speed is much faster than those at the top imagined. 'I think the world has changed quite a bit since last year,' confirmed Spencer Dale, BP's Chief Economist.[579] Which raises the question: a year earlier in 2017, how much of that significant level of change was on any C-suite register of risks or list of possibles to watch? The signs are that the answer was 'virtually none'.

We heard one leading independent expert encourage them to realise that 'change is not new; it has not just been discovered' especially by the energy business. They had to be phlegmatic. CEOs had to realise that changes now are nothing like what the sector faced in the past, especially when assets were expropriated during wars. But they had to renew themselves. Coming fast down the track, for example, is mass battery and power storage technology. 'What will batteries do to our business?' was a question he told them they had to think about. Had they adequately contemplated and gamed this option. So they had to ask themselves: 'How much are you prepared to disrupt the way you are thinking at the moment?' Despite 'a degree of uncertainty' with a multitude of scenarios which are likely to be wrong, he urged on them 'the need for a sense of calm' with 'a new sense of perspective'. He told them that they – CEOs – 'have to understand they are not soothsayers; they can't predict the future', even if that is what shareholders and the public might expect.

Instead CEOs need to assess realities and risks so that 'they understand the range of reasonable possibilities', then 'position the company with resilience against that range. That is not easy. But it is much more dangerous if you pick up one strand only.' They should 'focus on one or two things within the total range of possibilities and get them right. In the hope that whatever scenario plays out you are well positioned. Given the whole range of possibilities, no one can know what technology will win, what the balance is going to be.'

Certainly, there is a recognition of executive shortcomings up to now. 'As an industry, probably as a result of too much groupthink, we probably think around too narrow a range of potential outcomes,' said one CEO. The industry has been 'poor at having too narrow a prospective range of outcomes'. It had to scope far beyond just oil prices to 'technological dislocations that could happen, and therefore alternative bets you might want to make' along with 'political dislocations and how you hedge that', and 'if you can't do it yourself, what partnerships you need to form, whether with supply chain, technology providers or providers of capital to give you the resilience in those uncertain conditions.'

Overall, perspectives and horizons need to be broadened – and fast. 'You have to look at wider scenarios; bring in experience from different industries; how you measure and value not just the embedded position you have got, but the extrinsic value of the options you may have. There are lots of tools from other industries. The pace of change is increasing so you need to do that quickly.'

The battles will be for 'ideas and different ways of thinking,' said another CEO. Oil and gas companies need to do much more than energy. 'We need to attract young people with different skill sets. The next generation. New ideas, and very different ways for thinking, and ways they want their careers to go, and the world to work. We need to be able to attract that. We need fresh ideas. We need to do more. There is an enormous risk that the Next Gen will choose clean and green. Enormous? Yes! We must embrace change and attract young talent. The NextGen – if they do not like the company or what it stands for – the values – then they will not go there even if they are qualified and it is a great job.'

For the energy sector, even if there are big new investments in renewables, image and reputation are a problem. 'How do you recruit when there is a lot of fuss in the newspapers?' asked another CEO. 'It is around values and what you communicate – to be seen to be caring. And the environment and green agenda is very important. But will you be contributing to this transition?' was the challenge from another CEO. 'An organisation must be fluid and not hierarchical, which is stultifying for a young graduate,' urged a third CEO.

What about the way employees are treated during this disruption? How are they encouraged and not alienated? 'I find it so important that we are able to move our people along. Going out there. Getting rid of people who work for us and going out and recruiting new talent with new skills is not going to give us sustainability in the long run. We need to be able to transfer careers again and again and again. And this is a skill set that any company needs these days, where clearly we have not been good enough.' 'A vital reason for lifelong learning,' chipped in another CEO.

Even with the current scale of global disruption, there remain too many narrow minds in oil and energy which need to be broadened. 'The industry must start to collaborate with industries outside our own space. We spend too much time together instead of going out and looking at other things that may actually support us also. ... We are way too claustrophobic'.

But the major new challenge is to keep the public onside. Why? 'We are losing legitimacy with the public.' It is crucial 'to be able to explain your world view to your staff and to the outside world'. This is because the industry is under public scrutiny as it has not been before. 'It has to be right down through the company. It has to be believed through the company and believed by all social audiences.'

The criticism hit a raw nerve. 'Most companies are traditionally very cautious on communications,' said one CEO. 'We must let people communicate around their companies. Their skills. Must educate them to do that. We need proud employees to take part in discussions and talk about this industry.'

Many were reassured by the candid nature of this 75-minute exchange, which represented a new spirit of corporate frankness. 'We must be calm and be able to explain,' said a CEO. 'Energy always thinks its problems are unique to them,' said another. 'Oil and energy are now as outward-looking as they should be. What matters now is culture and values,' said a third. The volunteering of both these issues reflected our broader **Thinking the Unthinkable** findings. But companies had to transform fast because of the rapid impact of digitisation and the pressures for renewables. 'It is about humans; their individual feelings. We must undergo transformation to keep people motivated.'

But what are the unthinkables and unpalatables, the threats if oil, gas and energy companies don't grip the issues and don't act? 'The threat is of digital outsiders coming in and taking a significant part of the [your] market,' warned one influential voice. 'Google Energy? Amazon Power? I could see them coming in and being electricity distributors, bringing everything together, buying it all at the lowest cost and selling it on. Someone inside the industry should pre-empt and do it themselves.'

Overall, 'in this age of uncertainty, I would be wary of any company with a single view of the future. No CEO should pretend to know the future, but should focus on one or two things. Become a leader in one, two or three fields. Companies should not pretend they know it all,' advised the independent expert.

The oil, gas and energy industry have been warned. The lessons are there for all leaders and all industries.

End notes

[577] BP Energy Outlook 2018, BP, 20 February 2018.

[578] 'Total chief learns from oil industry's past errors' by Andrew Ward and David Keohane, Financial Times, 13 February 2018.

[579] 'BP says war on plastic will curb oil output', by Emily Gosden, Energy Editor, The Times, 21 February 2018.

39
'I JUST DON'T THINK HUMANS ARE DESIGNED FOR THIS'

Thinking the Unthinkable has hit and exposed a raw nerve of leadership concerns. We have found it remarkable how much, and how frankly, so many leaders at the top have opened up to us. This is especially true about their human inadequacies to accept and handle the new unthinkable challenges. How do they recalibrate themselves when the daily pressures and expectations are so massive, and increasingly so?

Every leader we approached for the project has wanted to talk. Even more remarkably they have carved out time in their usually manic schedules. None – literally none – have slammed the corporate door in our face. Quite the opposite. There has routinely been enthusiastic and active encouragement. This is the almost-universal tone of encouragement for the project. 'Find out more! Tell us more! Please find examples of the solutions we are looking for, and need urgently.'

But as we have written already, it is so easy to assume that a problem means there must be an instant solution. When it comes to finding ways to think unthinkables, the best we can offer so far is options and examples of who has done what, then how it has worked out or is working out (or not).

Almost all of our interviewing and conversations have remained confidential by agreement. That means no identification of who said what. It is a commitment we will not breach. And we have not done so. Every interview has confirmed not just the profound nature of the new challenges to leadership as already reported in detail. They have offered glimpses into the personal dilemmas and tensions for those at the top. How should they take on this stark new challenge to the conformity that got them to the top? As they share with us, in almost every case it is staring them in the eyes at minimum range.

How to handle this? We could share conversations with many leaders. Here we share, anonymously, the edited version of one very revealing meeting lasting well over an hour with the CEO of a major corporate. It highlights the vexatious nature of the challenge and its scale. What to do? How to do it? When to do it? It is not about clicking fingers and discovering an instant shaft of light and great, off-the-peg vision. And above all, what are the odds that the options chosen in search of a solution will produce any positives or progress?

Here goes.

CEO: 'Thinking the Unthinkable.' It's a great phrase. The problem with 'unthinkable' is that it's things that happen beyond your reference frame. And because of all the things you've been describing, more and more things are happening beyond people's reference frame. That's how I think about Thinking the Unthinkable.

And that's a capability problem. So if the world is behaving in a way that people can't understand ... then the risk envelope presents them with a series of issues that their training doesn't help. That creates risk, significant risk in itself. ... It's a leadership problem. It's a leadership capability and capacity problem.

Managing the thinkable is also becoming more difficult. Digitisation and the pace of change is creating new competitive landscapes, new products, new disruptions, at a rate that even regulators can't follow, they can't cope with. So the regulators are following problems and creating regulations after things have happened. ... This is even though they can see that this is happening, they can't actually do it fast enough.

The problem is simply [that] the pace of change is disrupting existing small companies. It's also creating such a spread of issues that a chief executive or a senior manager has to manage, even in the thinkable zone. That's also throwing up leadership capacity and capability issues.

TTU (Thinking the Unthinkable): We emphasise the human all through [our research and reporting], as opposed to arrows on a diagram.

CEO: I just don't think human beings are designed for this, which is probably the most fundamental way of expressing what you're expressing. … Now maybe that's a crazy thing to say. But I don't think so. At least if we are designed for it, we haven't learned how to be in it. So we haven't evolved, yet.

The hopeful thing is it's only a class of dinosaurs like me that can't evolve. And really we should just get out of the way because there's a whole bunch of people who have evolved who would be perfectly comfortable with all this, in which case …

TTU: We would not agree with 'dinosaurs' by the way, we would not use that kind of description at all.

CEO: I'm just saying maybe, just maybe, that's the issue. … That we've been trained in a certain way and actually the way we've been trained doesn't work anymore. … The younger people need to be revolutionary. But also older people need to leverage their experience in trying to moderate some of that. And I don't think that's changed fundamentally, but I have to think (to use your phrase, 'the unthinkable') that maybe it has.

TTU: Can I just put a clarification in there? We're actually saying we should talk about Thinking the Unpalatable. The evidence is usually there. The question is why it doesn't get through the system.

CEO: On average, globalisation has been good for the world. But it's left a whole bunch of people really behind and angry. And we've been guilty of the law of averages. On average, the world is better off. I think most economists would say they could prove it. Most people would say that more people are out of poverty than previously, all of that. But it's created in a very short time-space massive inequality and massive disruption to people's lives. [It is at] a pace which is so fast that your average human being can't adapt to it in their working lifetime.

So they end up on the street or their life completely disintermediated in some way, or their livelihood suddenly transported halfway round the world. Massive issue. And so this issue of pace and globalisation and … large numbers of people who have been left behind. … And the problem is the pace is getting greater and greater.

[ADDITIONALLY] climate change, on average, will be managed by mankind. I believe that. I think we are learning very fast how to manage it. But we will probably only get to the zone of the right solution, we won't get to the two-degree solution. ... Large numbers of people will have to adapt because of it. And it will impact a lot of people. ... And there will be large parts of the world that will have to adapt. That puts huge strain on communities, society...

[ADDITIONALLY] Respect for the global institutions that have guaranteed peace since the Second World War is decaying, or even evaporating. Almost to the point where they're operating in a bubble. That's greatly worrying because one of the moderators of all of this is respect for stability, respect for institutions, respect for individuals. And that feels like it's quite a lot weaker.

I don't know whether the respect for individuals is weaker just because the quality of leadership is not there or whether it's something else. But it just feels like everybody can criticise anybody.

[THE CEO CITES A TOUGH CORPORATE DECISION. IT AFFECTED A LARGE NUMBER OF CUSTOMERS. MANY VOICED COMPLAINTS.]

I can only hope that people at least respect that we're trying to do the right thing. But the hatred of companies, global institutions – and indeed the individuals that represent them – is a sign that this is just being undermined all the time.

TTU: Do you want to extend that to algorithms and AI [Artificial Intelligence]?

CEO: Well yes. Digitisation is all of the above. I think algorithms and AI; and starting to find patterns in things ahead of everybody else; and being able to spot social media moments before they've even hit the news and act on them. I mean, all of this.

What is the possible consequence of this? In the positive, I think there's just huge positivity around. ... And we mustn't forget that in all of this – economy progress, technology, reduction in the cost of lots of things, the spread of wealth globally. All of that is possible as a result of a lot of this. But the two outcomes that I fear are firstly social and/or societal breakdown, which would seem to me to be more probable of happening more often in more places at any particular moment. So one country will have it one day. Another country will have it the next day. But there's always going to be quite bad social breakdown occurring.

The second outcome which I fear is the risk of global conflagration of some kind. Another world war, because everyone's looking inwards. There isn't an institutional framework to stabilise it. The UN is doing as good a job as it can do. NATO is doing as good a job as it can do. But these are being threatened. And so I do worry for our children and grandchildren that we're careening, I think is the right American word, towards bad things, mainly because we can't prevent them in time because we can't think fast enough or join the dots fast enough.

It's not an inevitability. It becomes a massive accident of all of these things coming together. So I do worry about it.

[SO HOW IS THE CEO CONFRONTING THE UNTHINKABLES FACING LEADERSHIP? THE CEO TALKS OF THE VALUE OF 'UNUSUAL' PEOPLE BEING PART OF HIS TEAM. BUT THERE IS STILL THE POSSIBILITY 'WE'LL BE TRIPPED UP']

I've called us a [multi] billion … startup because I think that's actually what we are. It's a very, very big struggle for us. I mean, there's no question. What I'm excited about is we've got some people, either by luck or judgement, we've ended up with some really unusual people. Unusual people who may just give us a tiny chance of being successful. But I think there's a good possibility that, just like everybody, we'll get tripped up.

TTU: Can I ask you what you mean by 'unusual'?

CEO: I don't believe this is all generational. I think it's to do with the capability to get it. It's not generational purely.

TTU: We agree.

CEO: I think it's mainly generational, because … the younger generation are mainly only used to a particular set of tools, therefore they don't know anything else. So mainly it's a generational thing.

[THE CEO TALKS ABOUT A SENIOR TEAM MANAGER AS AN EXAMPLE OF HOW UNTHINKABLES CAN BE PREPARED FOR]

[Name] has invented a number of pretty extraordinary things, including the way to manage unstructured data. [More detail, but redacted] Now this is a solution which every company that's got legacy systems – which by the way is every company, pretty much – could find useful.

I got exposed to this when I went to visit his team and he's a bit of a maverick. But what he really wants is simply recognition and the chance to teach others and to help others. He's got lots of young people on his team. But he's not another generation.

And I've got a weird maverick … [details redacted] who's quite disruptive at times, but seeks things out like a pig looking for truffles.

TTU: I put that up there because that's the kind of thing which some of your peers will say: 'We've got no mavericks in the company anymore, we can't think differently.' And one of your peers said, in a meeting like this about a year ago, 'I need mavericks in the company, we've destroyed them in the last 20 years. What are we going to do, how are we going to get them? We've got to shake the tree.'

And I said, 'If you shake the tree, you're going to have no fruit left on it because actually mavericks are the visionaries.'

CEO: Now I think companies just need to find ways to break open the talent box and think about it in a different way. And I think one of the things that may have partly saved [company name] –….. is we've ended up taking about 35% out of the management and hired in about 15%. So a net 20% reduction. And we've brought into the company some really unusual new people.

I'm going to sound like – and am sounding like – we've got it sorted. We absolutely haven't. We're miles away from getting it sorted but there are just a few glimmers of hope in a business sense.

All of these are positives. What worries me isn't the positives. What worries me is: just as there are positive examples, there are negative ones. Like the risk of blockchain literally disintermediating our main business, removing it completely.

TTU: You've got to embrace it one way or the other. You've got to think about it not as an unthinkable but as an unpalatable. It's going to come.

CEO: Yes.

TTU: And you can't sort of say, 'We'll live without it.' You've got to embrace it and now is better than four years from now, or four months from now.

CEO: Well it's certainly better to embrace it than not, at any time, however late you are to the party. ... It's good to embrace it whenever you've figured out that you should.

TTU: Our interest is when you talk about 'unusual' new people ... because one of the words which even one of the chairmen of a very large company ... used was 'wacky'. What's the place for wacky people? Because shouldn't someone who's wacky be seen as a wise person? Even that language – which comes with no price whatsoever, or no cost – can make or define or break how you're going to approach this.

So I think for us, for the positive side, the way you talked about unusual new people, that's really helpful and really indicative of the way new options and solutions can come. And I didn't know this was where our discussion would go today. But I think that's indicative of how many companies are not prepared to go that far.

And you may say it was like this 30 years ago, but many companies are now facing something far more existential.

CEO: Why do you think that is? I mean why do you think it's different from 30 years ago?

TTU: Our findings are identical to what we could have said 20 or 30 years ago. ... The time compression means that it can become existential much quicker. ... When someone like [Indra Nooyi, CEO of PepsiCo] is saying, 'We're in danger of creating angry citizens and angry consumers,' that's rather what you're saying as well, from your own particular area ... It's just the way you tackle it. Because most people are saying to us, 'We're facing stovepipes of risk; outside of that, "the board don't want to know."'

CEO: Well we're the same. I've given you some examples where I think we're adapting. But we are so old fashioned in many ways as well. So we've got the same issues. The only thing that may have helped us is [when] we really got into a crisis situation [details redacted].

We had to … reassess the whole business model. Now maybe that will turn out to have been really fortunate, because if we had been sailing along and it was going alright, I suspect I would have come in and gone, 'Oh look at all this, all this cash flow. We can just make a few adjustments and it'll be alright.' And I could have got involved in some worthwhile initiatives like Thinking the Unthinkable and spending more time on it.

I do think that did help, strangely. Because we had to do some fundamental analysis of what the hell is the future of this company going to be? Because the fundamentals didn't look very good. But we are way [away] from where we need to be. I mean we've got silos that are totally stuck with entitlement cultures that are very difficult to shift … but great values. And I think that's going to be our saving grace. … Values are what controls the company when no one is looking.

One of the inventions that we've done … is we've just unveiled new values. It's taken two years – 18 months – of work. And the reason we did is that we didn't have a single set of values. And the one worry about not having a single set of values is – against this backdrop – how on earth do you stay coherent without it, and avoid importing risks?

And I think the single sets of values are really important. What I couldn't have expected is how well they've so far gone down. But it's very early days.

TTU: Internally?

CEO: Yes. It's very early days.

TTU: And with the board?

CEO: Yes, the board is fully behind it. … We're allowing people to have lots of conversations about them. But you won't find them on anyone's wall because we want people to have a proper conversation about them first. Then we're going to unveil them again, properly. But so far, people are relating to them in a way that I … It's really strange. We had top [redacted] people here together two months ago. The last time we did it was eight years ago. And I was expecting when we unveiled the values to that group that we would get, you know, the usual: a third of people who hated them; a third of people that were neutral; and a third of people that liked them. But it actually turned out to be … quite a bit higher than that. … I think it was 50:50 or something. But there weren't many people who said, 'I hate them,' or, 'I don't even think we're behaving that way.' Because we spent a couple of days on it.

And people were using unusual words. The most pessimistic was, 'Oh, these might actually work.' That was relief. Relief, yes. I am relieved. And we said, 'Why are you relieved?' 'Well, because you haven't totally screwed it up.' So people were really quite excited. But anyway, whether they work or not, the point is…

TTU: Did that take a lot of selling beforehand?

CEO: Actually no, it didn't take any selling. It took a lot of listening. And we basically involved [many hundreds of] people in telling us what they thought the values of the company were or should be. And the same themes kept coming up. We had a cross-section of the senior leadership who agreed to help discuss this in [a large number] of workshops across the company. And eventually the themes became very consistent.

We wanted three values but there were five themes. So we ended up recognising that … the values needed to be what the themes were, not what we thought.

TTU: How honest do you think people felt able to be?

CEO: So look, here's the other problem we've got. And I've caused it, if I can dare personalise it. … the one worry I have – the enemy within – is that people are actually now just going to say, 'It's not worth running the risk of speaking up because you'll just get fired.' And I don't think that's the way I am. But it's what many people perceive. So all of this change that we've driven has had some good aspects. Just like we've been talking about. Hopeful aspects anyway. But there's just as many dangerous aspects to it.

So that's really what we're dealing with at the moment.

TTU: But did you fire people or get rid of [number] people because they spoke up?

CEO: No. We actually went through a very laborious consultation process and listened to everybody. We were way too nice to people in some ways. But that doesn't matter. The perception is: is it safe to speak up? Now I don't think, just to be clear, it's the young generation or the frontline [job description] who are predominately thinking that, although some of them will obviously. I think the big problem is our junior and middle management.

[More details about the values initiative.]

We've had [details redacted] conversations with the top 50 about the evolving nature of these themes, before we finally [broadened into the outreach discussions] ... and involved half of them in shaping it with the organisation, listening. But now we've given the whole organisation three months to talk about them. ... I think it is a bit unnerving. You see the odd little whisper of them appear.

CEO'S COLLEAGUE: We opened it up to every employee. So not all of that is two way.

CEO: We haven't yet got to everyone's laptop. But the values are slowly seeping out. People have got the time and the space to conceptualise them for them and their teams. And of course enough people know about it that the teams are asking their bosses, 'Can we have a conversation about this?'

When we finally do launch them officially, I think they will have touched a very large proportion of the organisation. We stumbled upon it and then realised it was the right way. But it definitely wasn't the right way for me to just stand up on some pedestal and say, 'Oyez: here you are; here's the new values.' That wouldn't have worked.

TTU: Your use of the word 'stumble' is important, because we're not talking about definite solutions, we're talking about options. And what you came upon was an option which suddenly bore fruit, potentially. You're not sure yet whether it's going to work, but you're moving in that direction. Did you do it on the basis of other experiences which other companies have had, which you've heard about?

CEO: In part.

TTU: Many or just a handful?

CEO: I had some help from somebody who helped me with the values at [a previous employer]. We also had help from other organisations that consulted with us about how to do it. [A number of newly recruited senior executives added new perspectives.]

And it's about 50:50. People who are literally new [in the time the CEO has been there] and people who are not at all new, some of whom have been here since the new company was born.

I find that pretty helpful actually as a mix. I wouldn't want it skewed dramatically differently in either direction. But some of the key leadership team is below the executive committee and also ended up with quite a lot of change. And I think that helps because it helps with this antidote to this conforming – [that] there's [only] one way of doing it.

Now the risk of course that we run and I run is that we start out like this and then end up doing exactly what we fear, which is we create a new thing that everyone is conforming to and there's just one set of values. [As a result] we're launching a new code of conduct. Before you know where we are, in five years' time everyone will have forgotten to think because they'll all be conforming to the new things.

TTU: But the level of disruption by then will be probably even more unpredictable. I picked you up on that use of the word 'dinosaur' right at the beginning. Because one of the things which is very clear to us is that you've got to retain institutional understanding in order to push some of this stuff through.

CEO: Well not just to push it through. To form the right judgements about how to do it. [The CEO lists two senior executives who have been in the company at least ten years. The CEO says about one of them:] Now [name redacted] is not always right either. But [has] got enough institution experience that [name redacted] can feel it.

And if you don't have people like that, no matter how many mavericks and interesting people you have, you just end up with chaos.

TTU: So the sense of vulnerability and anxiety is clear. How clear is the question, and therefore the way ahead?

CEO: The challenge that I've got in all this is: what problem are we trying to solve together? What is the problem we're trying to solve? I always ask that.

There are two things about management. You've got to understand your current reality and you've got to understand what problem you're trying to resolve. Once you've got those two things, you can do something.

I think we're beginning to understand our current reality in this area – 'we' being the business community. I'm not sure I understand what problem we're trying to solve and who we are solving it for. Are we solving it so that we all, as companies, survive? Are we solving it for our shareholders? Are we solving something for society?

I don't know the answer to the problem statement. Do you have an answer? What problems are you guys trying to solve?

TTU: The human capacity of leaders to survive and thrive in this extraordinary, complex world. What it needs for leaders to be able to do.

CEO: You're planning on providing a toolkit? Okay. That would be very helpful. I would like to be connected in some way to what you're doing. I have no idea what that way is. I find it not only interesting; I think it's really fundamental. But I don't know, yet, what the problem is. Is it that leaders don't have the equipment? Is it that leaders don't have the confidence? Is it…?

I don't know what it is but there is a leadership vacuum building that needs something to fill it. I suspect many things will fill it over the next 20 years, unfortunately.

40
THINK 'MAVERICK AND WACKY': HOW TO CHANGE CULTURE, BEHAVIOUR AND MINDSET

Change isn't rocket science. But it is 'damn hard to do' as so many have confirmed to us. So, in order to think and take on unthinkables, can you eat an elephant in one mouthful? And if so, how do you do it?

Business schools and social scientists have been working for several decades to apply social science and systems theory to change culture. So why have so many designs not really worked? When it is attempted, culture change is preached and promoted. Yet it is often designed poorly with little achieved. Here is the rather caustic assessment of Satya Nadella, CEO of Microsoft: 'In the past whenever we have tried to have these cultural values, put up posters and what have you, I wasn't able to recall what the heck they meant or what they were. They were all corporate speak. I think a lot of us love to talk about culture. But it has to take organic roots.'580

So what new possibilities emerged for changing culture, mindset and behaviour from our extensive data and the case studies we have shared with you?

There are two core takeaways. Each of them recognises that the external environment demands transformation not just of the organisation but above all the minds that run it. This can be achieved by reacting immediately as a crisis unfolds, as happened at Safaricom. Or it can be achieved by acting proactively to address longer-term existential threats, as is being done at OCP or by PepsiCo.

Initiating radical change has to be conceived, then bought into and driven right from the top. In so many ways updating culture is a human challenge more than a systems challenge. Too often, consideration of that human bit is marginalised in favour of fancy diagrams and flowcharts with arrows and boxes. That is the inevitable and understandable assumption when there is the periodic rhetoric about 'reinventing the company'.[581] There is never enough about people. It is the human parts of the system and the flowcharts who must overcome their instinctive default to conformity. It is people who have to make re-invention possible culture change happen.

Do leaders have what is needed? We have to be careful about over-optimism on what is possible. There are plenty of myths about what bosses can really achieve as managers. Stefan Stern and Cary Cooper list 44 of them.[582] They refer to them as 'only 44 things' for bosses 'to get wrong'. Their first myth is that 'there is one way to lead or manage'. Myth 41 is that 'people hate change'. But while there may be myths about what bosses can do, the new scale and challenges of disruption are real. They cannot be dismissed as false or invented.

This brings us back full square to the three critical issues which we set out for you at the very start of this book; **culture**, **behaviour** and **mindset**. With them must come the four new ambitions: **purpose**, **values**, **courage** and **humility**. Change must be backed unquestioningly by the boards. It is a team risk, not an individual risk for just the CEO and chair.

Uncertainty and prevarication mean there will be no chance of pulling off change against a tsunami of disruption. It was unwavering personal vision and relentless determination that brought significant progress at DBS under Piyush Gupta, PepsiCo under Indira Nooyi, OCP under Mostafa Terrab and DNB under Rune Bjerke.

Engaging, motivating and energising staff in this transformation is critical. Wavering and incremental half measures have little chance of pulling off the scale of recalibration that is needed. Most of our profiled leaders or organisations have made significant progress because they actively engaged staff in identifying the problems and proposing answers.

Most important was not just that they were seen to listen. They took notes and, in many respects, took action. Above all there has been no fear of comeback or being marginalised professionally if they were radical or wrong with good intent. Critically, there have been incentives to take risks. That happens by being 'maverick', 'wacky' or even 'bonkers' in their ideas and approach if necessary.

Many inside companies and institutions are naturally sceptical and suspicious, of course. But led by Generation Z and the millennials, a defining number of employees enthusiastically become early adopters. They cotton on fast – literally. Bob Collymore, CEO of Safaricom, for example, noticed that after he swapped his grey socks for coloured ones, his core team started doing the same. Such change and bold statements of individuality can become infectious. They help change culture, mindsets and behaviour. And that's the way it needs to be.

So does the energy and determination of Gen Z and the millennials to mobilise the waverers until successive tides of enthusiasm grip much of the organisation. That is why focusing strongly on engaging and developing the potential of younger NextGen staff-members is so important. The palpable energy of the self-appointed facilitators for Le Mouvement in Morocco, or the dynamism of the BLAZERS in Kenya, or the NextGen at DBS in Singapore has become as infectious and radical as was needed for the challenge to disruption.

Bumps, setbacks and adversity should never matter that much. What do matter are the efforts and risk taking to push for change, even if there is no guarantee of assured success. Those maverick people and their wacky ideas must have a new acceptance. They will be found to be the main drivers for a new culture, mindset and behaviour, not liabilities.

Of course, there will always be resistance and scepticism. It will come especially from those of a certain generation whose natural instinct to conform is under threat, and therefore with it their career or job security. On that score there is no hiding the negatives if the chemistry fails and the risks are seen as not having been worth it.

In 2015 John Cryan was appointed CEO of the ailing Deutsche Bank. DB had gone from a fabled generator of cash to a new basket case of a bank. Cryan had been under instructions to change a culture and level of high-stakes risk-taking that had drained the bank of cash and its reputation. The hype had to be stopped. The approach of this 'bluff

Brit' was to come clean and be open. But it had the wrong impact. It was found to be ill conceived, so it backfired. 'Cryan is almost too honest. It's not good for morale. There's a phalanx of people interviewing [for jobs] with rivals.'[583] On a Sunday afternoon in April 2018 the Cryan way of resolving DB's crisis status came crashing down. The board sacked him. Within three weeks the new CEO Christian Sewing announced what for years would have been an unthinkable. Deutsche would no longer have ambitions to challenge rival banks and be a leading global investment bank.[584] Corporate finance and trading in the US would end.

The DB experience highlights the tension and dilemma. In pursuit of a new culture, how much do you have to just accept and put up with these tensions and private anxieties from those who work for you? The people either stay and engage, or they eventually drift away. But extraordinarily most do come to the other side of the comfort zone where they then become fully enthused and engaged.

To create the chemistry for success and the self confidence for thinking unthinkables there has to be good communication. It must be cross-silo, top-down and bottom-up, online or vigorous, vivacious and face-to-face as we saw with OCP's Café Culture, DBS's hackathons and Aviva's reverse mentoring. 'You need to have some passion and you need to have some, I would say, personal "skin" in the game, and you need to have stories. And I think that's what business leaders lack, you know, they just hide behind jargon, they hide behind numbers, and you think, "I just have no clue what this person is all about,"' said the Katherine Garrett-Cox, CEO of the British subsidiary of the Gulf International Bank of Bahrain.

In addition there should be informal referees, moderators or 'culture champions' throughout the organisation. Reverse mentoring may frighten many top executives. They fear what it will reveal. But the evidence is that they can achieve positive results. By their very presence the role of millennials will both invigorate and inspire. There must be an evolving set of new ground rules which are both implicit and explicit.

Similarly, as the OCP experience confirms, technological transformation must have a clear purpose, with new offerings for employees, customers or clients. Everyone in your organisation must be alert to the destructive possibility of creating the 'angry customers and angry consumers'. We highlighted this alert from PepsiCo's Indra Nooyi many pages back. They can switch loyalty and support via the swish of a few strokes on a handset keyboard from anywhere.

Courage and **humility** are key parts of the fierce resolve needed for an extraordinary determination to make change happen.[585] All of these are needed because there can never be a guarantee of success, and there can be a need to explain failure. Hence that priority for experimentation and trying out ideas in order to be prepped to take on unthinkables, whenever they arise.

End notes

[580] 'Microsoft hits refresh', *Wired*, November 2017.

[581] See for example the cover story and analysis 'Reinventing The Company', *The Economist*, October 24th–30th 2015.

[582] op cit. *Myths of management* by Stefan Stern and Cary Cooper.

[583] James Chappell, analyst at Berenberg quoted in 'How Deutsche Bank's high-stakes gamble went wrong' by Patrick Jenkins and Laura Noonan, *Financial Times*, November 9, 2017

[584] 'Deutsche Bank abandons global investment bank ambitions' by Olaf Storbeck, *Financial Times*, 27 April 2018.

[585] We borrow the title of Jim Collins's seminal paper 'Level 5 leadership: the triumph of humility and fierce resolve', *Harvard Business Review*, January 2001.

41

USING 'SMART COMMAND' TO UNCONFORM CONFORMITY

Let's remind you again that central to our findings is the following: the conformity which gets leaders to the top disqualifies them from understanding and thriving in a world of Black Swans, Black Elephants and Black Jelly fish. These are wicked problems for which there are currently no solutions, just options to try out and experiment with in the ways we have seen done in all the case studies, with varying degrees of success.

So, the heart of this book's takeaways is the fact that there is no alternative to confronting and then addressing that **conformity**, and with it the implications for **culture**, **behaviour** and **mindset**. As with this Red Alert, ignore it at your peril.

Can that be done? Yes, of course! After all, conformity is a psychological trait as old as human existence. Its origins are tribal. That is why it is so relevant to leaders in both corporates and government these days: they are overseeing tribes of workers and employees. They have 'tribal' loyalties, traditions and expectations. Even the millennials and GEN Z are tribal in their own distinctive ways.

'Culture evolved when people were in small tribes. If you didn't fit in with the tribe you didn't live,' John Childress told us. His core professional focus is as a consultant for how organisations address culture.[586] '[In a tribe,] if you were an outcast you did not survive, so your whole makeup is [focused on] "How do I fit in and belong?" And we still carry those genetic predispositions, or social predispositions.'[587] That explains in a very straightforward way why changing culture, mindset and behaviour is such a challenge.

Don't assume that taking on conformity in order to change culture is a revolutionary first. Challenging conformity is an ancient challenge. It goes back at least 2500 years to the teachings of the Chinese philosopher Confucius. His thinking inspired the concept of **Remonstrance.**

Remonstrance guides an official on how to take the risk of telling an Emperor respectfully that he may be wrong. The goal is to 'awaken' the leader to a better path. There was a moral duty to do so, despite the obvious uncertainties attached to crossing an ill-defined line of acceptability. Embracing Remonstrance should draw on the shared understanding and values that prevail in traditions and culture. But it is always a high risk. Any official at the court knew that if the Emperor was displeased, they risked death.[588]

Two millennia later, that same risk of challenging a forceful leader is not about being condemned to death. But there is a professional equivalent. It is about risking the same kind of career-limiting move (CLM) that is at the heart of our ten reasons why leaders and those who work for them find themselves unable to Think the Unthinkable.

Aron Cramer, President of Business for Social Responsibility, shared with us his definition of a CLM. It reads like a Rubik's Cube of contradictory pressures which can probably never be resolved as one, despite pressures or expectations to do so and somehow be perfect. 'That comes from questioning the objectives of your institution. It comes from being out of step with the social norms that exist inside institution. It comes from questioning superiors. And for CEOs it comes from questioning the objectives of public markets. You just can't do it.'[589]

But times are changing fast, as confirmed by the core new vulnerabilities from not thinking unthinkables. Leaders who previously seemed unassailable have had public rude awakenings born of an institutional and personal complacency. As Facebook experienced in 2018, they discover suddenly when 'shit happens' that they and their institution had been calibrated to only think of positives. As a core part of their FB tribal culture the possibility of negatives, whatever they might be, and their likely devastating impact was barely considered.[590] Addressing the new vulnerabilities from this culture of complacency and assumed invincibility was barely on the radar screen of those at the top. It was an unthinkable. That is until 'unthought-about' events worked like a giant pile driver on corporate credibility, thereby forcing the issue right to the top of the agenda in unavoidable, unexpected and potentially existential ways.

The experiences of two major figures among the many who have faced the unthinkable spotlight of public scrutiny is salutary. As well as Zuckerberg, there was Martin Winterkorn of Volkswagen. Zuckerberg still runs the company he created in his university dorm. Winterkorn was fired and now faces criminal charges in the US for conspiring to cover up VW's diesel emissions cheating. The indictment was filed in secret in March 2018. It was unsealed to coincide with the VW annual meeting on 3 May. The charges were viewed as a 'rare attempt to prosecute a CEO for company actions'.

What links them is their obsessive focus on growth. It led to a culture where the leaders and their strategy could not be challenged. 'Only Good News' was reportedly the secret label for the conference room of Facebook's Chief Operating Officer, Sheryl Sandberg. That was because good news was all she wanted to hear, as one jaundiced former insider revealed.[591]

It was the same story at VW. A week after the 'dieselgate' scandal broke in September 2015, employees received a letter urging 'a culture in which it's possible and permissible to argue with your superior about the best way to go'.[592] It was far too late. VW was already confronting the new reality that its diesel deceit had been exposed in the US. Why had the possibility – and more realistically the inevitability – of this defeat mechanism being discovered and exposed not been fully gamed and scoped at the highest executive levels inside VW years earlier? Had the question been asked and answered: What if the defeat mechanism and its skewing of emissions data were to be discovered one day? The apparent failure to do so with free debate and open disclosure seemed incredible.

The letter in question had been written by Bernd Osterloh, chief of the VW Works Council. He was a leading member of the Supervisory Board which subsequently faced merciless criticism for its passivity. At the same time, Michael Horn, CEO of VW America, told a US Congressional committee: 'This company has to bloody learn and use this opportunity in order to get their act together, and 600,000 people worldwide have to be managed in a different way. ... This is very, very clear.'[593] VW's survival seems to be assured after sales rebounded to record levels and the revenues from car sales kept increasing. Observers had detected shifts in the culture under the new CEO, Matthias Mueller, then he was ousted in April 2018.[594] The new CEO, Herbert Diess subsequently told shareholders at VW's annual meeting there would be a new corporate culture that is 'more open, honest and decent' with 'misconduct punished relentlessly'.[595] But the financial cost so far runs into tens of billions of dollars, with many more downside costs expected.

The culture in the banking sector has been in the public spotlight since the 2008 Financial Crisis. Now, the failings exposed by an inappropriate culture have been highlighted officially. Almost a decade later, in March 2018, the UK's Financial Conduct Authority (FCA) published a series of major essays on how to transform culture in the financial sector. The essays began with this damning comment: 'Culture in financial services is widely accepted as a key root cause of the major conduct failings that have occurred within the industry in recent history, causing harm to both consumers and markets.'[596]

Let us repeat and highlight this damning verdict from the FCA regulator. 'Culture ... is widely accepted as a key root cause of the major conduct failings.' This finding builds on the conclusions from our four years highlighting and charting unthinkables, along with their impact on leadership. But few wanted to hear or believe them. The language of that verdict from the FCA must not be ignored. Indeed, it must be embraced. What CEO or leader can now fail to grip the implications of such a blunt official assessment and warning?

Yet while there is a huge amount of deep analysis available on the impact of cultures and subcultures in organisations, there are no easy answers on how to change them. Hence our suggestion to consider locking onto the Thinking the Unthinkable Progressions: firstly in order to wake up to the reality of disruption, then to understand what your particular challenges are, then to grip the issue, experiment and learn from others.

This is what we urge can now take place through the Thinking the Unthinkable process of 'progressions' and also the concept of a new lily pad community of leaders which we have introduced to you. This book should be viewed as a catalyst for leaders to build both the new awareness and that community.

End notes

[586] *Culture rules!* (2017) by John R Childress, Principia Group.

[587] John R Childress interview, 22 March 2018.

[588] 'Remonstrance: the moral imperative of the Chinese scholar-official' by Anita Andrew and Robert Andre LaFleur, *Education About Asia* 19 (2) pp. 5–8. The co-authors thank Alan Chan, Dean of the Humanities and Social Sciences (HASS) faculty at Nanyang Technological University, for alerting us to the concept of Remonstrance.

[589] Interview, 1 July 2015.

[590] As Facebook's Head of News Partnerships, Campbell Brown, admitted at the FT Conference on the Future of News, op cit. Campbell Brown, March 22 2018. Confirmed too by Founder and CEO Mark Zuckerberg, op cit. 10 April 2018.

[591] *Chaos monkeys: obscene fortune and random failure in Silicon Valley* (2016) by Antonio Garcia Martinez. New York: Harper Collins.

[592] Bernd Osterloh and Michael Horn, quoted in 'Fear and respect: VW's Culture under Winterkorn' by Andreas Cremer and Tom Bergin, 10 October 2015.

[593] 'Board room politics at the heart of VW scandal', *Financial Times*, 4 October 2015.

[594] 'What went so right with VW restructuring?', *Financial Times*, 18 January 2018.

[595] 'Volkswagen CEO Herbert Diess urges more honest corporate culture', *Deutsche Welle*, 3 May 2018.

[596] *Transforming culture in financial services*, Financial Conduct Authority, 12 March 2018.

42
THE PUBLIC: ALWAYS QUESTIONING AND UNFORGIVING

Who carries responsibility?

Should leaders – whether corporate or political – carry blame if there are massive failings in what has now become a permanently disrupted world? The public, the shareholders, the voters and stakeholders all expect perfection, or something close to it. But in this time of new uncertainty it has to be accepted that this is not possible.

Tolerance, encouragement and an acceptance of responsibility are needed, not blame. That is because there are no easy answers. There is a profound and growing disconnect between public expectations and the perfection – or near perfection – they expect to be available and delivered. The signs are that this mismatch will widen.

The far-sighted Harvard Professor Ronald Heifetz wrote the same in 1994 in his book Leadership Without Easy Answers.[597] His big idea is **Adaptive Leadership**. He wrote presciently twenty four years ago: 'Today we face a crisis in leadership in many areas of public and private life. Yet we misconceive the nature of the leadership crisis. We attribute our problems too readily to our politicians and executives. We frequently use them as scapegoats. Although people in authority may not be a ready source of answers, rarely are they the source of our pains. ... Our current crises may have more to do with the scale, interdependence, and perceived uncontrollability of modern economic and political life.'[598]

Heifetz draws on his rich career as a psychiatrist and a cellist. He has devised a ground-breaking leadership education programme at Harvard. His course on 'Leadership Without Easy Answers' was described to us enthusiastically by Jason Blackstock. He is an inspirational expert in quantum physics who works to bridge the interface between science and global public policy. Jason stepped back in early 2018 as head of STEaPP, the department of Science, Technology, Engineering and Public Policy at University College London (UCL). He has assisted Ron Heifetz on the class. He described to us a dual approach. It is centred on knowing yourself and your biases. It is also important to understand the systems around you and the new realities of super-fast change. This corresponds precisely to what has been revealed in our ten takeaways after crunching the data from our hundreds of interviews and conversations for this **Thinking the Unthinkable** project.

'The goal is first to understand the culture and the external factors,' Jason told us. 'You do the class which is focused on the external dynamics first. Then you do the one that's internal. He [Heifetz] would advise that if you start with an internal lens you attribute far too much of the world to yourself. As opposed to the reality that, actually, you're … irrelevant for a lot of things. And you need to be able to interrogate the world around you better in order to understand how to make the most impact in that system.'[599]

Jason added: 'What makes the [course] so exceptional is [that] too many of the leadership programmes only do the "Try and understand yourself deeply" … without recognising that we are social creatures. And at the end of the day, much of you is just shaped by your interactions with other people. The roles that you take on are things that you have inherited from family, parents, gender, ethnicity, culture.'

'Adaptive Leadership' puts experimentation at its heart to address 'wicked problems.' These are problems which are hard to comprehend and are without obvious solutions. As we saw in the case studies, adapting is what has brought success for a CEO like Rune Bjerke after 11 years running the Norwegian e-bank, DNB. Bjerke's strategy is fuelled by improvisation and adaptation. Competitors are engaged not challenged. As he told us, they become 'frenemies'. In an era of wicked problems, such a culture is about being flexible and trying things out. This is especially the case when a bank like DNB is being forced by disruption to become a completely different 'non-bank' fintech concept in this new digital world, with all the unsettling implications for staffing and work practices in order to guarantee survival.

Hence the critical role of adaptability in changing culture, mindset and behaviour. 'Adaptive problems are often systemic problems with no easy answers,' says Heifetz. As our interview data confirms, in an atmosphere where those at the top confide that they are a mix of 'scared' and 'overwhelmed', the ways forward on culture, mindset and behaviour are certainly not easily devised in C-suites.

Indeed, the challenges are formidable. But as our case studies like OCP, DBS, Aviva and PepsiCo confirm, taking them on marks out the CEOs who will overcome immense risks to pull off both change of culture and survival. To achieve that, engaging, trusting and embracing the people who work for leaders at the top must be a no-brainer. So must evolving new purpose and values.

Heifetz agrees. But his analysis has been out there circulating for two decades. So why does it still not have more spontaneous traction in this new and turbulent period of unthinkables that are born of a different kind of disruption? 'Mobilising an organisation to adapt its behaviours in order to thrive in a new business environment is critical. Without such change any organisation would falter. Indeed, getting people to do adaptive work is the mark of leadership in a competitive world. The solutions to adaptive challenges reside not in the executive suite but in the collective intelligence of employees at all levels, who need to use one another as resources, often across boundaries, and learn their way to those solutions.'[600]

Like Heifetz, the leadership consultant Patricia Seemann is a trained medical doctor. Her 3am Group supports stressed senior executives who often struggle to handle the wicked problems that are the stuff of nightmares (hence the name '3am'). During six conversations in London, a snowy Swiss Alpine village, and over Skype, she generously shared her experience and wisdom. 'How the hell do you design a strategy in today's world? It used to be you could do one for three or five years. You cannot any more. You can set the general direction, and then you try out stuff and you constantly re-frame, re-frame, re-frame.'

What does this require? 'Huge, hugely iterative experimentation. ... Rather than having answers, you [as leader] ask questions. So, obviously, you are going to have to hire different kinds of people. If you are leading that way, your processes will be very different. They will be less about ticking boxes and more about giving people lead indicators for performance. ... The critical thing is to have an organisation that can learn incredibly quickly. So the whole topic of "learning organisation" that was big in the '90s is coming back with a vengeance. Learn faster than your competition. ... You then reallocate resources to where it is actually working. Withdraw it where it isn't. It is a much more evolutionary and much more organic way of managing your company.'

How can that reformed culture be achieved? 'This requires new leadership styles. You hire the right talent. You make sure that the processes in the company enable decision-making – such as make sure that people have the right information, that they know which hoops to jump through and such, that they all have access to the right kind of knowledge. And the technology – which is of course very important these days – supports the decision-making. And that there is a culture that supports this as well.'

For leaders, the relationship with those working for you must change. Right now, the followers of a leader expect the leader to have the answer. But if a leader is smart and understands the wicked territory in which he or she is operating, then the most productive attitude can be 'You know what: I don't have the answer!'

Patricia calls it 'smart command'. She defines it as 'command that listens: a command that is also in command of oneself'. The smart leaders who apply it are 'extremely skilled at attracting people to the right problems, making sure that they're not distracted, making sure that they have everything that they need to make the good decision'.[601]

The eminent British businesswoman Dame Helen Alexander endorsed that 'smart command' principle. As CEO of The Economist she transformed the business model and took the newspaper to the US market with huge success. She was the first female President of the Confederation of British Industry. For 24 years she sat on many boards as a director or chair until her death in 2017.

Dame Helen told us: 'Leadership is about listening, not just about speaking. And it's also about understanding the external environments – not just in your own organisation. A key quality of leadership is to keep one's antennae open to outside spheres – within the country, looking at what's going on in other companies, other models, other sectors and other countries. All the time being able to evaluate what resonates with the business that they're involved in. So that they are fully rooted in the business.'[602]

Dame Helen chaired the Port of London Authority. During her time, they developed the principle of 'Visible and Felt Leadership'. It was spun off from the health and safety policy. Board members were told they had to set an example. They must lead from the front and experience PLA jobs for what they are. They had to sit on reception for a day; they had to be seen on the docks or in boats with the pilots. The overriding principle was to develop highly sensitised antennae that ensured understanding of 'all the external issues affecting the business'.

We described to Dame Helen how one of our interviewees had told us that he was so busy that he didn't have the time to dictate emails or thoughts he had during the day. She responded sharply. That's 'utterly silly'. She added, 'It's just a matter of how the leader and organisation manages its leader's time. And if the organisation has got into a process of wall-to-wall meetings throughout the day, then that's something that has to change – maybe when his successor takes over!'

Another female chair was equally firm. When we first met Dame Judith Hackitt[603] she was Chair of the British Health and Safety Executive. Her target had been achieving systemic change to the culture, behaviour and mindset for how risks are addressed in the workplace. The culture overall was complacent and largely unimpressive. There had been a dehumanising of contacts and culture.

'Management systems in the workplace have become the comfort blanket of leaders. We have an approved management system, an accredited management system, yes. But how do you know? How do you know that that's covering the risks, the real risks to your business? You don't. And if you don't talk to people. ... And what I think has happened with this systematisation of all workplaces – it's all done in the ether and electronically and all the rest of it – is that we've lost a lot of what used to happen through human interaction of people just sitting and talking and saying, 'What would happen if ...? Have we thought about ...?'

Attitudes can often be wanting. Priorities are often inappropriate. 'I think [that] what you see is people fill their space with being busy. ... You've got people in organisations running huge risks, and at the same time, setting themselves goals and measuring things that are trivial and unimportant. And at worst, it's going to stop someone cutting their finger on a sheet of paper or whatever. It's bizarre.'

Dame Judith is an engineer by training. She has been a prominent advocate for the huge changes needed on leadership attitudes to risk. Those ambitions and fears were suddenly tested after the Grenfell Tower disaster when 71 residents were killed by a devastating fire[604] in a high-rise residential block in west London. She agreed to chair the first investigation into why building standards had failed and apparently been flouted.

In December 2017, her interim findings into Grenfell confirmed the scale of inadequate leadership on safety standards which she had already shared privately with this **Thinking the Unthinkable** project two years earlier. Her investigation had ferreted out deeply questionable attitudes and practices in the bidding and construction processes. She concluded: 'This is a call to action for an entire industry and those parts of government that oversee it. ... True and lasting change will require called a universal shift in culture too rebuild trust amongst residents of high-rise buildings. ... This change needs to start now.'[605]

The likelihood of a catastrophic fire in many of the UK's high-rise buildings had not been unthinkable. It had been unpalatable. Experts and officials feared that the inevitability was there, especially because of compromised building standards which insiders knew about as part of the design and budgeting process. But few within the profession had taken the risk of whistleblowing the likely horror of what would happen, and why.

It has been the same in Dubai. Five fires in prominent and iconic high-rise hotels and residences – some of the tallest buildings in the world – had been unthinkable, at least officially. Dubai was about promoting success and perfection. Therefore, the unthinkables of such fire horrors were never meant to happen. But they did, with revelations of improper building material and corners cut on oversight processes and materials used. This meant they were more combustible. They didn't snuff out a fire; they accelerated it.

The fires in Dubai and at Grenfell Tower are Black Swan events – low probability but catastrophic when they happen. Time and again in the aftermaths of such events it is clear from our own conversations with leaders and the inquiry reports that major risks were never considered. They were usually glossed over as unthinkable. They were the 'what ifs' which a narrow risk culture suggested would never happen, so they would not be considered. But as one insurance executive put it to us: 'There was never consideration of drone camera or TV news helicopter broadcasting live – in real time – from your factory fire.'[606]

End notes

[597] *Leadership without easy answers* (1994) by Ronald A Heifetz. Cambridge, MA: Harvard University Press.

[598] ibid. Professor Heifetz warned in an interview of a deficit of trust as people feel betrayed by politicians. 24 October 2017.

[599] Interview, 27 February 2018.

[600] op cit. Ronald A Heifetz and Donald L Laurie.

[601] Extracted from interviews with Patricia Seemann 2015–2017: 7 April, 19 April, 28 May, 1 July, 14 September 2015; 19 January 2017.

[602] Interview, 1 June 2015.

[603] Dame Judith Hackitt interview, 21 July 2015.

[604] 14 June 2017.

[605] *Interim report into the review of building regulations and fire safety*, Ministry of Housing, Communities & Local Government. The final report was published on 17 May 2018.

[606] Conversation with senior executive from a major US insurance company, 18 September 2017.

43

FIND THAT EMOTIONAL HOOK AND REWARD

How to overcome this ongoing culture of denial?

The focus of many executives continues to be on the conformity of box-ticking rather than coldly assessing the nature and scale of major risks. Here is one revealing survey by the US consultancy CEB (now part of Gartner). It highlighted a major risk mismatch which is fully in line with what we have discovered. It confirmed what Chief Risk Officers had quietly confided to this project. Many risks are simply not even thought about or entered on risk registers.

On the one hand, the companies which CEB sampled spent just 6% of their time addressing major strategic risks which could severely damage the business with a potential impact of 86%. On the other hand, the companies said that their audit teams spent half of their time (52%) on legal and financial risks. This was disproportionate. Their likely risk of impact was calculated at just 5%.[607] CEB concludes: 'An over-focus on process misses the fact that people are the biggest source of risk. and fails to make employees part of the solution.'

Airmic is the London-based risk managers association. John Hurrell was CEO for ten years until 2017. He expended considerable energy arguing for the culture on risk to be modified. He believed that organisations and above all those that lead them must be moved away from 'risk blindness'. And that meant from the board downwards. 'I think most boards realise that they live in a transparent world. Or they realise to a degree that they didn't ten years ago. And five years from now, they'll realise it much more. The very fact [is] that every time anything goes wrong; everything is in the open. ... You cannot ignore the fact you operate in a glass house now.'

There is an important emblematic example from Airmic's casebook. After a $100 million explosion at one of their factories a member discovered that the third line of defence was a simple $50 widget to cut the power off. It had failed. 'The person who had the authority to spend $50 to replace that was three lines up from the person who could spot that the problem had occurred. And it didn't get done. And our observation is that senior management don't trust their delegates as much they need to for this to be effective,' said John Hurrell.[608]

We asked why. 'I think that's cultural,' said John. Airmic's 'Roads to Resilience' report highlighted eight companies which are noticeably risk-aware.[609] As with the case studies for this **Thinking the Unthinkable** work, two central success factors are engaging staff and good communications. This must be done at all levels, with conversations about risks encouraged throughout the organisation. But doing that is so much easier to say than achieve. In principle a risk manager's role is to identify them then flag them up to the leaders. But a staggering 50% of those managers feel inhibited from doing so. They say that is because of myopia from their leaders, denial and above all an unwillingness to accept that unthinkables and unpalatables are likely to be hurtling down the track. Remarkably there seems to be a common culture of asking, 'Why list a risk if you don't see it or understand it?'

How can employees at all levels be encouraged to air their anxieties, especially those 'mavericks' with often-inspiring new thinking, but who conformist minds at the very top are likely to view as 'wacky'? Dame Judith Hackitt, the health and safety supremo, confirmed to us that this is a major question. Often a reluctance to give the answers needed shows how leaders continue to hold back when it comes to the dramatic changes needed for culture, mindset and behaviour. 'If you say those sort of things, and you are immediately ostracised for saying it, [then] that is as big a problem as if you're not rewarded for saying those things. ... The reward for being the maverick, for being the off-the-wall thinker, doesn't have to come in monetary terms. It can simply come in terms of people valuing the fact that you provide that, and that you have raised a concern that is worthy of more than just a "that won't happen" response.'[610]

Another Chair said: 'You do actually want to have, on a board, somebody who is willing to be [maverick and wacky]. And there are some people who are very outspoken, who think perhaps the unthinkable, who don't care a stuff as to how their colleagues actually view them on things, who are prepared to come up with things which, as you said, nine times out of ten are not wrong necessarily, but impractical. I call it that, rather than "wrong".'

Dame Helen Alexander always encouraged her one female NED [non-executive director] to give alternative perspectives at one company's board meetings. 'Is it because she's a woman? Is it because she's American? Is it because she's from the IT world? I don't know. But she has a different set of views.' The issue was not just gender balance. It is about ensuring not just that all voices are heard, but more importantly how unconventional ideas are aired.

Why this fast-growing emphasis on the value of gender diversity to overcome the pressing deficits in culture, mindset and behaviour? 'Women think differently. They bring a different perspective, they bring a different view of problems and how they can be solved,' said Dame Judith. 'And any woman who has spent any time in an organisation that is very much a male-dominated culture will have faced that challenge of either "How do I get myself heard?" or "Am I simply going to conform to the culture here and not be true to myself and provide the observations that I can?"'

And changing behaviour?

Alan Watkins is a consultant and physician. He is co-founder and CEO of Complete Coherence, a company which advises leaders on their performance and what to do about their failings. He describes 'ill-discipline in decision making, on big decisions. ... So, thinking the unthinkable goes round and round in circles.' He says that 'virtually all the companies I'm working with, it's the basic fundamental relationship with staff and how you get them collectively working together. ... That's one of the things you have to teach them. So, how do we unlock, and integrate, your cleverness and our cleverness, and bring that together in a more sophisticated answer that we can all get behind?'[611]

Tara Swart is a neuroscientist, medical doctor and executive advisor. She told us how she coaches leaders to address their sense of bewilderment.[612] There has to be a fuller understanding of how the brain addresses decision-making under acute stress. Much of it has not been used yet. The leaders need to build up their physical and mental resilience. This helps them develop new behaviours. They then use her neuroscientific knowledge to help them create new pathways in the brain, so that new behaviours become habit and replace the existing 'bad' habits.

The majority of Tara's clients are engineers, accountants and lawyers. They have enormous technical expertise. All have exceptional abilities to earn fees and revenue; that is how they have risen up the hierarchy. But now they are in senior roles, they need to use their emotional intelligence more effectively. She compares it to learning a new language. 'You can teach French to somebody, [so] you can teach emotional intelligence.'

As part of this search for a new culture, both Tara and Alan agree that exercise, nutrition and sleep are essential. Both shallow breathing associated with stress and the body always being stuck on 'red alert' can be transformed. But getting this message across is one thing; achieving such change on the scale that is needed is another.

There must be incentives. On one occasion Tara was Skyping an executive client. She noticed from her screen that he was getting seriously overweight. She told him: 'You must take some exercise.' He replied: 'I have a choice of doing three half-hour walks, or I get to see my son.' She persuaded him that he would be a better father to his son if he were fitter. Soon afterwards she heard from his colleagues that they were amazed how 'fast the fat came off his body' and how thin he became as her advice all suddenly 'clicked'.

Her big takeaway for changing culture, mindset and behaviour? 'It's about coming up with an emotional hook and reward.'

End notes

[607] op cit. 'Getting a handle on a scandal', Schumpeter column in *The Economist*, 31 March–6 April 2018.

[608] Interview, 21 July 2015, and subsequent conversations.

[609] *Roads to resilience*, Airmic, January 2014.

[610] op cit. Dame Judith Hackitt, 21 July 2015.

[611] Interviews, 1 March and 16 July 2016.

[612] Interview, 18 October 2017. Also presentation at Corinthia Hotel, London, 6 July 2017.

44

'SUCH GOOD CULTURE THAT WE INFECTED THE STAFF'

A toxic culture frequently suppresses all possibilities to create the right conditions to modify culture positively. To fix it, a leader must accept the scale and nature of it first, otherwise he or she will fail.

Making change happen requires the equivalent of 20/20 insights into how the organisation actually functions. That is not so easy today. Long gone are the days when a leader knew which buttons to press in their hierarchical organisation so that decisions and resulting instructions are carried out smartly. The command-and-control structures have morphed into highly complicated networks which include suppliers, sub-contractors and complex global supply chain networks. Inevitably, this means there is a huge range of subcultures and operating environments, and an already overwhelmed leader can't be across them all in the way they should be.

In a 21st century company – with all its 'silos' and global networks – this makes it very hard to identify the underlying drivers of culture, unwritten rules and human connections not written into the organisational charts. 'I started to make a list of what really drives the culture, which is how people behave on a regular, repeatable basis, and what they believe,' John Childress, consultant and author of the book Culture Rules![613] told us. 'Things started popping up that were not on the radar screen in most organisations.'

They include peer pressure, interpersonal relationships and crucially the role of informal leaders. There are also the embedded processes. 'The real critical examination of the policies and procedures that actually go on inside your organisation, whether it's budgeting process, whether it's meetings, whether it's hiring profiles, whether it's compensation formulas, whether it's review processes, all those things – nobody's taken a critical look at it in a long time.'[614]

The goal is to incentivise behaviour, as we saw at the insurance company Aviva where call centre staff were rewarded for solving problems, not merely taking calls quickly. It is not all about money. Recognition is often as important. Robert Chapman is the outspoken CEO of the US manufacturing company Barry-Wehmiller. He has made recognising employees' contributions central to a company culture that famously puts humans first. The group has successfully expanded to include a hundred companies round the world linked by the same business culture.[615]

Can there be a Wow! or Eureka moment in efforts to change culture?

Christiane Wuillamie offers critical pointers to how to achieve such moments on culture. She founded the IT services company CWB Systems in 1994. She grew it 100% year-on-year into a multi-million-pound enterprise before selling it in 2001. She sees her formula for success as having changed her own culture and leadership style. 'When you're a founder, you're pretty anal, autocratic, and think you're right all the time, until I discovered culture. We went through a culture transformation where the whole company went through experiential workshops based on our values. Every stage of the employee engagement process was linked to our values; from interviews, to on-boarding, to managing performance as well as exit. I also decided to ask for some volunteers to be our culture champions. Those are the kind of people who usually have a lot of what I'd call, some irritating, aspects, like overly creative, or the vocal shop steward who always complain. We channel their energy to being the leaders of our corporate culture. And when you turn those around, it's almost a magical effect.'[616]

Maintaining culture has to be seen as like watering a plant. It takes constant attention. But it brings positive results. 'We charged less, and we achieved 40% [profit],' said Christiane. 'That's a good culture margin. That is good culture, because what we did is that we don't use only our own resources, because we transform the client's staff. We just brought in the right kind of people to transform that staff.'

'You may think that's a clever commercial. But no. It's because we worked really hard at culture. We have such good culture that we infected the staff.'[617]

End notes

[613] op cit. *Culture rules!* by John R Childress.

[614] Interview with Christiane Wuillamie OBE and John R Childress, 22 March 2018.

[615] Bob Chapman and Barry-Wehmiller's cultural transformation story is described in *Leaders eat last* (2014) by Simon Sinek. London: Penguin. Also, *Everybody matters: the extraordinary power of caring for your people like family* (2015) by Bob Chapman and Raj Sisodia. London: Penguin.

[616] op cit. Interview with Christiane Wulliamie OBE and John R Childress, 22 March 2018.

[617] ibid.

45

DO YOU HAVE 'PURPOSE'?
IF SO, CAN YOU DEFINE IT?

Let's finally return to the word and concept **Purpose**. It emerged as a key new finding in our 2018 data crunch of leaders' anxieties and thoughts. They linked it closely to **Inclusivity/Diversity** and **Behaviour**.

For leaders, **Purpose** is the word of the moment. It is often used liberally in order to satisfy increasingly jittery shareholders and voters alike. It is designed to build new credibility and reduce scepticism about what companies and political institutions are really about.

Purpose is now the super-fashionable question to ask corporates about themselves. It is also the word that smart leaders want to be heard coming from their mouths and in company language.

But do those at the top who quote 'purpose' really appreciate what is required to justify its use?

A modest but growing number of leaders do realise there is pressure for defining the clear **purpose** of their company or institution. This means defining organisational **values** beyond just financial success and quarterly returns on capital. The new realisation is that purpose has to be 'lived'. It must never be about the kind of politically correct declaratory statements like Corporate Social Responsibility (CSR). CSR has become so commonplace, so devalued and so derided. Increasingly, customers and stakeholders see it as empty and unconvincing because of a conspicuous corporate failure to deliver more than politically correct words. CSR It was always loosely referred to in corporate and political statements, literature and annual reports in order to leave the right impression. But those who dug deeper found the commitment to such responsibility was often skin deep. Social responsibility was often labelled as lip service. It was derided as companies and institutions just going through the motions for show. Too often there was less genuine intent to be socially responsible than use of the phrase implied.

The same could easily happen to **Purpose**. Its fast-growing number of advocates give it a capital 'P' to denote what they call a 'socially-engaged conception of purpose that seeks to create value for a broad set of stakeholders.'[618]

But for the many reasons already detailed in this book, the new values bound up in this single word are both powerful and critical for the recalibration needed by leaders for thinking unthinkables. It is also going to be much more difficult to escape with honour if customers, shareholders and voters discover that **Purpose** is merely being used for window dressing without any genuine commitment to the concept.

Why is defining purpose so critical? 'Who are the leaders that are going to be successful tomorrow?' asked Paul Polman of Unilever.[619] They are 'the leaders that don't work for their own interest, but work for the common good. The leaders that can have a longer-term vision. The leaders that are driven by a deeper purpose so that they can take some more risks in doing so. So those are the ones that we need to nurture.'

Polman has seen off the naysayers and sceptics in Unilever. He remains a tireless advocate for putting a social purpose at the heart of the giant company's business strategy. He irritates many of his peers because of his relentless pressure on the issue. But gradually global events are encouraging more to join him, even if not so vocally or publicly yet.

Bound up in that one word 'purpose' is the idea that for companies to operate they need to be about much more than just shareholder value and quarterly numbers. It is about addressing inequalities and the growing disillusionment or anger of customers. Behind closed doors we have heard the deep concern of leaders. They accept that without a much more ambitious clarity of purpose the corporates, public service and political parties they work for will not retain the confidence of millennials and the Next Gen especially.

'It's only when you start to really press CEOs on precisely what is the purpose of their business that you realise that they often do not have a clear notion of it,' said Professor Colin Mayer of the Saïd Business School in Oxford. 'Or it often does boil down – in the case of publicly listed companies – to something about profit, rather than about companies producing goods and services that benefit us as customers and communities and, in the process, producing profits.'[620]

So increasingly companies will be expected to declare a set of goals beyond profits. More than ever, political parties will have to deliver on their promises to voters in elections. The days of assuming blind loyalty and allegiance are over. This must include how they engage with their workforce, suppliers, and wider society and the environment. But the fear remains that **Purpose** remains loose, convenient talk that often amounts to little more than declaratory or idealised statements. **Purpose** will only be mainstreamed when there is hard evidence that having strong values adds money and social value to the company. There is plenty of anecdotal evidence. But frequently this is not enough for hard-nosed investors, at least if they are looking for a hard-nosed return for their money.

Is there hard evidence yet on the new value of **Purpose**? Colin Mayer is leading the charge to find rigorous data on the Future of the Corporation through his work at Oxford Saïd and the British Academy. But he says: 'Until that's the case, it's going to be extremely difficult to persuade the investment community that they should be moving in this direction in a big way.'

This is despite the very clear signals on purpose now being sent by the public, which cannot and must not be ignored.

End notes

[618] *How can purpose reveal a path through disruption?* (2017) EY Beacon Institute.

[619] op cit. Paul Polman, 6 July 2015.

[620] Interview with Professor Colin Mayer. 1 May 2018.

46
IT'S THE GEOPOLITICS, STUPID

A final urging from Thinking the Unthinkable is to widen dramatically your perceptions. That means going well beyond largely conformist tram lines. It means embracing geopolitics with more than just politeness.

There has to be commitment and awareness. What happens in parts of the world that you have never visited, know very little about and probably rarely read of is now more important in this firmament of unthinkables than you probably even dare to imagine.

Ignore this at your peril.

Why? A remarkable reason why so many leaders expressed to us fear and the acute sense of being overwhelmed was their sense of powerlessness and inability to grip the implications of major geopolitical events. Geopolitics is defined loosely along the lines 'the studying of foreign policy to understand, explain and predict international political behaviour through geographical variables' or 'politics, especially international relations, as influenced by geographical factors'.

The narrowness of both vision, analysis and command of detail about unfolding global events surprised us. On occasions we were shocked. This is for the generation of leaders at the top. But the looming challenge for the millennials is even greater. It is also potentially more sinister.

Millennials have a new, exciting, roller coaster mix of instinctive anxiety and often untested wisdom. Many have deep and justified fears about the impact of climate change and the legacy being left to them by the current older generations. Our work has been constantly energised by talking and brainstorming with them in a host of different formats and locations.

But is there the experiential band width to appreciate the scale of adversity and threats to all they take for granted which this book has set out? After all, the NextGen are too young to have the battle scars from being forced to embrace such adversity. The increasingly backward leaning, retro nature of so many unthinkable geopolitical developments goes counter to so much of their natural optimism. It is very different from the deepening anxieties of those who grew up in a Cold War which had certain rules.

It is wonderful to have great start-up ambitions and to aspire to have a great idea which makes you super rich like Mark Zuckerberg of Facebook. But by his own admissions, Zuckerberg's wealth has not guaranteed him the fullest of wisdom. It generated a 'know-all' assumption of omnipotence and almost world domination. But the arrogance of being 'too idealistic and positive' meant he and Facebook became blinded to harsh realities like geopolitics.

Zuckerberg had to admit publicly to being too 'idealistic' and 'positive'. That is how he explained to the US Senate[621] the failures of him and his colleagues to scope the impact on their credibility from unthinkables or unpalatables on misuse of the personal data of up to 87 million account holders. But sinister forces in geopolitics now have to be assumed to be at work everywhere. They exploit what is fast being shown to be the naïveté of such idealism and positivism. They leave vicious ghosts, shadows and dark trails from their murky actions. For the next generation there is a massive cost to being naïve, 'positive and idealistic' about the true nature of these new threats. Being super connected in this digital world only a keystroke away with almost infinite access to information does not guarantee the vital understanding of global events, and their implications.

On geopolitics, throughout this Thinking the Unthinkable process we have found ourselves becoming wrapped in a paradox. We have had to ask frequently: how could two-thirds of leaders claim to a survey that they are super confident as confirmed by the PwC CEO Survey of January 2018? Yet at the same time they seemed to believe that the world beyond whatever is directly related to their work could be effectively marginalised, ignored or even deemed irrelevant.

Remember PwC Global chairman Bob Moritz's two sobering reflections from that survey. Firstly, many of these newly super confident CEOs don't know how to handle 'threats the business world is not used to tackling directly by itself'.[622] Secondly, CEOs 'fear wider social threats that they can't control ... in a fractured world'.[623] Both points were a warning to leaders: you are simply not broadminded enough, especially when it comes to the imperative to embrace geopolitics.

In other words, leaders are either too complacent, in denial or perhaps determined to kid themselves that everything is just fine. Yet both of these two shortcomings highlight an almost primeval new need to embrace the fast-changing realities of geopolitics far more energetically and willingly than is done currently. Geopolitics has profound implications for the ways business and governing are done, and in which the public expect leaders to lead. There is a certain cosiness that is convenient but also dangerous. It comes from leaders defining far too narrowly what is relevant for them and those that serve them in this new era of disruption. What they need to analyse and be aware of must be far broader.

Failure to institute this now carries a downright existential danger. The former US Secretary of State Condoleezza Rice reinforced that new imperative for having a far broader view. 'The top of the company has to be constantly vigilant about this. You know, one of the problems is nobody ever gets praise for stopping something that didn't happen. And so, your political risk people: . . . you feel like they are crying wolf. Listen to them. Get them into the board room. Get them into the C-suite. Be personally responsible as a CEO for understanding the risk environment. Because in this geopolitical environment, those risks are coming from multiple sources.'[624]

This means there is no option but to redefine the horizons of geopolitics. Not to do so is negligent. The lines of sight must be recalibrated. So must the assessments of risk. This may be out of the comfort zone for many leaders. But in so many ways this re-definition is not an option. It is a necessity. Everyone has to be worried about the implications of geopolitics. They cannot be ignored or waved away just because leaders claim not to understand them or see their relevance. They will affect us all in one way or another. The NextGen too have to come to terms with this.

For example, Russia's use of what it calls 'new generation warfare (NGW)' or 'political warfare'[625] may seem an obscure, distant irritation. But it is a far-wider challenge that goes well beyond the studious fascination of policy wonks and think tankers. These are existential geopolitical challenges to the nature of society as we assume it will remain. That is why geopolitical issues like these must be a wakeup call both for every leader and those they serve, whether that is customers or voters. Both kinds of warfare, and much more, are threatening the durability and stability of all that we take for granted.

So without creating alarm or derision, governments must find ways to alert their publics that geopolitics and threats from elsewhere could very swiftly affect their lives and the lives of every citizen. As with so many unthinkables, the assumption of positive can turn to negatives dramatically quickly. Towards the start of the third decade of this 21st century, geopolitical threats won't be happening on remote battlefields. They are more than likely to be digital and invisible. They could readily have a profound disruptive impact on so much that is just around us and taken for granted in the community where we live and work.

Supplies of the main utilities like electricity, gas and water are at risk. So is the reliability of phones or computers. This is not to be alarmist. The highest levels in the security services say that this is now far more sinister and uncertain than during the Cold War. Adversaries led by Russia have already revealed both their new capacities and their new intent to use them. Therefore smart governments and corporates which are seized of these new realities of geopolitics have taken action.

In August 2016, for example, the German Interior Ministry published a warning document that encouraged people to stockpile supplies of food for ten days and water for five days, and prepare for possible military conscription.[626] The alert was justified. But it was derided in large sections of the public and many parts of the media as merely Hamsterkaeufe – an invitation for hoarding and panic buying.[627]

The implication of these new geopolitical realties is that the stability and security of society is at risk. There has to be a new and wider definition of 'national security'. This means the credibility and effectiveness of leaders too. Very quickly the confidence of the public and next generation in those leading them could collapse. And the danger is that these growing geopolitical pressures will deepen what are already growing structural instabilities in society.

This is not just an alert generated originally by this **Thinking the Unthinkable** project based on what leaders confidentially told us. It has now been coming from some of the most senior global chairs and CEOs like Joe Kaeser of Siemens, Larry Fink of BlackRock, Steve Schwartzman of The Blackstone Group, Indra Nooyi of Pepsico and Paul Polman of Unilever. Others have also begun saying it, but not quite so publicly – at least not yet, and certainly not with the push that is needed.

So once again, in tune with the red alert on the cover and right at the start of this whole book: ignore their warnings at your peril. These leaders are not being alarmist to grab headlines. In their view the viability and survivability of society as we have come to know it – plus their huge business enterprises – is at ever greater risk. This is an existential threat, and it does not matter which generation you come from.

Remember the warning at the start of the book from Chris Donnelly from the Institute for Statecraft. 'The rate of change we are going through at the moment is comparable to that which happens in wartime. We have change at war rates, yet we think we are at peace.' This confirms the scale of recalibration needed, and the speed. It is about coming to new senses.

This why you must view the geopolitical implications of a new warfare as not being about weapons and kinetic explosive force as we currently know them. Neither is it about warfare as we currently think of it. It is about warfare to destabilise society in ways that have been revolutionised by the advent of AI, plus the use of sophisticated techniques to influence public opinion and to exploit social divisions. The report on the malicious use of AI warned of 'improved capacity to analyse human behaviours, moods, and beliefs on the basis of available data. These concerns are most significant in the context of authoritarian states, but may also undermine the ability of democracies to sustain truthful public debates.'[628]

The implication for geopolitics is this. At a time when established democracies are deeply divided with processes that are under threat, how can democratic and corporate procedures and systems be modernised to be able to cope with new existential threats that are hurtling towards us all? Whichever way they point, the eventual findings of the biggest investigation into Russian efforts to influence the 2016 US presidential election by Special Counsel Robert Mueller are likely to be political dynamite. One way or another it must be assumed that they will transform the thinking about external threats and the new geopolitics.

Remember what Chris Donnelly said next: 'The global pace of change is overcoming the capacity of national and international institutions.' Therefore in light of this new geopolitical reality, institutions and corporates must change.

In the US, to forestall further Russian malicious in the US mid term elections in November 2018, ordinary state-level election officials are attending intensive cyber security training sessions. The priority is to ensure that 'outside adversaries are not able to create a population of Americans that for the rest of their lives will believe the election was stolen from them,' Alex Stamos, Facebook's chief security officer told a cyber security bootcamp in Spring 2018.[629]

The new geopolitical threats are not just from Russia. There are multiple state-sponsored threats from many points on the global compass. Despite the new and extraordinary pace of détente, there remains sharp attention on North Korean expertise on cyber warfare. It is the same for concerns about Iran's growing digital prowess. China is under a tight spotlight because of the risk in the West from using technology supplied by companies like Huawei or ZTE. There are also the relentless commercial and political tentacles from the irrepressible 'Belt and Road' strategy.

The threats are not just from governments and business. There are also consumers and citizens. This is how Ciaran Martin, head of the UK National Cyber Security Centre, characterised the new geopolitics. 'We also see terrorists, hacktivists and lone operators, many of them operating in the propaganda space. And we are conscious, as so-called securocrats, of the risk of being seen to overstate a threat.'[630]

The challenge is not about the system. It is about human capabilities to accept and adapt what one CEO described as the multiple disruptions that are 'invading our existence'. This is why we remind you of the seven words we shared with you on page 20. They underpin the way forward for **Thinking the Unthinkable**. They are **culture, mindset, behaviour** plus a new **purpose** and **values** which can be achieved through greater **courage** and **humility**. Easy words. Much harder to achieve. But so vital.

Having held on tight through our analysis, now you can release the grip a little and allow the blood to circulate. This is the moment to Get Real in the face of the new unthinkables and unpalatables. Here are our suggestions for what to do.

End notes

[621] op cit. Mark Zuckerberg, 10 April 2018.

[622] op cit. Bob Moritz, 22 January 2018.

[623] op cit. PwC CEO Survey, 22 January 2018. To recap, they are 'extremely concerned' about geopolitical uncertainty (40%), cyber threats (40%), terrorism (41%), availability of key skills (38%) and populism (35%). Most tellingly, these threats outpace familiar concerns about business growth prospects such as exchange rate volatility (29%) and changing consumer behaviour (26%).

[624] Condoleezza Rice interviewed by Fox News, on 1 May 2018 about her book *Political risk how business and organisations anticipate global insecurity* (2018) Co-authored with Amy Zegart. London: Weidenfeld and Nicholson.

[625] op cit. *Modern political warfare* by Linda Robinson et al.

[626] 'So will die Bundesregierung im Kriegsfall reagieren' [in German], *Frankfurter Allgemeine*, 21 August 2016.

[627] 'Germans told to stockpile food and water for civil defence', *BBC News* website.

[628] op cit. *The malicious use of artificial intelligence*, 20 February 2018.

[629] 'America vs hackers' by Hannah Kuchler, *Financial Times*, 28/29 April 2018.

[630] Ciaran Martin, Chief Executive of the UK National Cyber Security Centre, speech at Billington Summit, Washington DC, 13 September 2016.

47

TAKEAWAYS FOR THE TAKE OFF

We remind you: our ambition in sharing this red alert must be to thrive on change and disruption, not to be destabilised and overwhelmed as many are.

Are you still holding tight?

Have we captured your professional anxieties? In doing so, have we actually reassured you that your fears are justified and that you are not alone?

Has this red alert opened your eyes and minds to where we have reached, and where you (and we) are all probably heading? It should have.

You kindly read this book to join us in understanding the acute stresses for leaders who feel they are operating blindfolded when confronting unthinkables. Look at the image on the front cover. Are you struggling for direction like those blindfolded leaders? Has the cartoonist correctly captured how you and your colleagues feel?

All of our red alert is based on hard evidence and data, not just a conspiratorial wish to promote controversy and polemics. Have we helped you think more actively about how you will think unthinkables? In this maelstrom of disruption, are you more content and at ease? Even reassured?

Are you now at one with the fact that the 'normal' you know and take for granted is vaporising fast and heading all you know in different directions? While increasingly anxious, are you at ease now because you realise more completely that the new normal is abnormal, and that your journey forward into the unknown of new disruptions is only just beginning?

We ask: do you now believe that is possible? If the answer is yes then we would like to know and celebrate what you have achieved, and how. Yes, we want to hear and to celebrate because so far you are in a tiny minority. Most leaders have got nowhere near that point yet! So please get in touch.

At the start of this book we wrote that the aim must be to thrive on this new scale of change, not be derailed by it. We urged that this unprecedented scale of disruption must create new positives and opportunities for you. But in order to thrive you also have to realise the sinister scale of what is unfolding, and the even more unthinkable direction in which things seem likely to travel next.

For the reasons we have laid out here – including the extensive evidence we have assembled – the new 'normal' – whatever it is – is sending bleak signals. Too many sinister unknowns and uncertainties now threaten the relatively stable and secure rhythm of life that most of us have been lucky enough to take for granted. Principles, nations and institutions are under threat and being shredded. 'Do not diminish or forget the danger of this moment,' warned former US Secretary of State John Kerry. 'Many seem to have lost the awareness of peace's fragility.'[631]

After all, a short time ago, who imagined that Putin's Russia would use a military nerve agent in a Western country, leading to further disturbance of an already increasingly strained geopolitical balance? Who thought that with all its clout and global ubiquity, Facebook's value and credibility would be felled by a massive commercial abuse of what is meant to be the confidential data of 87 million subscribers? Even FB's founder and CEO Mark Zuckerberg never believed that.[632]

But again, under the Al Jolson warning – 'You ain't heard anything yet' – the scale and nature of disruption must be assumed to be in its early stages. There is much more to come of disturbingly unknown scale and direction. It will further threaten stability and conformity. There is no evidence to suggest otherwise.

Are you locked in to the new reality? Are you ready? Are you prepared? Will you continue to hold tight?

If you disagree then we would appreciate very much hearing from you (via www.thinkunthink.org). That is the new process and community we have created for both sharing and debating these new leadership challenges in the face of the new disruption and uncertainty.

And if our conclusions from the evidence are wrong or need to be more nuanced, then please challenge us and share the reasons. We need to know why. That is because we follow the data, not our whims and assumptions.

As we said during the first impromptu coffee meeting at the very start of the project in 2014 we did not set out to find skewed evidence that conveniently fitted our hunch from 2014. We looked for evidence from leaders themselves. We asked them to volunteer their views. What were their private anxieties? What were they thinking? Huge numbers have been generous with their time and analysis. None – we repeat none – were reassuring.

We have converged that data and shared our analysis up to this point. A combination of what they said individually and what the aggregated data showed have framed what we wrote and where we took you in this book. They define what our takeaways are for you now. Soon you will be prepared for take-off into this new unknown of disruption. But you do not have to be on your own. You can join the expanding **Thinking the Unthinkable** process and community where you can exchange experiences and options.

After our hundreds of interviews and conversations, plus the search for examples and case studies, we do not believe there are off-the-peg solutions. Gone are the days when leaders can assume they will reach ready solutions in the lofty heights of their C-suite offices, then pass them down the executive tree for implementation. Instead there is an urgent imperative for new options to be created by experimentation and risk taking involving staff, contractors and stakeholders at all levels.

We remind you of Peter Ho's view which we cited right at the start. He is the distinguished former head of Singapore's civil service who spent his career pioneering new thinking about risk. For many of today's challenges he says 'there are no immediate or obvious solutions, because nobody can agree on what the problems are in the first place, never mind what the solution should be. Additionally, geopolitics is producing wicked problems, because of the inherent complexity of nations, governments, and politics.'[633] We have found no grounds to contest or modify this view – at least for the moment.

Peter Ho challenges the temptation to try to break down problems into bite sized chunks. 'More likely than not there will be different organisations managing only parts of the larger problem. This is because when we try to understand our complex world we often try to break it down into simpler subsets that are easier to understand it. We hope [that] when we aggregate it, we will produce results that approximate the real world.'[634]

Peter Ho advocates 'an approach in which information from all sources is shared across disciplines and across sectors. Then they need to be evaluated holistically. In other words, complex situations should be studied as a whole and not just in their parts. This approach helps to connect the dots by thinking broadly, then by considering how different events, drivers, and agents interact with each other. We can see the larger picture and obtain a better fix on the possible outcomes. In responding to wicked problems, such an approach is not just desirable, it is absolutely critical.'[635]

We share Peter Ho's vision that the dots have to be connected to make sense of the many challenges we are facing and will face in the near future.

This means that, 'the purpose of leadership in a wicked problem world has to change', according to Patricia Seemann[636] of the 3am Group. Nowadays it is about 'becoming the one figuring out what the best way is to frame problems, what the most important questions are to be asked'. This must involve a radically new approach and attitude that many leaders find hard to accept, let alone introduce. It involves engaging many more staff and stakeholders in decision-making. Barriers to sharing thinking and even maverick or wacky ideas must be removed. There must be open, risk free encouragement to share insights and hunches. Top down barriers to internal communications and open engagement must be removed. There must be an end to a deferential hierarchy by age and experience: often the youngest and latest into the organisation have the sharpest thoughts. Additionally, there needs to be direct access to the widest possible number of sensors and analysts, however unorthodox they might be.

In summary, there is an imperative to change fundamentally not just organisational systems but also human capacities. It means deep changes to 'the way we are structured, organised, the way we share information, the way we process information, the way we reward people, the way we take risk and analyse risk. [It is about] the way we organise what is up, what is strategic, what is not, what is tactical. Who has the right to do what, what type of control,'[637] said one exceptional leader currently in the throes of a top-to-bottom refit of an organisation distinguished by its extraordinary complexity.

This is exactly what we discovered in our case studies. They have confirmed how risk-taking and experimenting – when it happens - have led to important positives. But often, new disruptions then suddenly forced new handbrake turns to the left or right, followed by major reassessments which have then undermined experimental progress achieved. This is the adaptive approach that Piyush Gupta, CEO of the bank DBS in Singapore has taken. He was rebuilding and transforming the bank successfully. Then new realities meant he smartly had to switch it into thinking and reacting like a start-up.

Hopefully your own leaders' insights and thinking can now be added as new lily pads of hope or experience. Even allowing for commercial sensitivities, you can share them via our dynamic **Thinking the Unthinkable** e-community. That process will now be taken forward via a constantly updated digital platform which will be parallel to all we have shared in this book.

We wrote at the start: your aim should be to disrupt yourself. Your ambitions should create a new **culture, mindset** and **behaviour**, with new **purpose, values, courage** and **humility**. We urged you to bear in mind these seven words at all times as you read the book. That remains our core encouragement for you going forward.

Under the rubric of those seven key words we highlighted for you on the first page of the book, let's bring together these takeaways for you. They explain how you can change your **culture, mindset** and **behaviour** by following the TTU Progressions. They will generate new **purpose** and **values**. To do this requires **courage** and **humility**.

It is not quite the 'toolkit' suggested by the CEO in the final case study. But it is a series of steps and progressions that have been shown to be worthy of very serious consideration:

1. First you need to move out of the **status quo of conformity**. This is the root problem which we outline in this book. It is what leaders themselves told us is a key blocker. Conformity constrains. It prevents leaders from understanding both the scale of the disruption and how to handle it.

2. To unblock the blockers, you need to **understand the external reality** of the extraordinary, disrupted world which now threatens us all with so much that is new and unthinkable.

3. The parallel priority is to **understand and calibrate honestly your internal reality.** What blocks you or your organisation from dealing successfully with the new external and internal challenges you confront, often unexpectedly?

4. Having scoped them, **address your challenges**. Then establish new, imaginative and appropriate ways to deal with disruption. Be bold and brave. Create a new culture, mindset and behaviour.

5. This is not a single one-off process. You need to **continue iterating, experimenting and taking risks with unknowns in order to thrive on change**. You must adapt continually to varying circumstances. You must constantly work to understand how new challenges will affect you, then work up new ways that mean you can adapt and deal with them.

In this book we have shared with you our data and analysis of the external realities that threaten organisations and individuals. We have seen how companies, institutions and above all their people in our case studies have worked up adaptive ways to deal with unthinkables. This creates precedents and options for all leaders to test.

What now follows are the lessons and learning you can take away from what has been learnt so far.

Don't freak and push back at the prospect of digesting another list! This is the sharp and direct way to transmit our findings to you, especially including the positives.

GRIP THE EXTERNAL REALITIES
Move forward positively by . . .

- **Accepting**
  - that new realities and disruption are from a new world you have neither experienced nor prepared for.
  - that failure to think unthinkables could swiftly kill your company or institution.
  - that conformist cultures, behaviour and mindset do not produce the value which many will now want and expect.
  - that global, political and economic stability is not guaranteed.

- **Understanding**
  - that in the interests of self-preservation the instability of the new global geopolitics must now be at the heart of all your analysis and calculations.
  - that the survival of 'capitalism' and its methods are also not as guaranteed as you assume. Remarkably, this is confirmed by leading 'capitalists' themselves.

- **Acknowledging**
  - that algorithms and AI will have a profound impact on the nature and scale of all the human activity that you, your colleagues and those who work for you take for granted.
  - the likelihood that AI and new digital developments will generate significant joblessness, greater inequality, a hollowing out of the middle classes, and a widening of the gap between rich and poor. Above all it threatens a scale of social instability and national insecurity that both corporate and political leaders will find they are increasingly unable to control.

GRIP INTERNAL REALITIES : ADDRESS YOUR OWN CHALLENGES

You must be honest with yourself.

First you must understand what Is affecting you. Then you must grip what is blocking you from moving ahead with profound change. You must admit frankly what you face, and its scale. The challenge is the same as for an alcoholic who can only deal with alcoholism once he or she acknowledges having the addiction. Only then can you take the kind of positive action that should bring about the kind of significant change that is needed.

This will mean urgently modifying the culture, mindset and behaviour in your organisation. You will also make significant progress by focusing on purpose, values, courage and humility in the original and innovative ways we highlighted in our case studies.

Our recommendations to you can be achieved by embracing a new courage and humility as a leader. This must involve a very personal commitment.

This means significant change on the following.

PURPOSE AND VALUES:

- **Establishing** a clear purpose and values that allow you to escape the short-term pressure of shareholder value and quarterly numbers. Then you will develop a long-term sustainable strategy.
- **Realising**
  - you must modify culture, behaviour and mindset in probably dramatic ways.
  - that the next generation wants your organisation to have a new social purpose and values. The millennials expect this.
  - that if you don't have social purpose and values, the next generation will probably shun you and your products.

COURAGE:

- **Creating** processes and an atmosphere to think unthinkables. You will not have them yet.

- **Planning** for adversity, shock and events that have never been on your radar screen.

- **Working out** how to make sure they are always on that radar screen and monitored 24/7.

- **Taking** bold steps to invest in experimentation and redefining risk.

- **Labelling** it a success to have tried new ideas to engage unthinkables, and never even hinting at retribution or accusations of 'failure' if they don't work out.

- **Accepting** that being 'wacky' or 'maverick' are big positives to be nurtured and encouraged, not suppressed and marginalised.

- **Embracing** what you may regard as 'wacky', 'maverick' or 'bonkers' ideas that you never dared to consider.

- **Removing** any risk that speaking out or having new ideas could be a career limiting move.

- **Never** even hinting at retribution or accusations of 'failure' if new ideas to engage unthinkables don't work out. It must always be labelled a success to have tried.

- **Experimenting** and venturing outside the conformist comfort zone which made you a leader.

- **Developing** new, comfortable ideas and processes from those uncomfortable realities.

- **Incubating** a new startup culture, whether internal or at arm's length.

- **Regarding** as a possible friend any new competition that might kill you – 'Engage the Frenemy!'

HUMILITY:

- **Changing** how you lead. Stop assuming you have to be a superhero – it's just killing you!

- **Involving**, encouraging and engaging staff.

- **Harnessing** the insights, fears and resentments of the Next Generation.

- **Regarding** your staff as your consultants, not the big consulting contractors who listen to what you say, feed it back and then charge huge fees for your own ideas.
- **Listening** to staff and generations at every level. They probably have better ideas than you!
- **Removing** any risk that speaking out or having new ideas could be a career-limiting move.
- **Accepting** that customers, consumers, employees, contractors, shareholders, stakeholders and voters expect much more say in what you do and why.

If all of this seems daunting and overwhelming, then yes it is. We understand that. But it is in line with scale of disruption and unthinkables. But once again: please remember that you are not alone. So come together with your peers to share what you know and what you have tried. You will find that your anxieties are the same as those of the vast majority of leaders. Stability and reassurance must not be assumed to be guaranteed any more.

How can you gain some reassurance? Remember too that his book is just a drop-dead publishing moment. The dynamic process of research and investigating case studies continues. You can opt for positive engagement by becoming a lily pad in the infinite lily pond of new dynamic thinking about unthinkables. As you read this, the process and community for facilitating this are being scaled up to empower the sharing of experiences like yours. This will allow you and your leadership peers to no longer feel alone in being 'scared' or 'overwhelmed'.

Join us![638] Share your experiences and tell us more. Remain in touch and connected via www.thinkunthink.org. Many others want to know how you have either been licking your wounds or benefiting from massive new opportunities as you confront future disruption and challenges. And together you can all learn to think the unthinkable and thrive on change.

And remember what we wrote at the start. This is not just about current leaders. It is also for those who aspire to be leaders or care about why leadership is being so destabilised by the new scale and nature of disruptions. They must be warmly welcomes into this process.

End notes

[631] op cit. John Kerry, 8 July 2017.

[632] op cit. Mark Zuckerberg, 10 April 2018.

[633] op cit. Peter Ho, 17 July 2017.

[634] ibid.

[635] ibid.

[636] Conversation with Patricia Seemann, 19 May 2015.

[637] Off-the-record interview with leader of an international humanitarian organisation, 10 April 2015.

[638] www.thinkunthink.org

48
FINAL THOUGHT

Maybe this is all too much! Maybe you want to clear your addled mind.

OK. Don't confine yourself to the relatively safe space of a committee room or executive water cooler in your C-suite. Head instead for open spaces like the beaches, hills or mountains. A walk and offloading of fears and anxieties with your colleagues and peers will probably work wonders.

We have done just that with top executives, investors and a host of radical thinkers on risk in a setting below the peaks of Mont Blanc above the French town of Chamonix.[639] It is a fantastic non-PC concept which does not go down so well with corporate or government scrutiny committees. But in al fresco locations like this we have watched executives talk and listen. Their thinking has been refreshed in new ways. All of us have benefited and been invigorated by a couple of days with our bodies and brains at new altitudes of thinking and reflection.

The convivial solution we all discovered is not to be found in grand, worthy business books or tightly choreographed conferences, Davos-style, behind oppressive security. It is in meetings like the Summit of Minds with the opportunity to go walking – and talking. And walking is what the founder and organisers of that wonderful executive gathering in Chamonix believe is the solution that allows leaders to really think the unthinkable.

We agree.

Having read our book, you should read theirs![640] It will help liberate you to think unthinkables.

---

[639] Summit of Minds conference held in Chamonix in September each year.

[640] *Ten good reasons to go for a walk* (2017) [E-book] by Thierry and Mary Anne Malleret. Pennsauken, NJ: BookBaby.

APPENDIX

WHAT LEADERS TOLD US.

OUR METHODOLOGY FOR ANALYSING INTERVIEWS AND TRANSCRIPTS

Since 2014 the **Thinking the Unthinkable** project has collected qualitative data from many leaders and other sources. At the time of writing there are transcripts from more than a hundred formal interviews and nine contemporaneous notes of conversations. Additionally there are transcripts from about 40 public events and interviews on radio and TV programmes, plus some 60 handwritten notebooks from the conversations and chats which Nik and Chris had with leaders. Considerable resources have been used to ensure the accuracy of the data. All transcripts have been re-checked against the original audio recordings in 2017-2018. This dataset is being constantly increased and updated. A total of 2495 pages of text have been analysed. In social science research this is regarded as a large, 'meaty' dataset by any standards.

We set out to enrich and substantiate our initial findings published in February 2016 and to test our original working assumptions. We analysed the data using a combination of text mining,[641] discourse and content analysis. We then used multiple analytic methods to complement each other.[642] This process is known as triangulation.

The software programme was NVivo version 12 Plus. The NVivo tools enabled us to see 'the big picture fast'. Through a combination of its automatic insight features, and our own interpretation, we gained rich, granular insights from our dataset.

To authenticate and peer review our analysis, we consulted Dr Christina Silver, co-founder and Director of Qualitative Data Analysis Services (QDAS). She is a Research Fellow at the University of Surrey. She helped us challenge our own assumptions, plan the data analysis and then achieve our research aims through NVivo. Christina emphasised the importance of the initial planning phase in order to identify the themes for analysis and subsequent manual coding. This would ensure our findings were robust, and that we got the most out of NVivo's processing capabilities. She is continuing to provide ongoing advice to **Thinking the Unthinkable** on the use of NVivo for our data analysis.

The large and diverse data sample allowed us to increase the generalisability, external validity and reliability of our initial findings. Our project researcher, Didi Ogede, began by inputting and then manually coding 20% of the transcripts. She identified the words and phrases which reflected more than 60 key themes about leadership which we wanted to test against our original, more subjective findings published in February 2016 which identified nine priority emerging themes.

In a second phase of this process of evaluation, Didi then used NVivo's pattern-coding features[643] to identify the same themes among the remaining 80% of the dataset. She did not blindly accept NVivo's assessment. She reviewed all the data segments it suggested. Based on her initial careful coding, she then refined the results to 'clean' the data and ensure greater accuracy.

During the first round of analysis, coding focused on 26 themes. The results corroborated the nine key concepts we first identified in February 2016. In doing so they substantiated the overarching assertions and conclusions about the new vulnerabilities of leadership which we made at that time.

Our next stage of updated and statistically rigorous analysis concluded in April 2018. It identified 'short-termism' as a dominant concern among leaders. More than 80% of our sample (103 interviewees) mentioned it. In addition, 'institutional conformity' and 'groupthink' were highlighted by more than 65% of our sample. The themes of 'fear', 'risk aversion' and 'wilful blindness' were also frequently mentioned by 58–62% of the sample. 'Confused', 'cognitive dissonance' and 'overload' were also volunteered frequently (by between 46–54% of the sample) 'Fear of career-limiting moves' was raised by more than 40% of the sample. 'Behaviour' was referred to by more than 50% of our sample. Importantly, this indicated that leaders acknowledge certain behaviours and attitudes among themselves and within their organisations.

Only three out of the original nine themes did not emerge in the top 10 of our systematic re-analysis. They were 'overwhelmed', 'reactionary mindsets' and 'denial'. The latter two were not included in the initial coding (of 26 themes). 'Overwhelmed' was very close to making the top ten.

A second round of data analysis is the backbone for this book. It included all transcripts plus data from other sources (notes of conversations, radio & TV programmes, and public events). It showed again that 'short-termism' was a dominant concern. 60% of our leaders mentioned it. 'Confused' and 'fear' were volunteered by more than 48%. The next to be mentioned was 'Risk aversion'. Important new issues were 'inclusivity and diversity', and 'purpose' were also frequently mentioned.

Of significant importance is the fact that new themes emerged, led by 'purpose', and 'inclusivity and diversity', plus 'overwhelmed'. The new appearance of purpose, inclusivity and diversity since 2016 reflects the fast growing awareness on these issues by a growing number of leaders, especially in the corporate sector.

This time, four out of our initial nine themes were not in the top 10: 'fear of career-limiting moves', 'wilful blindness', 'reactionary mindsets' and 'denial'. (The latter two themes were not included in coding of the 26 themes, so they were not tested using our data.)

The difference in results is explained by two factors. First is the far-wider data sources included in this 2018 sample. Second is the fact that some characteristics in the original conclusions in 2016 were subjective aggregations of impressions by the authors. These phrases did not always fit neatly into the NVivo coding protocols. So the phrases were not coded for the NVivo data crunching process. This does not devalue what each phrase identifies. It does not mean it is no longer valid. It is a realistic acceptance that what makes a good descriptive cannot necessarily be matched in the data-coding process.

In conclusion, our analytic strategy facilitated by NVivo enabled us to refine and reinforce our initial hypothesis. We were also able to generalise our findings. Therefore we can be confident that the original subjective 'hunch' which catalysed this project from 2014 was largely correct. The issues for leaders have become wider, deeper and more negative than in 2014 and our interim study in 2016. There are therefore solid grounds to conclude that leaders continue to struggle and worry about their new vulnerabilities in this age of deepening disruption.

End notes

[641] Text mining is the analysis of data contained in natural language text. The application of text mining techniques to solve business problems is called text analytics.

[642] Ahmed, A and Sil, R (2012) 'When multi-method research subverts methodological pluralism – or, why we still need single-method research', *Perspectives on Politics* 10 (4) pp. 935–948.

[643] Pattern coding is a way of grouping summaries into a smaller number of sets, themes, or constructs.

ACKNOWLEDGEMENTS

World developments, the pace of change and unthinkables, plus the scale of global disruption mean that we had to make sure this book is as timely and up-to-date as is humanly possible. We have met our aim and ambition!

The 100,000 words were written in 12 weeks. The manuscript was edited and published in five weeks, with updates inserted in the manuscript as late as 16 May.

Nik and Chris achieved this not just by way of long days and nights of writing. The project started as an idea over coffee in early 2014. By mid 2018 there was significant backing from a growing team. They were hired to help meet the exponentially growing demand and expectations for the results of our ongoing research project and process.

First, we thank our publisher, Alex Sharratt of John Catt Educational. He and his colleagues rose brilliantly to the challenge of producing this book at a super-fast speed. They helped us disrupt the usual publishing timeframe. We applaud their enthusiasm, ambition and flexibility. Alex said 'Yes' to our ambitious ideas. Our editor Jonathan Woolgar and designer Rebecca Bafico worked calmly and at speed to ensure our manuscript became this book while the world around us kept being disrupted by unthinkables. Sarajane Woolf worked super-fast to complete the index.

Our agent Caroline Michel at Peter Fraser and Dunlop encouraged us to keep going when we discovered that conventionally minded publishers would not experiment with the super-fast aims we had. These include developing an e-platform in parallel with the book in order to sharpen its relevance as we took forward the concept as a living project. Thank you to Tessa David and Dan Heron at PFD for helping us to pull this off.

The **Thinking the Unthinkable** team is now a diverse, multi-generational group. Each member has played a vital role.

Our editorial consultant Sam Whipple brought his expertise in change management on a huge number of organisational and digital fronts. He ensured order and new confidence as we scaled up our work and structured the book.

Two millennials joined us in early 2018 for the heavy lifting and scaling up of the project. Rebecca Geach, our project coordinator, has provided vital support to implement Sam's plans on multiple and disparate fronts. We especially thank our researcher Didi Ogede for the quality of her analysis and energy. With a looming book deadline, she willingly allowed her life to be taken over by two intense months of data crunching, validating our interviews and challenging our interpretations. In support, our independent data adviser and reviewer Dr Christina Silver showed us that high-quality data analysis is about clarity of purpose and thinking. In addition, Gus Mitchell developed a research stream relating to the Cape Town water crisis.

Consultant Ali Willis joined us to work on our thought leadership progressions that respond to the requests from anxious leaders, corporates and institutions about 'How can you help us?' or 'What can you do?'

Our design consultants Carley Bowman and Jon Elliman worked long, intense hours to design the **Thinking the Unthinkable** branding. They also developed the innovative web platform www.thinkunthink.org that accompanies this book. It is a vital new tool that complements the book and the ebook/Kindle edition. It takes forward the whole new process we are developing for **Thinking the Unthinkable** into the future. Carley's additional role building the content has been especially valued.

In late 2017 our researcher Lydia Bethan Brown convinced us that we must jump in at the deep end and analyse all our data. Lydia initiated the first huge task of re-checking, line by line, more than 2500 pages of transcripts. This was led by our virtual PA, Christine Southam. Christine's company headed a small 'transcript taskforce' of Suzie Lacon, Julie Hudson and others in meticulous cross-checking. We now appreciate the full value of what seemed at the outset to be a terrifyingly huge piece of work to undertake. We now realise it was vital to strengthen the credibility of the results which first surprised, but now largely reassure so many leaders.

Our first millennial team member, Magda Dybał, gave us valuable support and new determination to scale up the project in late 2016. She taught us a great deal about embracing the start-up mentality. She also brought her formidable Polish network of contacts into play to help us create our database.

Zahid Mahmoud is an IT 'star'. He is always unflappable, developed our first website, and helped us overcome innumerable IT issues as the digital goal posts kept moving. Malissa Taylor Saks set us up on social media. Stiv Twigg shot and produced the videos we are still using to explain the project. Andy Łodziński curated animated graphics and edited our video. In our first three years, Vicky Townshend worked often day and night to transcribe our interviews with absolute discretion.

An important element of the projection of our findings is social media. Alex Just and his team from Pagefield Global Counsel of Nadia Asfour, Maxine Stott, and Kieran Nagendran provided the design then the spine of our daily profile via Twitter, Instagram, LinkedIn and Facebook.

Three people who tragically are no longer with us gave us enormous inspiration when so many others at top levels were sceptical and could not believe our findings. Dr Sylke Tempel was killed in a thunderstorm near Berlin. She was the first leading think tank editor to 'get' thinking the unthinkable. Sylke rushed our first article into the German foreign policy journal *International Politik* in January 2016. Thereby she put our findings on the leadership map. Dame Helen Alexander was the first woman CBI President. She made time before she began her cancer treatment to give one of our most encouraging and insightful conversations. Professor Jean-Pierre Lehmann of the IMD business School in Lausanne was an indefatigable advocate of all we were uncovering. He defied the professional sceptics and determinedly mentioned our findings in any article whenever he could until shortly before his death before Christmas 2017.

The engagement of Dr Noel Tagoe – then the Vice President for Education at CIMA (now the AICPA) – was critical when we produced our first draft in August 2015. He too defied the professional sceptics who could not believe our findings and wanted them ignored. He insisted our first interim findings had to be published in February 2016. Thank you again, Noel. We also thank Noel's former colleague Naomi Smith, who entertained us in several interviews as she guided us through culture and change in management accountancy.

Almost all of our hundreds of interviews and conversations were conducted anonymously. We would like to name so many for the extraordinary insights and frankness they have shared with us. However, that would breach our understanding with them. You know who you are. Thank you. And if at any time you would like to break cover as the mood around unthinkables changes, then please tell us.

Some we can thank, however, as we battled uphill against conformity and scepticism. Professor Lord Nicholas Stern and Lord Martin Rees have provided unswerving encouragement and support, especially when they detected that we were finding the going was tough. So have Professor Sir Cary Cooper, Dr Parag Khanna and Professor Sir Lawrence Freedman. We give special mention for the first time to Dame Mariot Leslie, a former senior ambassador and director of top portfolios at the Foreign and Commonwealth Office. It was her insight in 2015 that led us to modify the working title from *Thinking the Unthinkable* to *Thinking the Unpalatable*.

We have enormous appreciation for their flow of comments and thoughts especially Nick Stern for his foreword. Aniket Shah has been a millennial inspiration since we first made contact in 2015. We are thrilled by the two forewords that show how **Thinking the Unthinkable** is a challenge of multi-generational dimensions.

Dame Judith Hackitt generously gave us a two-hour interview on a scorching day. Her encouragement to keep pushing against the conventional thinking remains an inspiration.

Thierry Mallaret energised us with his extraordinary gathering of leaders in the French Alps. His Summit of Minds and his Monthly Barometer newsletters have helped those at the top re-assess how they work and think. We have benefited too. Ever since we began **Thinking the Unthinkable**, Patricia Seemann, has patiently shared and explained the best thinking on leadership and wicked problems. She has been hugely generous with her time and ideas. Sir Jeremy Greenstock and Nick Greenstock of Gatehouse Advisory Partners provided inspiration and cautionary advice on business strategy. Professor Colin Mayer of the Oxford Saïd Business School is a champion of Purpose for leaders. We have gratefully watched, monitored and moved forward in his slipstream of wisdom. Dr Andrew White, Associate Dean for Executive Education at Saïd has been equally encouraging, especially with his own new thinking on the 'twin peaks' threatening leadership. Norman Pickavence CEO of Tomorrow's Company has been ready to share new thinking on reconnecting leaders who are fearful of all that is now threatening.

These acknowledgements are not conceived as a roll call, even though they might read that way. But it is vital to recognise the many who have given or facilitated new insights for the project, especially because of the gatherings they have convened.

We mention especially Michael Ignatieff, Sean Cleary, Rick Haythornthwaite, Don McCutchan, Yoshi Hori at Globis in Tokyo, and Margery Kraus the founder and executive chair of APCO Worldwide. Her support has been enthusiastic throughout, especially with seminars and conference sessions she has initiated or so kindly introduced us to. Michael Roux bravely stimulated important new debate ahead of orthodoxy at the Australia Leadership Retreat in Hayman Island, then at the Gold Coast. Risto Penttilä did the same at successive European Business Leaders Conferences in Helsinki. So did the annual German Marshall Fund's Brussels Forum, the Lennart Meri conferences in Estonia, the GLOBSEC gathering in Bratislava, the ESPAS conferences at the European Commission, and the Bled Forum in Slovenia. London-based think tanks, including the Royal United Services Institute, Chatham House and IISS, always enriched our thinking and perspectives through their speaker and seminar programmes. Professor Mick Cox generously made available LSE Ideas for a top-level brainstorming. Until our interim report in 2016, the World Economic Forum warmly engaged on the issue. For three decades the Ditchley Foundation has stimulated our thinking through its weekend conference retreats in Oxfordshire. Nik expresses deep thanks to Kings College London and Nanyang Technological University in Singapore for extending him Visiting Professor status, which in a series of study periods opened his thinking to invaluable new perspectives and debate.

Chris wishes to thank two personal mentors. Charles (Chip) Hauss and his wife Gretchen are always hospitable hosts in Washington DC. Chip has been a tireless supporter and a fount of ideas. Chip went through the early manuscript and made many insightful suggestions. Pip Clarke of Complete Coherence generously gave coaching and mentoring to Chris in 2017 at a complex time for the project as it morphed from a partnership to a company. Pip's thoughtful advice and coaching insights on self-management, wellbeing and managing stress have been hugely helpful.

Chris also pays tribute to the wisdom of his cousin Mildred Masheder, now in her 101st year. She was an enthusiastic mentor in her slightly younger days. At the start of the project, Mildred encouraged Chris to keep going on and to continue to ask probing questions of leaders. A number of key ideas that are now embedded in our thinking work came out from lively conversations with her. Chris also thanks his cousins, Mani and Hartwin Busch and Christopher and Julie Langdon, and his sister Fruzan Bethell-Langdon. They have all suggested books to read and provided ideas to keep him firmly grounded. Similarly, Rob Spain, Charles Mathieson and Professor Mbulu Madiba have all helped sharpen thoughts.

Chris and Nik could have achieved none of this without the understanding, forbearance and support of their families. Chris thanks his wife who has chosen not to be mentioned by name. Having lived for years with Nik often away on assignments for the BBC and ITN, Nik's wife Judy endured his long absences once again – this time over a laptop in his attic study at almost all hours or on research trips.

Finally, it goes without saying that the remaining errors and deficiencies in the book are solely the responsibility of the co-authors.

Nik Gowing and Chris Langdon, 18 May 2018